TORPEDOES

A LIST OF REFERENCES TO MATERIAL IN THE NEW YORK PUBLIC LIBRARY

COMPILED BY

WILLIAM A. ELLIS
TECHNOLOGY DIVISION

NEW YORK
1917

NOTE

This list contains the titles of works in The New York Public Library on Oct. 1, 1917. They are in the Reference Department of the Library, in the Central Building at Fifth Avenue and Forty-second Street.

REPRINTED WITH SUPPLEMENT DECEMBER 1917
FROM THE
BULLETIN OF THE NEW YORK PUBLIC LIBRARY
OF OCTOBER 1917

form p-307 [x11-11-17 2c]

TORPEDOES

A LIST OF REFERENCES TO MATERIAL IN THE NEW YORK PUBLIC LIBRARY

COMPILED BY WILLIAM A. ELLIS

GENERAL

1. Harvey torpedo. (Engineering, London, v. 9, 1870, p. 180, 241; v. 11, 1871, p. 35–36, 124; v. 13, 1872, p. 352, 412; v. 14, 1872, p. 262; v. 24, 1877, p. 391–392.) **VDA**
Invention of John Harvey.

2. The Lay torpedo. (Army and navy journal, New York, v. 13, 1875, p. 182, 293, 595, 610, 674; v. 14, 1876, p. 766, 783, 802; v. 15, 1877, p. 15; v. 16, 1879, p. 657; v. 20, 1883, p. 737, 995; v. 25, 1887, p. 697.) †† **VWA**

3. Notes on torpedoes. (Army and navy journal, New York, v. 7, 1869–70, p. 261, 325, 560, 628–629, 733; v. 8, 1870, p. 94; v. 9, 1871–72, p. 82, 106, 817; v. 10, 1872–73, p. 110, 537, 654, 730, 802, 811; v. 11, 1873–74, p. 126, 206, 222, 230, 254, 297, 313, 342, 358, 392, 446, 456–457, 505, 523; v. 12, 1874–75, p. 200, 284, 473, 506; v. 14, 1876–77, p. 283, 799, 823; v. 15, 1877, p. 254, 285, 327; v. 16, 1878, p. 86, 87, 103; v. 19, 1882, p. 501; v. 20, 1882–83, p. 263, 873; v. 21, 1884, p. 813; v. 23, 1886, p. 500, 619, 682, 873, 1015; v. 24, 1886, p. 75, 440; v. 25, 1888, p. 515; v. 28, 1891, p. 754, 875; v. 29, 1891–92, p. 254, 434, 477, 513; v. 30, 1893, p. 545; v. 31, 1893, p. 43; v. 32, 1894–95, p. 85, 115, 162, 207, 405; v. 33, 1896, p. 657; v. 36, 1899, p. 449; v. 41, 1904, p. 775, 1071; v. 42, 1904–05, p. 128, 256, 392, 477, 771, 1267, 1327; v. 43, 1905, p. 147; v. 45, 1908, p. 996; v. 46, 1908–09, p. 140, 572, 583; v. 48, 1910–11, p. 119, 187, 1512; v. 50, 1913, p. 1309; v. 52, 1914–15, p. 263, 364, 427, 776, 871, 1133, 1229, 1361, 1393, 1624, 1649.) †† **VWA**

4. Notes on torpedoes. (Engineer, London, v. 45, 1878, p. 171, 402; v. 84, 1897, p. 423; v. 95, 1903, p. 40, 471; v. 105, 1908, p. 665; v. 107, 1909, p. 428; v. 109, 1910, p. 40, 66, 196, 348, 472, 573; v. 110, p. 197.) **VA**

5. Notes on torpedoes. (Engineering, London, v. 8, 1869, p. 227; v. 10, 1870, p. 286, 473; v. 11, 1871, p. 321, 394, 463; v. 12, 1871, p. 30, 114, 155, 322; v. 14, 1872, p. 34, 366; v. 17, 1874, p. 114, 400, 447; v. 25, 1878, p. 64, 179, 388; v. 28, 1879, p. 36, 177; v. 29, 1880, p. 127, 498; v. 30, 1880, p. 272, 296, 322; v. 31, 1881, p. 434, 486; v. 33, 1882, p. 142, 218, 297; v. 36, 1883, p. 92, 543; v. 43, 1887, p. 234,

369; v. 50, 1890, p. 532; v. 51, 1891, p. 344; v. 55, 1893, p. 165, 223, 625; v. 70, 1900, p. 5; v. 74, 1902, p. 147, 610, 674; v. 76, 1903, p. 353.) **VDA**

6. Notes on torpedoes. (Institution of Naval Architects, Transactions, London, v. 13, 1872, p. 42, 258; v. 23, 1882, p. 9; v. 29, 1888, p. 184–187, 191; v. 32, 1891, p. 12, 21, 30–31; v. 36, 1895, p. 183; v. 52, 1910, p. 7.) **VXA**

7. Notes on torpedoes. (Marine engineer, London, v. 10, 1888, p. 203; v. 13, 1891, p. 447; v. 17, 1895, p. 197; v. 18, 1896, p. 205; v. 19, 1897, p. 14, 96, 223; v. 20, 1898, p. 68; v. 24, 1903, p. 433; v. 25, 1903, p. 330; v. 26, 1904, p. 256; v. 31, 1908, p. 39.) **VXA**

8. Notes on torpedoes. (Scientific American, New York, v. 10, 1863, p. 362; v. 50, 1884, p. 49; v. 52, p. 276; v. 53, p. 19, 50, 149, 342; v. 54, p. 73, 117, 166; v. 55, p. 48, 88, 280, 336–337, 387; v. 56, p. 25, 185, 309, 370, 389; v. 57, p. 114; v. 58, p. 2, 33, 243, 376; v. 59, p. 311, 358; v. 60, p. 183, 228, 324; v. 61, p. 32, 102, 135, 178; v. 62, p. 182, 185; v. 64, p. 9, 374; v. 65, p. 161–162, 273; v. 66, p. 147, 164, 184; v. 67, p. 323; v. 68, p. 23, 262; v. 69, p. 137, 261, 323, 354–355, 387; v. 70, p. 21, 230; v. 71, p. 44, 164, 213, 263, 310, 354, 375–376; v. 72, p. 108, 178, 184, 251, 261; v. 73, p. 185, 364, 377; v. 74, p. 83; v. 76, 1897, p. 99; v. 77, 1897, p. 376; v. 79, 1898, p. 76, 211; v. 80, 1899, p. 92, 244–245; v. 81, 1899, p. 358; v. 82, 1900, p. 35, 151, 247; v. 83, 1900, p. 52, 151, 194, 244; v. 85, 1901, p. 119, 166; v. 86, 1902, p. 60, 84, 94, 204; v. 87, 1902, p. 124, 290, 443; v. 88, 1903, p. 238, 374; v. 89, 1903, p. 190; v. 90, 1904, p. 40, 271; v. 91, 1904, p. 244, 461; v. 94, 1906, p. 286; v. 97, 1907, p. 413; v. 101, 1909, p. 313; v. 109, 1913, p. 278; v. 112, 1915, p. 117; v. 114, 1916, p. 95, 575.) **VA**

9. Notes on torpedoes. (Scientific American supplement, New York, v. 1, 1876, p. 453; v. 6, 1878, p. 2193, 2208–2209, 2223, 2301, 2462.) **VA**

10. Notes on torpedoes. (United States Naval Institute, Proceedings, Annapolis, v. 27, 1901, p. 436–437, 839–840; v. 28, 1902, p. 162–163, 439; v. 30, 1904, p. 882–883; v. 31, 1905, p. 727–730, 1014; v. 32, 1906, p. 1606–

General, continued.

1607; v. 33, 1907, p. 418, 875–876; v. 34, 1908, p. 1338; v. 35, 1909, p. 309, 985; v. 36, 1910, p. 625, 903; v. 38, 1912, p. 345; v. 39, 1913, p. 395, 872, 1357; v. 40, 1914, p. 1192, 1508, 1821; v. 42, 1916, p. 268, 967.) **VXA**

11. **Torpedo** experiments. (Engineering, London, v. 18, 1875, p. 126, 165, 269, 439; v. 19, 1876. p. 214, 354, 500; v. 21, 1878, p. 185; v. 22, 1879, p. 367–368; v. 29, 1886, p. 462; v. 32, 1889, p. 93–94, 116; v. 39, 1896, p. 143–145, 636; v. 40, 1897, p. 258, 475; v. 41, 1898, p. 256; v. 42, 1899, p. 478.) **VDA**

12. **Torpedo** experiments in England. (Army and navy journal, New York, v. 12, 1874–75, p. 41, 104, 110, 186, 206, 265, 270–271, 318, 327, 334, 715–716; v. 13, 1875–76, p. 22, 30, 755; v. 14, 1877, p. 383; v. 15, 1877–78, p. 79, 546; v. 17, 1879, p. 266; v. 19, 1881, p. 35; v. 20, 1882, p. 979; v. 24, 1887, p. 925, 939–940; v. 25, 1888, p. 905.) **†† VWA**

13. **Torpedo** experiments and practice (United States). (Army and navy journal, New York, v. 11, 1873, p. 30, 167, 375; v. 12, 1874, p. 23, 58–59; v. 13, 1875, p. 74; v. 15, 1877, p. 135; v. 16, 1878, p. 7, 253; v. 20, 1882, p. 422; v. 24, 1886, p. 156; v. 49, 1911–12, p. 43, 1599; v. 52, 1914–15, p. 265, 1002, 1532.) **†† VWA**

14. **Torpedoes** or submarine explosive instruments. (Engineer, London, v. 22, 1866, p. 168; v. 23, 1867, p. 242; v. 31, 1871, p. 49; v. 34, 1872, p. 78.) **VA**
Invention of C. A. McEvoy of London.

15. The **Whitehead** torpedo. (Army and navy journal, New York, v. 13, 1876, p. 650, 679, 746; v. 14, 1876, p. 142; v. 15, 1877, p. 79, 299; v. 17, 1879, p. 143, 586, 607; v. 18, 1881, p. 747, 774, 1077; v. 21, 1883, p. 341.) **†† VWA**

1630

16. **Hanzelet,** Jean Appier, called. La pyrotechnie de Hanzelet, Lorrain, ou sont representez les plus rares & plus appreuuez secrets des machines & des feux artificiels. Propres pour assieger battre surprendre & deffendre toutes places. Pont à Mousson: I. & Gaspard Bernard, 1630. 4 p.l., 264 p. 8°. **VOG**
This work contains interesting data on floating and land mines, bombs, rockets, and artificial fire for lighting battlefields, etc.

1641

17. **Collado,** Luys. Prattica manuale dell' artigliera. Opera historica, politica, e militare. Milano: Filippo Ghisolfi & Gio. Battista Bidelli, 1641. 8 p.l., 328 p. illus. 4°. **† VWW**

1644

18. **Mersenne,** Marin. De nauibus sub aqua natantibus. (In his: F. Marini Mersenni Minimi cogitata physico mathematica, in quibus tam naturæ quam artis effectus admirandi certissimis demonstrationibus explicantur, Pariis, 1644 ⎣part 1⎦. p. 207–208.) **OKC**
The author gives Cornelis Jacobsz Drebbel the credit of inventing the submarine.

1648

19. **Wilkins,** John. Mathematicall magick. Or, The vvonders that may be performed by mechanicall geometry. London: printed by M. F. for S. Gellibrand, 1648. 7 p.l., 295 p. illus. 16°. **PBC**
Concerning the possibility of framing an ark for submarine navigations. The difficulties and conveniences of such a contrivance, p. 178–190.

1650

20. **Siemienowicz,** Kazimierz. Artis magnae artilleriae. Pars prima... Amsterodami: apud Joannem Janssonivm, 1650. 8 p.l., 284 p., 2 l., 22 pl. f°. **† VOG**
Gives data on bombs, rockets, and floating mines.

1676

21. **Binning,** Thomas. A light to the art of gunnery...either in sea or land-service ... London: printed by J. D. for W. Fisher and R. Mount, 1676. 8 p.l., 3–172 p., 4 charts, 3 pl. 4°. **VWW**
Gives receipts for making petards, grenades, fire arrows, rockets, fire trunks, fire barrels, and mines; also receipts for the illumination of trenches and battlefields.

1699

22. **Fernandez de Medrano,** Sebastian. El perfecto artificial, bombardero y artillero, que contiene los artificios de fuegos marciales, nuevo uzo de bombas, granadas, y practica de la artilleria, y mosquete, &c. Brusselas: L. Marchant, 1699. 8 p.l., 196 p., 2 l., 10 pl. 16° in eights. **VOG**
Notes on bombs, rockets, and grenades.

1745

23. **Orval,** Perrinet d'. Essay sur les feux d'artifice pour le spectacle et pour la guerre. Par Mr. P. d'O. ⎣i. e., Perrinet d'Orval.⎦ Paris, 1745. xii p., 2 l., 224 p., 13 pl. 12° in eights. **VOG**
Notes on rockets and mines.

1762

24. La Machine infernale. (Recueil de planches, sur les sciences, les arts libéraux, et les arts méchaniques, avec leur explication, Paris, 1762, v. 1, Art militaire, Fortification, planche 11, fig. 6.) **†† * AP**

1764

25. Bélidor, Bernard Forest de. Oeuvres diverses de M. Belidor, concernant l'artillerie et le génie. Amsterdam: Arkstée & Merkus, 1764. 1 p.l., xxxix, 396 p., 7 pl. 8°. **VWW**

For descriptions of mines see p. 94–191, 320–391; for descriptions of bombs, p. 238–319.

1776

26. Bélidor, Bernard Forest de. M. Belidor's new method of mining. (In: Robert Jones, Artificial fireworks, London, 1776, p. 157–178.) **VOG**

27. Jones, Robert. Artificial fireworks, improved to the modern practice, from the minutest to the highest branches... Also, Mr. Muller's Fireworks, for sea and land service... London: J. Millan, 1776. 3 p.l., 193 p., 8 pl. 2. ed. 8°. **VOG**

28. Vallière, Jean Florent, marquis de. Dissertation on mines, and their advantages in the defence of places. (In: Robert Jones, Artificial fireworks, London, 1776, p. 178–186.) **VOG**

18 — ?

29. Torka, Johann. ₁Seeminen.₁ (In his: Die Wunder der Technik, Berlin ₁18 — ?₁, p. 446, 451.) **V**

30. —— ₁Torpedos.₁ (In his: Die Wunder der Technik, Berlin ₁18—?₁, p. 450–460.) **V**

1810

31. Fulton, Robert. Torpedo war, and submarine explosions. New York: printed by William Elliot, 1810. 57(1) p., 1 l., 5 pl. ob. 8°. **Reserve**

32. —— —— New York: printed by W. Eliot, 1810. New York: Reprinted, W. Abbatt, 1914. 55 p., 5 pl. 4°. (Magazine of history with notes and queries. Extra number. no. 35.) **IAG (Magazine)**

The original pamphlet was reviewed in the *Proceedings* of the United States Naval Institute, Annapolis, Md., v. 12, 1886, p. 252–254, *VXA*.

33. Sur les moyens proposés par Robert Fulton, pour la destruction des vaisseaux de guerre et la défense des ports et des rades. illus. (Société d'encouragement pour l'industrie nationale, Bulletin, Paris, année 9, 1810, p. 170–182.) **VA**
Detailed description of Fulton's torpedo.

33a. Use of the torpedo in the defence of ports and harbors; communicated to the Senate, February 26, 1810. 11th Congress, 2d session. illus. (In: American state papers, Washington, 1834, v. 14, Naval affairs, v. 1, p. 211–226.) *** SBE**

1811

33b. Experiments on the practical use of the torpedo, communicated to the House of Representatives, February 14, 1811. 11th Congress, 3d session. illus. (In: American state papers, Washington, 1834, v. 14, Naval affairs, v. 1, p. 234–244.) *** SBE**

1820

34. Griswold, Charles. Submarine navigation. (American journal of science and arts, New Haven, v. 2, 1820, p. 94–100.) **OA**
Gives account of David Bushnell's submarine or torpedo and the attack on the British fleet in New York harbor, August, 1776, by Ezra Lee.

1825

35. Cutbush, James. Of the American turtle. (In his: System of pyrotechny, Philadelphia, 1825, p. 515–521.) **VOG**
Gives a very interesting account of David Bushnell's submarine or torpedo and the attack on the British fleet in New York harbor in August, 1776.

36. —— Of the combustible substances used in, and the manner of preparing a fire-ship. (In his: System of pyrotechny, Philadelphia, 1825, p. 507–512.) **VOG**

37. —— Of the torpedo. Of the marine incendiary kegs, etc. (In his: System of pyrotechny, Philadelphia, 1825, p. 521–525.) **VOG**

Notes on Fulton's torpedo. Attempt of a Mr. Mix to destroy the "Plantagenet" in Lynnhaven harbor in July, 1813; also attempt of a Mr. Penny of Easthampton, Long Island, to destroy a British battleship.

38. Montgéry, de. Notice sur la vie et les travaux de Robert Fulton. Paris: Bachelier, 1825. 1 p.l., 70 p. 8°. **AN p.v.26, no.19**
Includes notes on torpedoes.

39. —— Traité des fusées de guerre, nommées autrefois rochettes et maintenant fusées à la Congrève. Paris: Bachelier. 1825. 2 p.l., 364 p., 6 diagrs. 8°. **VWS**
Gives data on submarines and torpedoes.

1825, continued.

40. Worcester (2. marquis), Edward Som-
erset. ⟨Torpedoes.⟩ (In his: The century
of inventions of the marquis of Worcester,
London, 1825, p. 12–14.)   **V**

Description of a bomb or torpedo for sinking ships;
also methods of protecting ships from torpedoes.

1840

41. Memorial of a committee of the military convention at Norwich, Vermont,
praying the revision ʻand alteration of the
system of the military defences of the
United States. Feb. 24, 1840. ⟨Washing-
ton, 1840.⟩ 26 p. 8°. (U. S. 26. cong.
1. sess. Sen. doc. 238; serial 358.)   *** SBE**

This ʻmemorial prepared by Captain Alden Part-
ridge, president of Norwich University, gives valuable
suggestions for the training of the "citizen soldiery"
applicable at this time; also data on the use of the
fireship and of Greek fire; also an interesting description of the fireship invented by Uriah Brown. The
proposed ship, seventy-five feet long, was to be so
constructed as to float low in the water. Its sides
and decks were to be protected by heavy iron plates
set at such angles that no shot fired at it could strike
at a greater angle than 15 degrees, thus causing the
shots to ricochet without penetrating the deck or sides.
The chief use of the boat was the firing of a liquid
composition through tubes passing through orifices in
the deck which on coming in contact with the air
would instantly take fire.

1862

42. Collier, Francis J.   Magnetic torpedoes. (Scientific American, New York,
new series, v. 6, 1862, p. 230.)   **VA**

Brief note.

43. Holman, H. R.   Harbor defence-tor-
pedoes. (Scientific American, New York,
new series, v. 6, 1862, p. 38.)   **VA**

Brief note.

44. Submarine infernal machine.   illus.
(Scientific American, New York, new
series, v. 5, 1862, p. 101.)   **VA**

Torpedo work on the Potomac river.

45. Submarine torpedoes — infernal machines. illus. (Scientific American, New
York, new series, v. 6, 1862, p. 164–165.) **VA**

Notes on the work of Robert Fulton and Lord
Cochrane.

1863

46. Demijohn torpedoes.   (Scientific
American, New York, new series, v. 8, 1863,
p. 19.)   **VA**

Abstracted from the *Pittsburgh dispatch.*

47. Destruction of the U. S. S. "Housa-
tonic" by a torpedo. (Scientific American.
New York, new series, v. 10, 1863, p. 165.)
VA

48. Explosion of a submarine **torpedo**
(Scientific American, New York, new
series, v. 8, 1863, p. 7.)   **V**

Destruction of the U. S. S. Cairo, Dec. 11, 1862.

49. The **"Monitor"** torpedo. (Scientific
American, New York, new series, v. 9, 1863
p. 56.)   **VA**

50. A **New** rebel torpedo. illus. (Scientific American, new series, v. 9, 1863. p.
388.)   **VA**

Report of William N. Jeffers on test.

51. The **New** torpedo in Charleston harbor. illus. (Scientific American, New
York, new series, v. 9, 1863, p. 164, 229.) **VA**

1864

52. Doty. On the torpedoes used by the
Confederate States in the destruction of
some of the Federal ships of war, and the
mode of attaching them to the rams.
(British Association for the Advancement
of Science, Report, Bath, 1864, Notices and
abstracts, p. 185–186.)   *** EC**

Also abstracted in *Army and navy journal,* New
York, v. 2, 1864, p. 138–139. †† *VWA.*

53. Experiment with torpedoes. (Engineer, London, v. 18, 1864, p. 146.)   **VA**

Experiment in the Scheldt near Antwerp.

54. New rebel torpedo. illus. (Scientific
American, New York, new series, v. 11,
1864, p. 228.)   **VA**

55. New torpedo. illus. (Engineer, London, v. 18, 1864, p. 254.)   **VA**

Invention made at Richmond, Va.   Abstracted
from *Scientific American.*

56. The **Rebel** torpedoes. illus. (Scientific American, New York, new series, v.
10, 1864, p. 390.)   **VA**

57. Torpedo planting by the Confederates.
(Army and navy journal, New York, v. 1,
1864, p. 653.)   **†† VWA**

58. Torpedoes. (Engineer, London, v. 18,
1864, p. 194.)   **VA**

Notes on invention used in Confederate navy.

59. Torpedoes used by the rebels. illus.
(Scientific American, New York, new
series, v. 11, 1864, p. 21.)   **VA**

1865

60. American torpedoes in England. (Scientific American, New York, new series,
v. 13, 1865, p. 350.)   **VA**

Invention of W. Beardslee.

1865, continued.

61. Comstock, C. B. ₁Use of land torpedoes by the Confederates at Fort Fisher.₁ illus. (War of the rebellion: a compilation of the official records of the Union and Confederate armies, Washington, 1895, series 1, v. 46, part 2, p. 215–217.) **IKC**
Letter to General R. Delafield.

62. The **Electrical** torpedo. (Scientific American, New York, new series, v. 13, 1865, p. 113.) **VA**
Note on the work of Nathaniel J. Holmes in England.

63. A **New** torpedo. (Engineer, London, v. 19, 1865, p. 253.) **VA**
Brief note on invention by a Swedish engineer.

64. Rye, William Brenchley. England as seen by foreigners in the days of Elizabeth and James the First. Comprising translations of the journals of the two dukes of Wirtemberg in 1592 and 1610. London: J. R. Smith, 1865. cxxxii p., 1 l., 3–300 p., 5 pl., 2 ports. 8°. **CN**
Has a reference to Cornelius Drebbel on p. 61, and an extensive biographical account of his activities on p. 232–242.

65. Torpedo invented by Donald McKay. (Army and navy journal, New York, v. 3, 1865, p. 89.) **†† VWA**

66. Torpedo invented by G. Davies, London. (Engineer, London, v. 19, 1865, p. 159.) **VA**

67. The **Torpedo** ship. (Scientific American, New York, new series, v. 12, 1865, p. 39.) **VA**
Brief note.

68. Torpedoes. (Army and navy journal, New York, v. 3, 1865, p. 728–729.) **†† VWA**
A new type of torpedo used in France.

1866

69. History of a torpedo boat. (Army and navy journal, New York, v. 3, 1866, p. 562; v. 4, 1866, p. 18.) **†† VWA**
Note on Confederate boat constructed at Mobile.

70. Holmes, N. J. Torpedo defences. (Royal United Service Institution, Journal, London, v. 10, 1866, p. 402–414.) **VWA**
With discussion, p. 414–416.
Gives valuable historical notes on torpedo warfare during the Civil war; also the development of the torpedo.

71. A **New** torpedo. illus. (Engineer, London, v. 22, 1866, p. 422.) **VA**
Invention of Mr. M. Nebol of New York.

72. Torpedo boats for harbor defence. (Army and navy journal, New York, v. 3, 1866, p. 457.) **†† VWA**

73. Torpedo experiments in England. (Scientific American, New York, new series, v. 14, 1866, p. 407–408.) **VA**

74. Torpedoes. (Engineering, London, v. 1, 1866, p. 333–334.) **VDA**
Notes on the work of Holmes and Maury.

75. Torpedoes for war. (Engineer, London, v. 21, 1866, p. 368.) **VA**
Notes on invention of H. J. Holmes and Lieut. Maury.

76. Vauvert, Maxime. Toulon. — Expérience de torpilles. illus. (Le monde illustré. Paris, v. 18, 1866, p. 196–197.) ***DM**

1868

77. Nouvelles torpilles. (Cosmos, Paris, série 2, v. 3, 1868, p. 27.) **VA**

78. Torpedoes. illus. (Engineer, London, v. 25, 1868, p. 1–2, 19–20, 35.) **VA**
Notes on torpedoes at the International Exhibition, Paris; Austrian torpedoes; experiments by Mallet, N. J. Holmes, Baron d'Ebner; the toposcope.

79. Torpedoes in France. (Engineer, London, v. 25, 1868, p. 260.) **VA**

1869

80. Gilmore, Arthur H. Anti-torpedo vessel. (Royal United Service Institution, Journal, London, v. 13, 1869, p. 33.) **VWA**

81. Hamilton, John Randolph. The American navy; its organization, ships, armaments and recent experiences. (Royal United Service Institution, Journal, London, v. 12, 1869, p. 243–271.) **VWA**
Valuable data on the use of torpedoes during the Civil war.

82. Jervois, W. F. Drummond. Coast defences, and the application of iron to fortification. illus. (Royal United Service Institution, Journal, London, v. 12, 1869, p. 548–569.) **VWA**
Notes on torpedoes and submarine mines.

83. Patents on torpedoes issued to Frederick N. Gisborne of London. (Engineer, London, v. 27, 1869, p. 58; v. 28, 1869, p. 44.) **VA**

84. Torpedoes. (Van Nostrand's engineering magazine, New York, v. 1, 1869, p. 632–635.) **VDA**
From *Pall Mall gazette.*

85. Torpedoes in war. (Army and navy journal, New York, v. 6, 1868, p. 35. 534, 600, 788.) **†† VWA**

1870

86. The **Austrian** torpedo. (Van Nostrand's engineering magazine, New York, v. 2, 1870, p. 325–326.)   **VDA**

87. **Captain** Harvey's torpedo. (Van Nostrand's engineering magazine, New York, v. 3, 1870, p. 657–658.)   **VDA**

88. **Fishing** up torpedoes. (Engineer, London, v. 30, 1870, p. 343.)   **VA**
Plan proposed by C. W. Merrifield.

89. **Harvey** torpedo. (Engineering, London, v. 9, 1870, p. 180, 241.)   **VDA**
The first article is reprinted in *Van Nostrand's engineering magazine*, New York, v. 2, 1870, p. 512–514, *VDA*.

90. **Harvey's** Seetorpedo. (Dingler's polytechnisches Journal, Augsburg, Bd. 197, 1870, p. 127–129.)   **VA**

91. The **Torpedo**. (Army and navy journal, New York, v. 7, 1870, p. 564.) †† **VWA**
Editorial.

92. **Torpedo** war. (Engineering, London, v. 9, 1870, p. 25–26.)   **VDA**
Valuable historical article. Notes on work of Bushnell and Fulton, and the use of torpedoes in the various American wars.

93. **Torpedoes**. (Engineer, London, v. 30, 1870, p. 72.)   **VA**
Experiments made at Plymouth, Eng., by Admiral Sir H. Codrington.

1871

94. **Beal**, S. Description of a Chinese torpedo. (Royal United Service Institution, Journal, London, v. 15, 1871, p. 728–730.)   **VWA**
Invention of John Lewis, an American.

95. **Braham**, Philip. Working torpedoes. illus. (Engineering, London, v. 12, 1871, p. 89.)   **VDA**
Abstract of paper read before the British Association, Section G.
Reprinted in *Van Nostrand's engineering magazine*, v. 5, 1871, p. 467–468, *VDA*.

96. **Callender**, M. L. Floating marine torpedoes. illus. (Van Nostrand's engineering magazine, New York, v. 4, 1871, p. 237–240.)   **VDA**
Also printed in *American artisan*, v. 12, 1871, p. 99–100, † *VA*.
Paper read before the New York Society of Practical Engineering, Jan. 18, 1871.

97. **Electrically** exploding torpedoes. (American artisan, New York, v. 12, 1871, p. 344.)   **VA**
Invention of Capt. Andrew Noble.

98. **Ericsson's** torpedo. (Army and navy journal, New York, v. 9, 1871, p. 339, 371.) †† **VWA**

99. The **Fish** torpedo. (Engineer, London, v. 32, 1871, p. 381.)   **VA**
Editorial.

100. **Fuses** for torpedoes. illus. (Engineer, London, v. 31, 1871, p. 46.)   **VA**
Used in the French navy.

101. **Harvey**, Frederick. Instructions for the management of Harvey's sea torpedo. London: E. & F. N. Spon, 1871. 43 p., 13 pl. 8°.   **VWS**

102. **Morshead**, W. Torpedoes. (Engineer, London, v. 31, 1871, p. 150; v. 33, 1872, p. 298.)   **VA**
Letters stating that on Oct. 20, 1860 he suggested the employment of electricity for the guiding of "explosive vessels."

103. **Self-propelling** submerged torpedoes. (Engineer, London, v. 31, 1871, p. 258, 328.)   **VA**
Patents issued to George W. Rendel.

104. **Stotherd**, Richard Hugh. Defensive submarine warfare. (Royal United Service Institution, Journal, London, v. 15, 1871, p. 705–733.)   **VWA**
Gives historical notes on torpedoes and their use during the Civil war.

105. A **Torpedo** cruise. (Army and navy journal, New York, v. 9, 1871–72, p. 30, 399, 737.) †† **VWA**
Experiments with the Harvey torpedo. From the London *Broad Arrow*.

106. **Torpedo** experiments. (Army and navy journal, New York, v. 9, 1871, p. 106.) †† **VWA**
Experiments conducted by Gen. Humphreys.

107. **Torpedoes**. (Engineer, London, v. 32, 1871, p. 223, 408, 424.)   **VA**
Letters by J. Haddan, Philip Braham, A. Alexander and Geo. Warsop.
Notes on the fish torpedo invented by R. Whitehead.

108. **Torpedoes**. (Van Nostrand's engineering magazine, New York, v. 4, 1871, p. 107–108.)   **VDA**

109. **Torpedoes** in oil wells. (Engineer, London, v. 31, 1871, p. 411.)   **VA**
Invention of a Mr. Roberts in Pittsburgh. Abstracted from the *Scientific American*.

110. **Weir**, Robert. Submarine torpedoes. (Van Nostrand's engineering magazine, New York, v. 4, 1871, p. 128–132.)   **VDA**
Abstract of paper read before the New York Society of Practical Engineering.

1872

111. **Harvey**, John. On the construction of vessels, in relation to the changed modes of naval warfare. (Institution of Naval Architects, Transactions, London, v. 13, 1872, p. 3–5.)   **VXA**
Notes on use of torpedoes in Civil war. Use of the "invisible shell," by Capt. Warner in 1844.

1872, continued.

112. Harvey's sea torpedoes in Italy. (Army and navy journal, New York, v. 9, 1872, p. 606–607.) †† **VWA**

113. Kirkland, William A. The rival torpedoes. (Army and navy journal, New York, v. 10, 1872, p. 314–315, 363, 406–408, 426.) †† **VWA**
Notes on the Ericsson and the Lay torpedoes. Letter by John L. Lay, p. 340.

114. Magneto-electric torpedo firer. (Engineer, London, v. 34, 1872, p. 69.) **VA**
Account of machine exhibited at the Copenhagen exhibition.

115. Merrifield, C. W. The effect of torpedoes on naval construction. (Institution of Naval Architects, Transactions, London, v. 13, 1872, p. 6–12.) **VXA**
Reprinted in *Engineer*, London, v. 33, 1872, p. 226, *VA; Engineering*, London, v. 13, 1872, p. 198–199, 212–213, *VDA; Journal of the Society of Arts*, London, v. 20, 1872, p. 363–365, *VA; Van Nostrand's engineering magazine*, New York, v. 7, 1872, p. 137–140, *VDA*.

116. Moerath, J. N. On the protection of vessels against torpedoes. illus. (Institution of Naval Architects, Transactions, London, v. 13, 1872, p. 1–2.) **VXA**
Also printed in *Engineer*, London, v. 33, 1872, p. 245, *VA; Journal of the Society of Arts*, v. 20, 1872, p. 362–363, *VA*.

117. Sprokkelingen op torpedo-gebied. Eerbiedig opgedragen aan de nog te benoemen torpedo-commissie van zee- en landmacht-officieren. Nieuwediep: L. A. Laureij, 1872. 36 p. 12°. **VXM p.v.3, no.3**

118. Stotherd, Richard Hugh. Notes on torpedoes, offensive and defensive. Washington: Gov. Prtg. Off., 1872. 1 p.l., [4]–5 p., 1 l., (1)2, (1)8–318 p., 4 diagr., 8 pl. illus. 8°. **VXV**

119. Torpedoes. (Engineer, London. v. 33, 1872, p. 31, 42, 84, 114, 150, 208.) **VA**
Correspondence between A. Alexander and A. M. regarding the assertion that General Paixhan proposed over fifty years previously to sink ships by submarine shell rockets.

120. Torpedoes for defence. (Army and navy journal, New York, v. 9, 1872, p. 736–737.) †† **VWA**

1873

121. Admiral Porter's report on monitors and torpedoes. (Army and navy journal, New York, v. 11, 1873, p. 472.) †† **VWA**

122. Alas, Genaro. Memoria sobre la defensa de las costas presentada al concurso anual de 1871 á 1872. Madrid: Imprenta del Memorial de ingenieros, 1873. 206 p., 1 l. 4°. (Memorial de ingenieros, Madrid, tomo 28, 1873.) **VWA**

123. Bucknill, J. Townsend. Description of the torpedo boats "Fortune" and

"Triana," U. S. navy. (Royal United Service Institution, Journal, London, v. 17, 1873, p. 539–542.) **VWA**
Notes on torpedoes.

124. Ericsson, John. Movable torpedoes. illus. (Army and navy journal, New York. v. 10, 1873, p. 339–340, 371–372.) †† **VWA**
Reprinted in *Engineering*, London, v. 15, 1873, p. 107–108, 175, *VDA*. The author's letter to the Secretary of the Navy is on p. 26.

125. —— The torpedo question. (Army and navy journal, New York, v. 10, 1873, p. 407, 422, 455.) †† **VWA**

126. The Ericsson torpedo. (Engineer, London, v. 35, 1873, p. 21.) **VA**

127. Ericsson's aggressive torpedo. (Army and navy journal, New York, v. 10, 1873, p. 732–733; v. 11, 1873, p. 56.) †† **VWA**

128. The Offensive use of torpedoes in naval warfare. (Engineer, London, v. 35, 1873, p. 159.) **VA**
Also printed in *Van Nostrand's engineering magazine*, New York, v. 8, 1873, p. 511–513, *VDA*, and in *Army and navy journal*, New York, v. 10, 1873, p. 535, †† *VWA*.
Notes on the Whitehead and Harvey torpedoes.

129. Palmer, Francis Ingram. Descriptive account of an horizontal-acting and disconnecting spur-torpedo-ram, fitted with auxiliary needle-torpedo thrusts; also, a dome-shaped, double roller one gun turret. Invented and designed by F. I. Palmer. [London: W. W. Head, pref. 1873.] 2 p.l., 73(1) p., 19 l., 6 pl. f°. † **VXV**

130. Seccombe, W. E. On a proposed torpedo catcher. (Institution of Naval Architects, Transactions, London, v. 14, 1873, p. 223–229.) **VXA**

130a. Steam torpedo launch constructed by Messrs. Yarrow & Hedley. illus. (Engineer, London, v. 35, 1873, p. 51.) **VA**

131. The Torpedo question. (Army and navy journal, New York, v. 10, 1873, p. 558.) †† **VWA**
From the *Broad arrow*.

132. The Torpedo question in England. (Army and navy journal, New York, v. 11, 1873, p. 136.) †† **VWA**

133. United States. — Ordnance Office, Navy Department. Notes on movable torpedoes. 1873. [Washington, 1873?] 32 p., 2 pl. 8°. **VXM p.v.2, no.2**

134. Vandevelde. Torpilles et défenses sous-marines. Rapport sur les appareils et expériences relatifs aux torpilles fabriquées à l'arsenal d'Amsterdam. Traduit par E. Garnault. Paris: A. Bertrand [1873]. 1 p.l., 168 p., 12 pl. 8°. **VXV**

135. Y. The torpedo question. (Army and navy journal. New York, v. 10, 1873, p. 438–439.) †† **VWA**

1874

136. Abbot, Henry Larcom.   Torpedoes for harbor defence. (Army and navy journal. New York, v. 11, 1874, p. 394, 410; v. 17, 1879, p. 121, 465–466.)   †† **VWA**

137. Aggressive torpedoes. illus. (Army and navy journal, New York, v. 12, 1874, p. 307–308.)   †† **VWA**

138. Barber, Francis M.   Lecture on drifting and automatic movable torpedoes, submarine guns, and rockets. Newport, R. I.: U. S. Torpedo Station, 1874.   40 p., 12 diagr.   8°.   (United States. — Ordnance Bureau, Navy Department.)
                    VXV p.v.1, no.2

139. —— Lecture on the Whitehead torpedo. Newport, R. I.: U. S. Torpedo Station, 1874.   39 p., 7 diagr.   8°.   (United States. — Ordnance Bureau, Navy Department.)   **VXV p.v.1, no.3**

140. Electrical warfare. (Army and navy journal, New York, v. 11, 1874, p. 606, 825.)
                    †† **VWA**

141. Ericsson pneumatic torpedo.   illus. (Engineer, London, v. 38, 1874, p. 468.) **VA**

142. Ericsson pneumatic torpedo.   illus. (Scientific American, New York, new series, v. 31, 1874, p. 390.)   **VA**

143. Hawksley, George. Torpedoes. (Engineer, London, v. 37, 1874, p. 237.)   **VA**
Letter outlining his invention of Sept. 2, 1860.

144. Hennebert, Eugène.   Les torpilles, par le major H. de Sarrepont ¡pseud.¡. Paris: J. Dumaine, 1874.   xii, 320 p. illus. 8°.   **VXV**
Extrait du *Journal des sciences militaires.*

145. Holmes, N. J.   Electric torpedoes. (Army and navy journal, New York, v. 11, 1874, p. 574.)   †† **VWA**

146. Merrell, John P.   Lecture on galvanic batteries and electrical machines, as used in torpedo operations. arranged in three parts. Newport, R. I.: U. S. Torpedo Station, 1874–75.   3 parts.   8°.   (United States. — Ordnance Bureau, Navy Department.)   **VXV p.v.1, no.5**
Part 1. Galvanic batteries. 1874. 30 p.
Part 2. Frictional and magneto-electric machines. 1874. 20 p., 3 diagr.
Part 3. Dynamo-electric machines. 1875. 40 p., 4 diagr.

147. The Torpedo attack on the Oberon at Stokes bay. illus. (Engineer, London. v. 38, 1874, p. 133–134, 152, 176, 185, 232, 271–272.)   **VA**
A series of experiments.

148. A Torpedo detector.   (Engineer, London, v. 37, 1874, p. 148.)   **VA**
Notes on the Wilde electro-magnetic induction machine.

149. A Torpedo detector.   (Van Nostrand's eclectic engineering magazine, New York, v. 10, 1874, p. 536–538.)   **VDA**

150. Torpedo explosions at Woolwich. (Engineer, London, v. 37, 1874, p. 85, 139, 209.)   **VA**

151. Torpedoes a century old.   (Army and navy journal, New York, v. 11, 1874, p. 426.)
                    †† **VWA**
Also printed in *Engineer*, London, v. 37, 1874, p. 174, *VA.*
Invention of John Cross of London, who about 1776 proposed a plan "to keep off all troublesome enemies, who dare presume to disturb their peace" and to end the American Revolution.

152. The Whitehead torpedo. (Engineer, London, v. 37, 1874, p. 141.)   **VA**
Series of experiments.

1875

153. Abbot, Henry Larcom.   Notes on electricity, in its applications to submarine mining. ¡New York:¡ Battalion Press. 1875–76. 2 p.l., ii–iii, 123 l., 13 pl. 8°. **VXV**
Proof ed. At head of title: Confidential.

154. American torpedo vessel.   (Engineer, London, v. 39, 1875, p. 420.)   **VA**
Brief note on the "Alarm."

155. Barber, Francis M.   Lecture on submarine boats, and their application to torpedo operations. Newport, R. I.: U. S. Torpedo Station, 1875.   39(1) p., 8 diagr. 8°.   (United States. — Ordnance Bureau, Navy Department.)   **VXV p.v.1, no. 4**

156. Converse, George Albert.   Notes on torpedo fuzes. Newport, R. I.: U. S. Torpedo Station, 1875. 31 p., 5 pl. 8°. (United States. — Ordnance Bureau, Navy Department.)   **VXV p.v.1, no.6**

157. Dawson, W.   Offensive torpedo warfare.   (Royal United Service Institution, Journal, London, v. 15, 1875, p. 86–91.)
                    VWA
Valuable notes on the use of torpedoes during the Civil war.

158. High speed torpedo launch built by Yarrow & Hedley. (Engineer, London, v. 39, 1875, p. 100.)   **VA**

159. Hill, Walter N.   Notes on explosives, and their application in torpedo warfare. Newport, R. I.: U. S. Torpedo Station, 1875. 60 p., 2 diagr. 8°. (United States. — Ordnance Bureau, Navy Department.)
                    VXV p.v.1, no.1

160. Lindsay, Charles.   Plan for protecting ships (at anchor), blockading a port from attacks by outrigger Whitehead, or Harvey torpedoes. (Royal United Service Institution, Journal, London, v. 19, 1875, p. 527–531.)   **VWA**

1875, continued.

161. Maritime attack by torpedoes. (Engineer, London, v. 39, 1875, p. 370–371.) **VA**
Also printed in *Van Nostrand's eclectic engineering magazine*, v. 13, 1875, p. 252–257, *VDA*.
Notes on the Whitehead torpedo.

162. A Monster torpedo. (Engineer, London, v. 39, 1875, p. 178.) **VA**
Brief note on experiments at Toulon.

163. Navigating torpedoes. (Manufacturer and builder, New York, v. 7, 1875, p. 219.) **VA**
Invention of Denayroùsse.

164. The **Oberon** submarine mine experiments. illus. (Engineer, London, v. 39, 1875, p. 361.) **VA**
Also printed in *Army and navy journal*, New York, v. 12, 1875, p. 715–716, †† *VWA*.

165. Submarine boats. Engineer, London, v. 40, 1875, p. 157.) **VA**
Gives data on torpedoes.

166. Torpedo ship "Vesuvius." illus. (Engineering, London, v. 19, 1875, p. 375–376.) **VA**

167. Woolley, A. Sedgwick. On spar torpedo warfare. (Institution of Naval Architects. Transactions, London, v. 16, 1875, p. 147–154.) **VXA**
Abstracted in *Engineering*, London, v. 19, 1875, p. 303–304, 306, 318, illus., *VDA*; *Engineer*, London, v. 39, 1875, p. 316–317, illus., *VA*.
Notes on Bushnell's torpedo and the use of torpedoes during the Civil war.

1876

168. Abbot, Henry Larcom. Approved matériel of the U. S. defensive torpedo system. As devised by H. L. Abbot. ₁New York:₁ Battalion Press, 1876–77. 2 p.l., ii, 93 l., 2 pl. 8°. (Part 2.) **VXV**
Proof ed. At head of title: Confidential.

169. The **Admiralty** torpedo school. (Engineer, London, v. 42, 1876, p. 446.) **VA**
Brief note.

170. Barnaby, N. On ships of war. illus. (Institution of Naval Architects, Transactions, London, v. 17, 1876, p. 1–12.) **VXA**
Defence against torpedoes, p. 3–5.

171. Bradford, Royal Bird. Suggestions on torpedo outfits of the vessels of the navy. Report on the torpedo fittings of the U. S. S. Intrepid. Washington: Gov. Prtg. Off., 1876. 21 p., 4 pl. 8°. (United States. — Ordnance Office. Navy Department.) **VXM p.v.2, no. 3**

172. Circuit closers. illus. (Engineering, London, v. 21, 1876, p. 96–98, 153, 184–185, 224–225, 404–406, 475–477, 549–550.) **VDA**

173. Fish torpedoes. (Engineer, London, v. 42, 1876, p. 289.) **VA**
Brief note.

174. Locomotive torpedoes. (Engineer, London, v. 42, 1876, p. 259.) **VA**

175. Notes on torpedoes: charge cases. illus. (Engineering, London, v. 22, 1876, p. 67–68.) **VDA**

176. The **Oberon** experiments. illus. (Engineer, London, v. 42, 1876, p. 14–15.) **VA**

177. Offensive torpedo warfare. (Engineer, London, v. 42, 1876, p. 11.) **VA**
Notes on the Harvey, Spar and Whitehead torpedoes.

178. Recent trial of the Lay torpedo. illus. (Scientific American supplement, v. 1, 1876, p. 337.) **VA**

179. Signalling and firing apparatus ₁for torpedoes₁. illus. (Engineering, London, v. 22, 1876, p. 303–304, 306.) **VDA**

180. Torpedo accidents ₁at Woolwich and Portsmouth₁. (Engineer, London, v. 41, 1876, p. 472, 484.) **VA**

181. Torpedo steam launches. (Engineering, London, v. 19, 1875, p. 165–166, 366–368; v. 20, 1875, p. 236.) **VDA**
For the Swedish, Danish and Austro-Hungarian governments.

182. ₁**Torpedoes** for defence of harbors.₁ illus. (Engineering, London, v. 22, 1876, p. 459–460, 534–535.) **VDA**

183. Torpedoes at the International Exhibition. Philadelphia. (Engineering, London, v. 23, 1877, p. 54–55.) **VDA**

184. Torpedoes at the ₁International₁ Exhibition, Philadelphia. (Scientific American supplement, New York, v. 1, 1876, p. 388; v. 2, 1876, p. 479.) **VA**

1877

185. Abel's mechanical primer. (Engineering, London, v. 24, 1877, p. 83–84.) **VDA**

186. Alliman, A. L. Torpedoes and torpedo warfare. (Engineer, London, v. 44, 1877, p. 367.) **VA**
Brief of lecture delivered before Kings College Engineering Society. Notes on David Bushnell, Robert Fulton, and Samuel Colt.

187. Allison, R. Torpedoes. (Engineer, London, v. 43, 1877, p. 446.) **VA**
Note on the torpedo invented by the author and Capt. C. J. Norton.

188. Basarow, A. Vorlesungsversuch über Torpedos. (Deutsche chemische Gesellschaft, Berichte, Berlin, Jahrg. 10, 1877, p. 25–26.) **PKA**

189. Capt. McEvoy's spar torpedoes. (Engineer, London, v. 43, 1877, p. 340.) **VA**

1877, continued.

190. Donaldson, John. The Thornycroft torpedo-vessels; their construction, armament, etc., and the results of certain experiments that have been made with them. (Royal United Service Institution, Journal, London, v. 21, 1877, p. 611–632.)   **VXA**
Notes on torpedoes and their use during the Civil war.

191. The **Early** history of torpedoes. (Royal Society of Arts, Journal, London, v. 25, 1877, p. 881–882.)   **VA**

192. Electric batteries for torpedoes. illus. (Engineering, London, v. 24, 1877, p. 161–162.)   **VDA**

193. Electric fuses, jointers, signalling, etc., for torpedoes. illus. (Engineering, London, v. 24, 1877, p. 219–220.)   **VDA**

194. Electro-contact torpedoes. illus. (Engineering, London, v. 23, 1877, p. 157–158.)   **VDA**

195. Electro-mechanical torpedoes. illus. (Engineering, London, v. 23, 1877, p. 214–215, 455–456.)   **VDA**
With illustration, p. 216.

196. The **English** torpedo system. (Army and navy journal, New York, v. 14, 1877, p. 646–647.)   †† **VWA**

197. Ferris, John. Notes on the removal of the hull of the ship "Forest" by extempore torpedoes. illus. (Royal United Service Institution, Journal, London, v. 21, 1877, p. 1133–1134.)   **VWA**

198. Gakuma, G. Torpedoes. (Scientific American, New York, new series, v. 36, 1877, p. 337.)   **VA**

199. Gun, ram and torpedo. (Army and navy journal, New York, v. 14, 1877, p. 834.)   †† **VWA**

200. Manufacture of the Harvey torpedo. illus. (Scientific American, New York, new series, v. 36, p. 402.)   **VA**

201. Mechanical torpedoes. (Engineering, London, v. 23, 1877, p. 406–408, 456.)   **VDA**
Mathieson's, McEvoy's, and Singer's torpedoes.

202. Moisson. Des explosions au sein de l'eau. (Revue maritime et coloniale, Paris, v. 52, 1877, p. 744–770; v. 53, 1877, p. 86–120.)   **VXA**
Abridged in Institution of Civil Engineers, *Minutes of proceedings*, London, v. 50, 1876–77, p. 299–300, *VDA*.
Explosions under water with reference to torpedoes.

203. The **Moveable** torpedo and the European war. (Army and navy journal, New York, v. 14, 1877, p. 672–673.)   †† **VWA**

204. Pott, Constantin. Die Entwicklung des Seeminen- und Torpedowesens, und dessen gegenwärtiger Stand in den ver-schiedenen Staaten. (Mitteilungen aus dem Gebiete des Seewesens, Pola, Bd. 5, 1877, p. 426–435.)   **VXA**

205. Protection of ships from torpedoes. (Engineer, London, v. 44, 1877, p. 117, 150.)   **VA**

206. Russian torpedoes. (Engineering, London, v. 24, 1877, p. 19.)   **VDA**

207. Scott, Michael. On improved ships of war and their defence against torpedoes. (Institution of Naval Architects, Transactions, London, v. 18, 1877, p. 37–49.)   **VXA**
Notes on effect of exploding torpedoes.

208. The **Steam** launch and the torpedo. (Army and navy journal, New York. v. 14, 1877, p. 688–689.)   †† **VWA**

209. Stone, Charles A. A general description of the ordnance and torpedo outfit of the U. S. S. "Trenton." (United States Naval Institute, Proceedings, Annapolis, v. 3, 1877, p. 89–93.)   **VXA**

210. Torpedo armament of various wars. (Royal United Service Institution, Journal, London, v. 21, 1877, p. 1137–1144.)   **VWA**

211. Torpedo boats. (Engineer, London, v. 44, 1877, p. 419–420.)   **VA**
Notes on torpedoes, p. 420.

212. Torpedo defence. (Army and navy journal, New York, v. 15, 1877, p. 201, 267.)   †† **VWA**
Editorials.

213. Torpedo defence. illus. (Engineering, London, v. 24, 1877, p. 279–280.)   **VDA**

214. Torpedo experiment in Germany. (Engineer, London, v. 44, 1877, p. 88.)   **VA**
Brief note.

215. Torpedo launch warfare. illus. (Scientific American, New York, new series, v. 36, 1877, p. 239, 246.)   **VA**

216. Torpedo launches. illus. (Engineering, London, v. 23, 1877, p. 428–429, 448–450.)   **VDA**
Also printed in *Van Nostrand's engineering magazine*, New York, v. 17, 1877, p. 125–128, *VDA*.

217. Torpedo range at the Royal arsenal canal. (Engineer, London, v. 43, 1877, p. 411.)   **VA**

218. Torpedo warfare. (Illustrated London news, v. 70, 1877, p. 556–558.)   ✱**DA**
Note on the "Alarm" designed by Admiral David Porter, U. S. N. Whitehead torpedo. Illustration of torpedo vessel used by the Russians on the Danube river; American torpedo-vessel Alarm.

219. Torpedo warfare. (Illustrated London news, London, v. 71, 1877, p. 227–229.)   ✱**DA**
Illustrations: Suspension torpedoes in a rapid river; Punshon's floating torpedo; Turkish self-acting torpedo; Towing of Harvey's torpedo against an enemy; Hall Macdonald rocket; and Outrigger torpedo.

1877, continued.

220. Torpedo warfare. illus. (Scientific American, New York, new series, v. 37, 1877, p. 39–40.) **VA**

221. Torpedoes at sea. (Engineer, London, v. 43, 1877, p. 184.) **VA**

222. Torpedoes in Turkey. (Engineer, London, v. 44, 1877, p. 105.) **VA**

223. Torpedoes in the United States. (Engineer, London, v. 43, 1877, p. 4.) **VA**

224. Die **Torpedos** im russisch-türkischen Kriege. (Mittheilungen aus dem Gebiete des Seewesens, Pola, Bd. 5, 1877, p. 365–371, 460, 508–510, 579; Bd. 6, 1878, p. 22–27, 116–117, 284–285.) **VXA**

225. Ueber Torpedoboote und Torpedos. (Mittheilungen aus dem Gebiete des Seewesens, Pola, Bd. 5, 1877, p. 474–478.) **VXA**

226. The **United States** torpedo steamer Alarm. illus. (Scientific American, New York, new series, v. 36, 1877, p. 159, 162.) **VA**

1878

227. Chardonneau, F. Des torpilles russes sur le Danube, à Soulina et à Batoum. (Revue maritime et coloniale, Paris, tome 57, 1878, p. 156–171; tome 59, 1878, p. 75–101.) **VXA**
Also printed in the *Journal* of the Royal United Service Institution, London, v. 22, 1879, p. 735–745, 1049–1065, *VWA.*

228. Harvey's improved torpedoes. illus. (Scientific American supplement, New York, v. 5, 1876, p. 1792.) **VA**
Abstracted from *Engineering.*

229. Modern torpedo warfare. illus. (Scientific American, New York, new series, v. 38, 1878, p. 82.) **VA**

230. A **"Momentum"** torpedo. (Scientific American, New York, new series, v. 38, p. 49.) **VA**
Invention of Commodore John A. Howell, U. S. N.

230a. R., L. Le bateau-torpille Yarrow. illus. (La nature, Paris, année 6, semestre 1, 1878, p. 412–414.) **OA**

231. Recent torpedo experiments. (Scientific American supplement, New York, v. 6, 1878, p. 2252.) **VA**

232. Recent torpedo experiments in England. illus. (Scientific American supplement, New York, v. 5, 1878, p. 1908.) **VA**

233. Russian torpedo boats. illus. (Scientific American, New York, new series, v. 38, p. 338.) **VA**
Brief description, well illustrated.

234. Spar torpedoes. (Engineering, London, v. 25, 1878, p. 14–15, 16, 127–128, 130, 208–209.) **VDA**

235. Der **Spieren-Torpedo** McEvoy. (Mittheilungen aus dem Gebiete des Seewesens, Pola, Bd. 6, 1878, p. 131–133.) **VXA**

236. Steel torpedo boats. (Scientific American supplement, New York, v. 5, 1878, p. 1837–1838.) **VA**
From *Iron.*

237. The **Telephone** and the torpedo. (Royal Society of Arts, Journal, London, v. 26, 1878, p. 887–888.) **VA**

238. Telephonic torpedoes. (Army and navy journal, New York, v. 16, 1878, p. 87) **†† VWA**
Invention of Capt. C. A. McEvoy.

239. Torpedo attack and defence. (Engineer, London, v. 45, 1878, p. 239–240.) **VA**

240. Torpedo operations in the Black sea. (Army and navy journal, New York, v. 16, 1878, p. 271.) **†† VWA**

241. The **Whitehead** torpedo. illus. (Scientific American, New York, new series, v. 39, 1878, p. 9.) **VA**

1879

242. Alliman, A. L. Torpedoes and torpedo-launches. (Engineer, London, v. 47, 1879, p. 80.) **VA**
Note on address before the King's College Engineering Society, Jan. 24, 1879.

243. Blake, Homer C. Torpedoes. (New York Evening Post, March 17, 1879.) ***A**
Abstracted in *Army and navy journal,* New York, v. 16, 1879, p. 593–594, †† *VWA.*

244. Brossard de Corbigny. Du rôle de l'électricité dans les défenses sous-marines. illus. (La lumière électrique, Paris, tome 1, 1879, p. 89–91, 128–131, 185–187; tome 2, 1880, p. 25–28, 45–46.) **VGA**

245. Chabaud-Arnault, Charles. De l'emploi des torpilles comme arme des canots à vapeur contre les bâtiments. (Revue maritime et coloniale, Paris, tome 62, 1879, p. 5–28.) **VXA**
Also printed in *Proceedings* of the United States Naval Institute, v. 6, 1880, p. 79–98, *VXA; Journal* of the Royal United Service Institution, London, v. 23, 1879, p. 1038–1055, *VWA;* and in *Van Nostrand's engineering magazine,* New York, v. 24, 1881, p. 180–193, *VDA.*

246. An **Electric** torpedo balloon. (Army and navy journal, New York, v. 17, 1879, p. 382.) **†† VWA**
Invention of Frank Peppard.

1879, continued.

247. Ericsson's aggressive torpedoes. (Army and navy journal, New York. v. 17, 1879, p. 162–164.)   †† **VWA**
Also printed in Institution of Civil Engineers, *Minutes of proceedings*, v. 59, 1879, p. 425–426, *VDA.* Abstracted in *Engineer*, London, v. 48, 1879, p. 286. *VA.*
Notes on the invention of Capt. John Ericsson.

248. Experiments on torpedo explosions. (In: United States. — Engineer Department. Annual report of the chief of engineers, 1879. Washington, 1879. 8°. 1879, part 1, p. 35–38.)   **VDDA**
Abstracted in Institution of Civil Engineers, *Minutes of proceedings*, London, v. 64, 1881, p. 449–450, *VDA.*

249. The **Herreshoff** torpedo launch. illus. (Scientific American, New York, new series, v. 40, p. 210.)   **VA**

250. Lancirversuche mit Whiteheadtorpedos in England. (Mittheilungen aus dem Gebiete des Seewesens, Pola, Bd. 7, 1879, p. 243.)   **VXA**

251. The **Lay** torpedo. (Scientific American, New York, new series, v. 41, p. 249.)   **VA**

252. The **Most** recent torpedo boats and their influence on marine architecture. (The Builder, London, v. 37, 1879, p. 106.)   † **MQA**

253. New French torpedo boats. (Scientific American supplement, New York, v. 8, 1879, p. 3034.)   **VA**

254. New torpedo experiments by Capt. Ericsson. illus. (Scientific American, New York, new series, v. 41, 1879, p. 257.)

255. Reactions-Offensiv-Torpedo. (Mittheilungen aus dem Gebiete des Seewesens, Pola, Bd. 7, p. 48–50.)   **VXA**

256. Real órden de 19 de abril de 1879, aclarando la intervención que en el servicio de torpedos corresponde á la marina, artillería é ingenieros. (Memorial de ingenieros, Madrid, tomo 34, parte oficial, 1879, p. 69–70.)   **VWA**

257. Torpedo ram "Polyphemus." (Scientific American supplement, v. 8, 1879, p. 3051; v. 12, 1881, p. 4631, 4727.)   **VA**

258. Torpedo warfare.   (Engineering, London, v. 27, 1879, p. 156–157.)   **VDA**

259. Torpedo work in the United States. (Engineer, London, v. 48, 1879, p. 340.) **VA**
Editorial.

260. Weeks torpedoes. (Army and navy journal, New York, v. 16, 1879, p. 515.) †† **VWA**
Invention of Asa Weeks.

261. Zur Torpedoboot-Taktik. (Mittheilungen aus dem Gebiete des Seewesens, Pola, Bd. 7, 1879, p. 217–224.)   **VXA**
Translated in *Journal*, Royal United Service Institution, London, v. 24, 1881, p. 112–118, *VWA.*
On torpedo-boat tactics.

1880

262. Ardois y Casaus, Federico. Fragata "Sagunto." Ligeras consideraciones sobre la defensa de este buque contra los botes-torpedos y torpedos auto-móviles. (Revista general de marina, Madrid, tomo 7, 1880, p. 897–905.)   **VXA**

263. Barber, F. M.   The progress of torpedo warfare. (United Service, Philadelphia, v. 3, 1880, p. 278–298.)   **VWA**

264. The **Camera** and the torpedo. (Photographic news, London, v. 24, 1880, p. 197.)   **MFA**

265. Diaz, Manuel.   Los torpedos en los buques. (Revista general de marina, Madrid, tomo 6, 1880, p. 767–783; tomo 7, 1880, p. 17–29.)   **VXA**

266. Fremantle, Edmund R. Naval tactics on the open sea with the existing types of vessels and weapons. (United service, Philadelphia, v. 3, 1880, p. 77–124, 187–202.)   **VWA**
Notes on the use and power of the torpedo.

267. Krummholz, E. Vertheidigung einer Flotte gegen Torpedoboots-Angriffe. (Mittheilungen aus dem Gebiete des Seewesens, Pola, Bd. 8, 1880, p. 241–252.) **VXA**

268. The **Lay** torpedo. illus. (Engineer, London, v. 49, 1880, p. 243–244.)   **VA**
Invention of John Lewis Lay, an American engineer.

269. Der **Lay'sche** Torpedo auf der Schelde. (Mittheilungen aus dem Gebiete des Seewesens, Pola, Bd. 8, 1880, p. 179–180.)   **VXA**

270. Montojo, Antonio. Experiencia del bote-torpedo "Lay." (Revista general de marina, Madrid, tomo 6, 1880, p. 687–692.)   **VXA**

271. Peruvian torpedo practice. (Nautical gazette, New York, v. 13, 1880, p. 154.)   **VXA**

272. R. Breves consideraciones sobre torpedos ofensivos. (Revista general de marina, Madrid, tomo 7, 1880, p. 261–265.)   **VXA**

273. —— Noticias interesantes referentes al estudio de los torpedos. (Revista general de marina, Madrid, tomo 6, 1880, p. 237–242.)   **VXA**

274. —— Torpedo Lay. (Revista general de marina, Madrid, tomo 6, 1880, p. 676–686.)   **VXA**

1880, continued.

275. Sims new submarine torpedo. (Nautical gazette, New York, v. 13, 1880, p. 150.)
VXA

276. Stschensnowitsch. Ueber die Verwendung der Torpedowaffe auf Torpedobooten und Schlachtschiffen. (Mittheilungen aus dem Gebiete des Seewesens, Pola, Bd. 8, 1880, p. 201–219.) **VXA**

277. Thornycroft, John Isaac. On torpedo boats and light yachts for high speed steam navigation. (Institution of Civil Engineers, Minutes of proceedings, London, v. 66, 1880, p. 87–178.) **VDA**
Gives valuable notes on torpedoes.

278. Torpedo-boat progress in 1879. (Iron, London, v. 15, 1880, p. 19–20.)
3 – † VA

279. Torpedo investigations. (Scientific American, New York, new series, v. 42, 1880, p. 74.) **VA**

280. Torpedo warfare at Portsmouth. (Marine engineer, London, v. 1, 1880, p. 149.) **VXA**
A series of experiments.

281. Towing and discharging torpedoes from torpedo boats. illus. (Engineer, London, v. 50, 1880, p. 477.) **VA**

1881

282. Abbot, Henry Larcom. Report upon experiments and investigations to develop a system of submarine mines for defending the harbors of the United States. Washington: Gov. Prtg. Off., 1881. 444 p., 19 diagr., 7 pl. 4°. (United States.— Engineer Department. Professional paper 23.) **†† VWI**

283. Donaldson, John. The further developments of the Thornycroft torpedo vessels. illus. (Royal United Service Institution, Journal, London, v. 25, 1881, p. 387–411.) **VWA**

284. The **Ericsson** "Destroyer." (Marine engineer, London, v. 3, 1881, p. 16–17.)
VXA
Notes on the work of David Bushnell, Robert Fulton, Samuel Colt, W. B. Cushing, and John Ericsson.

285. Ericsson's torpedo system. (Engineering, London, v. 32, 1881, p. 331–332.)
VDA
From *American machinist*, New York, v. 4, Sept. 24, 1881.
Reviewed by William W. Kimball in United States Naval Institute, *Proceedings*, Annapolis, v. 7, 1881, p. 339–341, *VXA.*

286. The **Lay-Haight** torpedo. (Army and navy journal, New York, v. 18, 1881, p. 1009, 1074; v. 26, 1889, p. 1020.) **†† VWA**

287. Pietruski, M. von. Improvisierte Torpedos und improvisierte Schutzmittel zur Abwehr von Torpedoangriffen. (Mittheilungen aus dem Gebiete des Seewesens, Pola, Bd. 9, 1881, p. 325–349.) **VXA**

288. Ein Raketentorpedo. (Mittheilungen aus dem Gebiete des Seewesens, Pola, Bd. 9, 1881, p. 628–629.) **VXA**

289. A Rocket torpedo. (Scientific American, New York, new series, v. 45, 1881, p. 131.) **VA**

290. Scandinavian experiments with submarine mines. (United States Naval Institute, Proceedings, Annapolis, v. 7, 1881, p. 121–154.) **VXA**
Translated from the Danish by Lieut. W. H. Beehler, U. S. N.

291. Scheidnagel, Leopoldo. Desarrollo de los principios físicos ó sean las bases, en que se ha fundado la combinación de los elementos, que constituyen el material orgánico reglamentario, para una línea defensiva de minas hidráulicas segun la propuesta descrita en el capítulo VII de la obra Minas hidráulicas defensivas. Madrid: Imprenta del Memorial de ingenieros, 1881. 38 p., 1 diagr. 4°. (Memorial de ingenieros, Madrid, anno 36, 1881, parte 1.) **VWA**

292. Torpedo accident at Newport, R. I. (Army and navy journal, New York, v. 19, 1881, p. 99, 101, 119.) **†† VWA**

293. Torpedo accidents at Hobson's Bay. (Engineering, London, v. 31, 1881, p. 434–435, 486–487.) **VDA**

294. Torpedo apparatus exhibition. (Telegraphic journal and electrical review, London, v. 9, 1881, p. 448.) **VGA**

295. The **Torpedo** boat Destroyer. (Scientific American, New York, new series, v. 45, 1881, p. 353.) **VA**
First public exhibition of Capt. Ericsson's "Destroyer."

296. Towing and discharging torpedoes from torpedo boats. (Scientific American supplement, New York, v. 11, 1881, p. 4298.) **VA**

1882

297. Bradford, Royal Bird. History of torpedo warfare. Newport, R. I., 1882. 90 p. 8°. **VXV**

298. —— Notes on movable torpedoes. Newport, R. I., 1882. 178 p. 8°. **VXV**

299. —— Notes on the spar torpedo. Newport, R. I., 1882. 98 p. 8°. **VXV**

300. —— Notes on towing torpedoes. Newport, R. I., 1882. 43 p. 8°. **VXV**

1882, continued.

301. Brennan's torpedo. (Engineer, London, v. 54, 1882, p. 26.)   **VA**

Abstracted in *Army and navy journal*, New York, v. 20, 1882, p. 61, †† *VWA*.
Notes new devices for steering.

302. Converse, George Albert. Electrical fuses. Theory, materials, construction, measurement, circuits, etc. [Lectures supplementary to "Notes on torpedo fuses" by Lieut. G. A. Converse, 1875.] [Newport, R. I.? 1882?] 65 p. 8°.   *** C p.v.1489, no.1**

303. A Curious torpedo. (Scientific American, New York, new series, v. 47, 1882, p. 97.)   **VA**

304. Défense des côtes au moyen des torpilles. illus. (Le Génie civil, tome 2, 1882, p. 521.)   **VA**

305. Holmes torpedo finder. illus. (Engineering, London, v. 33, 1882, p. 343.)   **VDA**

With illustration on p. 357.

306. The Lay torpedo. (Engineering, London, v. 34, 1882, p. 630.)   **VDA**

307. The Lay torpedo. (Scientific American, New York, new series, v. 47, 1882, p. 5.)   **VA**

308. Moors, H. The sea-cell as a possible source of danger in torpedo experiments. (Royal Society of Victoria, Transactions, Melbourne, v. 18, 1882, p. 71–81.)   *** EC**

Abstracted in Institution of Civil Engineers, *Minutes of proceedings*, London, v. 71, 1882, p. 521–522, *VDA*.

309. Torpedo boat for the Italian government. illus. (Scientific American, New York, new series, v. 46, 1882, p. 330.)   **VA**

310. Torpedo warfare. illus. (Scientific American supplement, New York, v. 14, 1882, p. 5659–5660.)   **VA**

From the *Engineer*.
Notes on mines.

311. Towing and discharging torpedoes. illus. (Scientific American supplement, New York, v. 13, 1882, p. 5177–5178.)   **VA**

Historical notes on the torpedo and submarine.

1883

312. Discharging torpedoes. (Engineer, London, v. 53, 1883, p. 291.)   **VA**

313. Earth torpedoes. (Army and navy journal, New York, v. 21, 1883, p. 321.)
†† **VWA**

314. English torpedo experiments. (Scientific American, New York, v. 49, 1883, p. 67.)   **VA**

315. Firing torpedoes. (Scientific American, New York, v. 48, 1883, p. 327.)   **VA**

Brief note.

316. Graydon's torpedo system. (Army and navy journal, New York, v. 20, 1883, p. 906.)   †† **VWA**

Invention of Lieut. J. A. Graydon, U. S. N.

317. Guerout, Aug. Le système de torpilles du capitaine MacEvoy. illus. (La lumière électrique, Paris, tome 9, 1883, p. 202–204.)   **VGA**

318. The Lay torpedo. (Scientific American, New York, v. 48, 1883, p. 50.)   **VA**

319. Locomotive torpedoes. (Army and navy journal, New York, v. 20, 1883, p. 1017–1018.)   †† **VWA**

320. McEvoy's torpedo system. (Engineering, London, v. 35, 1883, p. 433–434.)
VDA

Also published in *Scientific American supplement*, v. 15, 1883, p. 6215, *VA*.

321. Noel, G. H. On certain points of importance in the construction of ships of war. (Institution of Naval Architects, Transactions, London, v. 24, 1883, p. 1–20.)
VXA

Torpedo defence, p. 8–10.

322. On sea-going torpedo boats. (Scientific American, New York, v. 48, 1883, p. 261.)   **VA**

Abstract of paper read before the Institution of Naval Architects by J. A. Normand.

323. Richard, Gustave. Application de l'électricité à la direction des torpilles offensives. illus. (La lumière électrique, Paris, tome 10, 1883, p. 22–24, 41–45, 74–78, 113–116.)   **VGA**

324. Sleeman, C. The Lay and other locomotive torpedoes considered for the purpose of coast defence, and also as the armament of ships, torpedo and submarine boats. (Royal United Service Institution, Journal, London, v. 27, 1883, p. 39–71.)
VWA

Abstracted in *Army and navy journal*, New York, v. 20, 1883, p. 1017–1018, †† *VWA*.
Description of the Lay, Ericsson, Brennan and Whitehead torpedoes.

325. Torpedo boats. illus. (Scientific American supplement, New York, v. 15, 1883, p. 6139.)   **VA**

From *L'Illustration*.
Notes on torpedoes in the French navy.

326. Torpedo boats in collision. (Scientific American, New York, v. 48, 1883, p. 243.)   **VA**

327. Whitehead and American torpedoes. (Army and navy journal, New York, v. 20, 1883, p. 635.)   †† **VWA**

1884

328. Automatic torpedoes. (Scientific American, New York, v. 51, 1884, p. 272.)
VA

Invention of George E. Haight of Hartford, Conn.

1884, continued.

329. Canet's apparatus for launching torpedoes. illus. (Engineering, London, v. 37, 1884, p. 230–231.) **VDA**

330. Chabaud-Arnault, Charles. Les torpilles à bord des navires et des embarcations de combat. (Revue maritime et coloniale, Paris, tome 82, 1884, p. 269–329.) **VXA**

Translated by Commander William Bainbridge Hoff in *Army and navy quarterly*, New York, v. 1, 1885, p. 91–117, *VXA.*

331. An **Electric** torpedo boat. (Scientific American, New York, v. 51, 1884, p. 100, 163.) **VA**

Invention of Professor J. H. L. Tuck.

332. Heinz, Julius. Die Bewegungsverhältnisse des Fischtorpedos. (Mittheilungen aus dem Gebiete des Seewesens, Pola, Bd. 12, 1884, p. 585–614.) **VXA**

333. Improved torpedo boat. illus. (Scientific American, New York, v. 50, 1884, p. 242.) **VA**

334. Improved torpedo launching apparatus. illus. (Scientific American supplement, New York, v. 17, 1884, p. 6991.) **VA**

335. Kingsford, H. Electrical grapnel for submarine cables and torpedo lines. illus. (Scientific American supplement, New York, v. 17, 1884, p. 6859.) **VA**

336. Our naval torpedo service. (Scientific American, New York, v. 51, 1884, p. 416.) **VA**

Notes on the work of Admiral T. O. Selfridge, U. S. N.

337. The **Pneumatic** dynamite gun for torpedo launches. illus. (Scientific American supplement, New York, v. 18, 1884, p. 7113–7114.) **VA**

338. Richard, Gustave. Le torpilleur de Nordenfelt et le gouvernail de M. Pugibet. illus. (La lumière électrique, Paris, tome 13, 1884, p. 249–250.) **VGA**

339. —— Les torpilleurs automobiles de Lay et de Williams. illus. (La lumière électrique, Paris, tome 14, 1884, p. 443–449.) **VGA**

340. Torpedo boat guns. (Scientific American, New York, v. 17, 1884, p. 6826–6828.) **VA**

Description of the Hotchkiss gun.

341. Torpedo boats. (Scientific American supplement, New York, v. 18, 1884, p. 7083.) **VA**

Brief historical review.

342. ₁**Torpedo** boats for the Danish and Russian governments.₁ illus. (Scientific American supplement, New York, v. 17, 1884, p. 6764–6765.) **VA**

343. Torpedo equipment of the British navy. (Engineer, London, v. 58, 1884, p. 482.) **VA**

344. Torpedo experiments in China. (Marine engineer, London, v. 6, 1885, p. 252.) **VA**

Experiments made by Capt. F. Harvey at Nankin.

345. Torpedoes for defence and attack. illus. (Engineering, London, v. 38, 1884, p. 364, 369–370.) **VDA**

Notes on J. S. Williams' plan.

346. Torpedoes and torpedo boats. (Marine engineer, London, v. 6, 1884, p. 201–203.) **VXA**

See also notes on p. 1, 196.

347. Das **Torpedowesen** in der deutschen Marine in seiner organisatorischen und materiellen Entwickelung. Berlin: E. S. Mittler u. Sohn, 1884. 16 p. 8°.
VXM p.v. 4, no. 6

348. Williams' system of coast defense by electrical torpedoes. illus. (Scientific American supplement, New York, v. 18, 1884, p. 7451–7452.) **VA**

For note on this invention see *Army and navy journal*, New York, v. 22, 1884, p. 272, †† *VWA.*

349. Yarrow, A. F. Torpedo boats having special reference to those built by Messrs. Yarrow & Co. (Royal United Service Institution, Journal, London, v. 28, 1884, p. 603–628.) **VWA**

1885

350. Accident causé par une torpille. (Cosmos, Paris, nouv. série, tome 2, 1885, p. 449.) **VA**

351. Aerial torpedoes. (Engineering, London, v. 39, 1885, p. 657–658.) **VDA**

Abstract of address by F. Gower before the Royal United Service Institution.

352. Autobiography of a Whitehead torpedo. illus. (Engineering, London, v. 39, 1885, p. 127–128, 155–157, 177–181, 205–206, 233–236, 257–260, 279–281, 306–307, 333–334, 383–385, 414–415, 521.) **VDA**

A very complete series of articles.

353. Bailly, B. La torpille intelligente, système Berdan. illus. (Cosmos, Paris, nouv. série, tome 2, 1885, p. 344–346.) **VA**

Protected by net.

354. Bateau-torpilleur sous-marin, système Goubet. illus. (Le génie civil, tome 8, 1885, p. 130–132.) **VA**

355. Beantwortung der von Vice-Admiral Hornby gestellten Fragen über Minen und Drahttaubarricaden. (Mittheilungen aus dem Gebiete des Seewesens, Pola, Bd. 13, 1885, p. 686–690.) **VXA**

1885, continued.

356. The **Berdan** torpedo. illus. (Army and navy journal, New York, v. 23, 1885, p. 128, 415–416; v. 24, 1887, p. 860; v. 25, 1888, p. 976.) †† **VWA**
Invention of General H. Berdan.

357. The **Berdan** twin torpedo. illus. (Scientific American, New York, v. 53, 1885, p. 192, 196.) **VA**
Notes on attack on ships protected by netting.

358. Bertrand. Exposition de l'école des torpilles. (La lumière électrique, Paris, tome 16, 1885, p. 365–366.) **VGA**
Account of the exhibits at the International Electrical Exposition, Philadelphia, 1884.

359. The **Brennan** torpedo. (Engineering, London, v. 39, 1885, p. 612.) **VDA**
Brief note.

360. British experimental evolutions with torpedoes and war ships. illus. (Scientific American supplement, New York, v. 20, 1885, p. 8008–8009.) **VA**
Use of torpedo nets.

361. Chabaud-Arnault, Charles. Die Verwendung der Torpedos an Bord der zur Schlachtflotte gehörigen Schiffe und Boote. (Mittheilungen aus dem Gebiete des Seewesens, Pola, Bd. 13, 1885, p. 69–113.) **VXA**
Translated from *Revue maritime et coloniale.*

362. The **Defense** of ports by means of electric torpedoes. illus. (Scientific American supplement, New York, v. 19, 1885, p. 7655–7656.) **VA**
From *La Lumière électrique.*

363. Encore une nouvelle torpille. (Cosmos, Paris, nouv. série, tome 1, 1885, p. 596–597.) **VA**

364. The **French** dispatch torpedo boat "La Bombe." illus. (Scientific American, New York, v. 53, 1885, p. 103.) **VA**

365. Gallwey, E. P. The use of torpedoes in war. illus. (Royal United Service Institution, Journal, London, v. 29, 1885, p. 471–496.) **VWA**
Abstracted in *Scientific American supplement,* v. 21, 1886, no. 536, p. 8554–8556, *VA,* and *Engineering,* London, v. 39, 1885, p. 268–270, *VDA.*

366. La **Guerre** aux torpilleurs. (Cosmos, Paris, nouv. série, tome 2, 1885, p. 338.) **VA**

367. Hayes, M. P. Torpedoes and torpedo boats considered as a sole means of defense for seaboard cities. (Scientific American supplement, New York, v. 20, 1885, p. 8010.) **VA**

368. Hobart-Hampden, Augustus Charles. The torpedo scare. illus. (Blackwood's magazine, Edinburgh, v. 137, 1885, p. 737–747.) *** DA**
Abstracted in *Army and navy journal,* New York, v. 22, 1885, p. 979–980, †† *VWA.*

369. Hogane, J. T. A torpedo reminiscence. (Scientific American, New York, v. 52, 1885, p. 357.) **VA**
Use in the Confederate navy.

370. Howell torpedo. (Army and navy journal, New York, v. 23, 1885, p. 68, 396; v. 26, 1889, p. 391, 532; v. 29, 1891–92, p. 205, 296, 313, 341; v. 34, 1896, p. 160, 207.) †† **VWA**
Brief notes.

371. Illustration of new "Berdan" torpedo. (Graphic, London, v. 32, 1885, p. 288.) *** DA**

372. Lartige, de. Nos torpilles dans les mers de Chine. illus. (Cosmos, Paris, nouv. série, tome 1, 1885, p. 150–152.) **VA**

373. Machine guns for repelling torpedo attacks. illus. (Engineering, London, v. 39, 1885, p. 281–284.) **VDA**

374. Nets versus torpedoes. (Scientific American, New York, v. 53, 1885, p. 181.) **VA**

375. New English fleet of torpedo boats. (Scientific American, New York, v. 52, 1885, p. 373; v. 53, 1885, p. 212.) **VA**

376. A **New** torpedo. (Engineering news, New York, v. 14, 1885, p. 244.) **VDA**
Invention of General Berdan.

377. Normand, J. A. Étude sur les torpilleurs. Paris: Gauthier-Villars, 1885. 28 p. 4°. **VXV**

378. Nos torpilleurs. (Cosmos, Paris, nouv. série, tome 1, 1885, p. 624.) **VA**

379. A **Novel** torpedo boat, "David Bushnell." (Scientific American, New York, v. 53, 1885, p. 341.) **VA**

380. Paulson's self propelling and steering torpedo. illus. (Scientific American supplement, New York, v. 19, 1885, p. 7673–7674.) **VA**
Invention of Richard Paulson.

381. R. Paulson's self-propelling torpedoes. illus. (Engineering, London, v. 39, 1885, p. 145, 169.) **VDA**

382. Sleeman, C. Torpedo-boat warfare. (Army and navy quarterly, New York, v. 1, 1885, p. 237–252, 284–300.) **VXA**

383. Sogenannte Tagesfragen. Erwiderung auf einen Artikel der Revue des deux mondes "Torpilleurs et canonnières" von einem Seeofficier. Braunschweig: Goeritz und zu Putlitz, 1885. 42 p. 8°. **VXM p.v.4, no.4**

384. Soulages, C. C. La défense des ports au moyen de torpilles électriques. (La lumière électrique, Paris, tome 15, 1885, p. 124–126.) **VGA**
Also in *Scientific American supplement,* New York, v. 19, 1885, p. 7655–7656, *VA.*

1885, continued.

385. A **Submarine** torpedo boat. illus. (Scientific American, New York, v. 53, 1885, p. 406.) **VA**

386. **Szígyártó**, W. Automobiles Minensystem für veränderliche Niveaustände. (Mittheilungen aus dem Gebiete des Seewesens, Pola, Bd. 13, 1885, p. 113–117.) **VXA**

387. Los **Torpederos** en un combate naval. (Revista general de marina, Madrid, tomo 17, 1885, p. 419–425.) **VXA**
Translation from *Engineering*.

388. **Torpedo** boats in war. (Scientific American supplement, New York, v. 19, 1885, p. 7896.) **VA**
From *Engineering*.

389. A **Torpedo** catcher. (Engineering, London, v. 40, 1885, p. 512.) **VDA**

390. **Torpedo** observing station. illus. (Scientific American supplement, New York, v. 19, 1885, p. 7656.) **VA**
From *La nature*.

391. **Torpedo** operations at Corfu. illus. (The Graphic, London, v. 32, 1885, p. 258.) ***DA**
Illus., p. 264.

392. The **Torpedo** scare. (Engineering, London, v. 40, 1885, p. 62.) **VDA**
Editorial.
Abstracted in *Army and navy journal*, v. 23, 1885, p. 38, †† *VWA*.

393. **Torpedo** swimmers — old and new. (Scientific American, New York, v. 52, 1885, p. 304.) **VA**
Notes on David Bushnell's boat and its use in the Revolution.

394. **Torpedo** warfare. (Marine engineer, London, v. 7, 1885, p. 87–89, 118; v. 8, 1887, p. 362; v. 18, 1896, p. 112.) **VXA**
A valuable historical review of the use of the torpedo in war.

395. **Torpedoes** for the Austrian navy. (Scientific American, New York, v. 52, 1885, p. 134.) **VA**
Abstracted from *La nature*.

396. **Torpille** guidée sur un parcours de 3 milles. (Cosmos, Paris, nouv. série, tome 1, 1885, p. 509.) **VA**
Also printed in *Le génie civil*, Paris, tome 7, 1885, p. 31, *VA*.

397. **Torpille** portée. (Cosmos, Paris, nouv. série, tome 1, 1885, p. 524.) **VA**

398. Une **Torpille** terrestre. (Cosmos, Paris, nouv. série, tome 1, 1885, p. 401.) **VA**

399. **Torpilles** terrestres. (Cosmos, Paris, nouv. série, tome 1, 1885, p. 482.) **VA**

400. Un **Torpilleur** coulé. (Cosmos, Paris, nouv. série, tome 2, 1885, p. 227.) **VA**

401. Un **Torpilleur** français. (Cosmos, Paris, nouv. série, tome 1, 1885, p. 512.) **VA**

402. Le **Torpilleur** 68. (Cosmos, Paris, nouv. série, tome 1, 1885, p. 428.) **VA**

403. **Torpilleurs** et cuirassés. (Cosmos, Paris, nouv. série, tome 1, 1885, p. 339–340.) **VA**

404. **Torpilleurs** japonais. (Cosmos, Paris, nouv. série, tome 1, 1885, p. 541.) **VA**

405. **United States.** — Fortifications Board. Report of the committee...upon torpedoes, stationary and movable, and torpedo boats. Committee no. 2. Washington: Gov. Prtg. Off., 1885. 1 p.l., 5 p. f°. †† **VXC** p.v.9, no. 5

406. **Volunteer** torpedo corps. (Engineer, London, v. 59, 1885, p. 404.) **VA**

407. **Wallace** torpedo. (Army and navy journal, New York, v. 23, 1885, p. 341.) †† **VWA**
Invention of Gen. Lew Wallace.

408. The **Weeks'** rocket torpedo. (Army and navy journal, New York, v. 18, 1881, p. 1093; v. 22, 1885, p. 937.) †† **VWA**
The first article is abstracted from the Providence, R. I., *Evening Bulletin* of July 26, 1881.

1886

409. **Bourgois**, Siméon. La guerre de course. La grande guerre et les torpilles. Paris: [G. Chamerot,] 1886. 71 p. 8°. **VXV**
Repr.: La nouvelle revue, 1886.

410. **Construction** of torpedo boats. (Scientific American, New York, v. 54, 1886, p. 275.) **VA**
Illustrations showing the various steps of the construction work.

411. La **Cuestión** de los torpederos. (Revista general de marina, Madrid, tomo 19, 1886, p. 455–459.) **VXA**
Translated from *Le Yacht*.

412. **Dubassov**, T. W. Die Taktik der Torpedoboote. (Mittheilungen aus dem Gebiete des Seewesens, Pola, Bd. 14, 1886, p. 65–89.) **VXA**
Also in *Revista general de marina*, Madrid, tomo 18, 1886, p. 407–423, *VXA*.

413. **French** naval maneuvers. illus. (Scientific American, New York, v. 55, 1886, p. 150.) **VA**
Notes on anchoring torpedoes.

414. **French** torpedo boat experiments. (Engineer, London, v. 61, 1886, p. 213.) **VA**
Brief notes on torpedo experiments.

415. **French** torpedo experiments. (Scientific American, New York, v. 54, 1886, p. 209.) **VA**

1886, continued.

416. Hall's fish torpedo. (Army and navy journal, New York, v. 23, 1886, p. 899.)
†† **VWA**
Invention of Lieut. Martin E. Hall.

417. Harris, Robert Hastings. The change in the conditions of marine warfare owing to the introduction of the ram, the torpedo, and the submarine mine, etc. illus. (United Service Institution, Journal, London, v. 30, 1886, p. 419–499.) **VWA**

418. Jaques, William Henry. Paper on naval torpedo warfare. Prepared for the use of the select committee of the United States Senate on Ordnance and War Ships. With papers by Lieutenant Commander F. M. Barber and Lieutenant E. W. Very. ₁Washington: Gov. Prtg. Off., 1886.₁ 147–191 p., 1 diagr. 8°. **VXM p.v.4, no.5**

419. ―― Torpedoes for national defence; a practical and concise review of these weapons...together with the results obtained at official trials, and a description and comparison of the Sims, Whitehead, and Howell... New York: G. P. Putnam's Sons, 1886. 49 p., 1 pl. illus. 12°. **VWS p.v.2A**

420. Land torpedoes. (Engineering, London, v. 41, 1886, p. 135–136.) **VDA**
Abstract of address delivered by Major M. T. Sale before the Royal United Service Institution, Jan. 27, 1886.

421. Le Roy, A. Parte de mar del torpedero francés núm. 61. Traducido por Emilio Hediger. (Revista general de marina, Madrid, tomo 19, 1886, p. 218–236.) **VXA**

422. Lisbonne, E. Torpilleurs d'Elbing. — Woodite. illus. (Le génie civil, Paris, tome 10, 1886, p. 46–47.) **VA**

423. ―― Torpilleurs des marines anglaise, française, italienne, allemande et russe. (Le génie civil, Paris, tome 10, 1886, p. 113–114.) **VA**

424. Manceau, Claude. Obus-torpilles et canons pneumatiques. illus. (Le génie civil, Paris, tome 9, 1886, p. 279–282.) **VA**

425. A New travelling torpedo. (Scientific American, New York, v. 54, 1886, p. 230.) **VA**
Note on work of R. Paulson.

426. Normand, J. A. Estudios sobre torpederos. Traducido por Emilio Hediger. (Revista general de marina, Madrid, tomo 18, 1886, p. 76–99.) **VXA**

427. On board a torpedo boat. illus. (Scientific American supplement, New York, v. 21, 1886, p. 8679–8680.) **VA**
Notes on the Whitehead torpedo.

428. Paulson, R. Paulson's electrical automatic torpedo. (Royal United Service Institution, Journal, London, v. 30, 1886, p. 535.) **VWA**

429. Puente y Patron, Ricardo Fernandez de la. Memoria sobre el torpedero "Retamosa." (Revista general de marina, Madrid, tomo 19, 1886, p. 182–210.) **VXA**

430. Riondel, A., conde. Propiedades marineras de los torpederos. Travesía de los puertos del océano á Tolon. (Revista general de marina, Madrid, tomo 19, 1886, p. 131–134.) **VXA**
Translated from *Cosmos* by S. Ll.

431. Russian prizes for torpedo defence. (Engineering, London, v. 41, 1886, p. 210.) **VDA**

432. The Sims torpedo. (Engineering, London, v. 41, 1886, p. 139.) **VDA**

433. The Sims torpedo. (Scientific American supplement, New York, v. 21, 1886, p. 8377.) **VA**

434. Sturdee, Sir Frederick Charles Doveton. The changes in the conditions of naval warfare, owing to the introduction of the ram, the torpedo, and the submarine mine, having regard to chiefly the following points in our own and foreign navies, viz.: — training of personnel; construction and protection of matériel; and attack and defence of ships and harbours. illus. (Royal United Service Institution, Journal, London, v. 30, 1886, p. 367–418.) **VWA**

435. Torpedo balloons. illus. (Scientific American supplement, New York, v. 22, 1886, p. 9031.) **VA**

436. A Torpedo cannon ball. (Scientific American, New York, v. 55, 1886, p. 309.) **VA**
Invention of Captain Coudray.

437. A Torpedo cannon ball. (Army and navy journal, New York, v. 24, 1886, p. 338.) †† **VWA**
Brief note.

438. A Torpedo catcher. (Scientific American, New York, v. 54, 1886, p. 52.) **VA**
Invention of John Samuel White.

439. A Torpedo catcher. illus. (Scientific American supplement, New York, v. 21, 1886, p. 8413–8414, 8567–8569.) **VA**

440. Torpedo experiments at Portsmouth. (Illustrated London news, London, v. 89, 1886, p. 509.) *** DA**

441. Torpedo experiments at Portsmouth upon the resistance. (United States Naval Institute, Proceedings, Annapolis, v. 12, 1886, p. 641–642.) **VXA**
From the *London Times*, Sept. 18, 1886.

1886, continued.

442. Torpedo vessels and their equipment. (Engineer, London, v. 62, 1886, p. 374.) **VA**
Notes on torpedoes.

443. Torpedoes. (Engineering, London, v. 42, 1886, p. 500, 575, 621–622.) **VDA**
A series of editorials on the value of torpedoes in war. Abstracted in *Army and navy journal*, New York, v. 24, 1886, p. 435, †† *VWA*.

444. Torpedoes eighty years ago. (Scientific American, New York, v. 55, 1886, p. 358.) **VA**
Notes on Robert Fulton's *Torpedo war and submarine explosions*, New York, 1808–10.

445. Torpedoes v. the "resistance." (Army and navy journal, New York, v. 24, 1886, p. 380.) †† **VWA**

446. Torpilleur sous-marin à déplacement variable par développement télescopique. (Le génie civil, Paris, tome 10, 1886, p. 199.) **VA**

447. Whitehead torpedoes. (Naval annual, Portsmouth, 1886, p. 474–475.) **VXA**

1887

448. Berdan torpedo boat. illus. (Scientific American, New York, v. 56, 1887, p. 326.) **VA**
Invention of Gen. Berdan.

449. The **Brennan** torpedo. (Army and navy journal, New York, v. 25, 1887–88, p. 133, 745; v. 26, 1889, p. 1031.) †† **VWA**

450. The **"Brennan"** torpedo. illus. (Engineering, London, v. 43, 1887, p. 601–603; v. 44, 1887, p. 2–4, 124.) **VDA**
Abstracted in *Army and navy journal*, New York, v. 24, 1887, p. 1003–1004, †† *VWA*.

451. The **Brennan** torpedo. illus. (Scientific American supplement, New York, v. 24, 1887, p. 9704–9706.) **VA**

452. British torpedo boat no. 79. illus. (Scientific American supplement, New York, v. 23, 1887, p. 9271–9272.) **VA**

453. A **British** torpedo fleet. (Scientific American, New York, v. 56, 1887, p. 401.) **VA**

454. C., J. Canon pneumatique à dynamite et obus-torpille du lieutenant Zalinski, de la marine États-Unis. illus. (Le génie civil, Paris, tome 12, 1887, p. 70–71.) **VA**
Abstract from *Scientific American*.

455. Concas y Palau, Víctor María. Torpedero de 2ª clase, construido para servir de tipo en la marina inglesa. (Revista general de marina, Madrid, tomo 21, 1887, p. 786–789.) **VXA**

456. —— Torpederos de mar. Sus pruebas é ideas corrientes sobre ellos en Inglaterra. (Revista general de marina, Madrid, tomo 21, 1887, p. 264–286.) **VXA**

457. Dixon, Jesse. Plans of moorings protected by netting against torpedo attack, to be utilized more especially by a blockading squadron. illus. (Royal United Service Institution, Journal, London, v. 31, 1887, p. 758–763.) **VWA**

458. Effect of a torpedo on an ironclad. illus. (Scientific American, New York, v. 56, 1887, p. 136.) **VA**

459. Experiencias de torpederos en la Báltico. (Revista general de marina, Madrid, tomo 21, 1887, p. 790–793.) **VXA**
Translated from *Le Messager de Cronstadt*.

460. The **Fish** torpedo. illus. (Scientific American supplement, New York, v. 23, 1887, p. 9449–9450.) **VA**
Data on the Whitehead torpedo.

461. Hughes, W. S. Modern aggressive torpedoes. illus. (Scribner's magazine, New York, v. 1, 1887, p. 427–437.) *** DA**
Abstracted in *Army and navy journal*, New York, v. 24, 1887, p. 883–884, †† *VWA*.

462. Lisbonne, E. Torpille Brennan. illus. (Le génie civil, Paris, tome 11, 1887, p. 235–236.) **VA**

463. Mahan, D. H. A new method for carrying and lowering, and for detaching boats; also a suggestion for defending ships against auto-mobile torpedoes. (United States Naval Institute, Proceedings, Annapolis, v. 13, 1887, p. 397–404.) **VXA**
Proposed defence against auto-mobile torpedoes, p. 403.

464. Mercader, Pedro. Viaje del torpedero "Orión" por los mares del Norte, canal de la Mancha y golfo de Gascuña. (Revista general de marina, Madrid, tomo 20, 1887, p. 3–23.) **VXA**

465. New British torpedo experiments. (Scientific American supplement, New York, v. 24, 1887, p. 9592–9593.) **VA**

466. New torpedo boat for the Spanish government. illus. (Scientific American, New York, v. 36, 1887, p. 169.) **VA**
Description of "El Destructor."

467. Novel method of protecting vessels against torpedo attack. (Scientific American, New York, v. 56, 1887, p. 231.) **VA**

468. Pneumatic dynamite torpedo gun. illus. (Engineering, London, v. 43, 1887, p. 344–345, 350.) **VDA**

469. Report of torpedo attack and defenses of U. S. S. "Tennessee." (United States Naval Institute, Proceedings, Annapolis, v. 13, 1887, p. 266–268.) **VXA**
Experiments made Sept. 16, 1886.

470. Sánchez de León, Baldomero. Torpederos. Visita á los talleres de construcción en Sestri (Génova) y al arsenal de Spezia. (Revista general de marina, Madrid, tomo 20, 1887, p. 333–337.) **VXA**

1887, continued.

471. A **Steam** propelled torpedo. illus. (Scientific American supplement, New York, v. 23, 1887, p. 9435–9436.)   **VA**
Invention of Edward C. Peck.

472. Steam torpedoes. (Scientific American, New York, v. 56, 1887, p. 164.)   **VA**

473. Los **Torpederos** blindados. (Revista general de marina, Madrid, tomo 20, 1887, p. 83–88.)   **VXA**
Translation of communications to *Le Yacht* by J. A. Normand and E. Lisbonne.

474. Torpederos ingleses. (Revista general de marina, Madrid, tomo 21, 1887, p. 108–138.)   **VXA**

475. Torpedo boat catchers. (Scientific American supplement, New York, v. 23, 1887, p. 9290.)   **VA**
From the *Engineer.*

476. A **Torpedo** boat flotilla attacks the Atlanta. illus. (Scientific American, New York, v. 57, 1887, p. 255, 258.)   **VA**
Sham battle off Newport, R. I.

477. Torpedo boats armed with pneumatic dynamite guns. illus. (Scientific American, New York, v. 56, 1887, p. 137.)   **VA**

478. Torpedo coast defence. (Army and navy journal, New York, v. 25, 1887, p. 128.)   **†† VWA**
Editorial.

479. Torpedoes. (Naval annual, Portsmouth, 1887, p. 482–500.)   **VXA**
A very complete article giving a description of the various types of torpedoes.

480. ¡**Torpedoes** in oil wells in Canada.¡ (Scientific American supplement, New York, v. 54, 1887, p. 9765.)   **VA**

481. Torpedoes and warships. (Engineering, London, v. 43, 1887, p. 186–187, 328.)   **VDA**

482. Torpedos automóviles modernos. (Revista general de marina, Madrid, tomo 21, 1887, p. 486–493.)   **VXA**
Extracts from *Le Yacht*, translated by E. Vallarino.

483. United States. — Engineer School of Application. Report upon trials with submarine mines executed jointly by Sweden, Norway & Denmark. 1874–1876. Translated from the Danish by Mr. C. W. E. Oxholm. Willets Point: Battalion Press, 1887. 2 p.l., 109 p., 1 pl. 4°. (Professional papers. v. 2, no. 8.)   **VWI**

484. Weyl, C. Torpederos y buque protector. (Revista general de marina, Madrid, tomo 21, 1887, p. 75–79.)   **VXA**
Translated from *Le Yacht* by E. Vallarino.

485. Y. Torpederos. (Revista general de marina, Madrid, tomo 21, 1887, p. 582–586.)   **VXA**

486. Zalinski, E. L. The pneumatic dynamite torpedo gun. (Military Service Institution of the United States, Journal, New York, v. 8, 1887, p. 169–196.)   **VWA**

1888

487. Aerial torpedo thrower, the Graydon air gun. (Scientific American supplement, New York, v. 26, 1888, p. 10794–10795.) **VA**
Invention of James Weir Graydon.

488. Barnaby, Nathaniel. Armour for ships. (Institution of Civil Engineers, Minutes of proceedings, London, v. 98, 1888–89, p. 1–81.)   **VDA**
Notes on torpedoes, p. 57.

489. The **Berdan** torpedo system. (Engineering, London, v. 45, 1888, p. 125–126.)   **VDA**

490. Bermejo, Segismundo. Informe referente á las experiencias verificadas, bajo la dirección de dicho jefe, por la División de Torpederos durante los meses de abril, mayo y junio, en cumplimiento de la real orden de 27 de marzo de 1888. (Revista general de marina, Madrid, tomo 23, 1888, p. 527–569.)   **VXA**

491. Bourgois, Siméon. Les torpilleurs; la guerre navale et la défense des côtes. Paris: Librairie de la Nouvelle revue, 1888. viii, 356 p., 1 l. 12°.   **VXV**

492. Clark, N. B. Gyroscopic torpedoes. illus. (United States Naval Institute, Proceedings, Annapolis, v. 14, 1888, p. 606.)   **VXA**

493. Demoulin, Maurice. Nouvelles machines marines, des bâtiments à grande vitesse, des torpilleurs et des embarcations à vapeur. Paris: E. Bernard & Co., 1888. 2 v. 4° and f°.   **† VXHG**
Text and atlas.

494. The **French** torpedo boat Coureur. (Scientific American, New York, v. 59, 1888, p. 10.)   **VA**

495. A **German** torpedo catcher. (Engineer, London, v. 65, 1888, p. 452.)   **VA**

496. Grenfell, Hubert. The position of the torpedo in naval warfare. (Royal United Service Institution, Journal, London, v. 32, 1888, p. 539–563.)   **VWA**
Abstracted in *Engineering*, London, v. 45, 1888, p. 416–417, *VDA; Engineer*, London, v. 65, 1888, p. 367, *VA; Scientific American*, New York, v. 59, 1888, p. 96–97, *VA; Mittheilungen aus dem Gebiete des Seewesens*, Bd. 17, p. 1–11, *VXA.*

497. Hennebert, Eugène. Les torpilles. Paris: Hachette et Cie., 1888. 2 p.l., 324 p. 2. ed. 12°. (Bibliothèque des merveilles.)   **VXV**

1888, continued.

498. Howell locomotive torpedo. illus. (Engineering, London, v. 45, 1888, p. 58–60.) **VDA**

Gives table of comparative qualities of various torpedoes.

499. The **Howell** torpedo. illus. (Engineer, London, v. 66, 1888, p. 144–145.) **VA**

Abstract in *Scientific American supplement*, New York, v. 27, 1889, p. 11272–11273, *VA.*

500. The **Howell** torpedo. illus. (Scientific American, New York, v. 59, 1888, p. 243–244.) **VA**

501. Inside and outside of a torpedo vessel — H. M. S. Rattlesnake. illus. (Scientific American, New York, v. 58, 1888, p. 383, 390.) **VA**

502. Jaques, William Henry. Torpedoes, torpedo vessels, and torpedo warfare. [Washington, 1888.] 8 p. 8°. (U. S. 50. cong., 1. sess. Sen. misc. doc. 160; serial 2517.) ***SBE**

Reprinted in *Engineering*, London, v. 46, 1888, p. 617–618, *VA.*

503. Land torpedo boats. (Scientific American, New York, v. 58, 1888, p. 20.) **VA**

504. Locomotive torpedoes. (Engineer, London, v. 65, 1888, p. 147.) **VA**

Notes on the Whitehead, Howell, Lay and Brennan torpedoes.

505. Machine guns and torpedoes. (Army and navy journal, New York, v. 26, 1888, p. 237.) **†† VWA**

Abstracted from the *Admiralty gazette,* Nov. 3, 1888.

506. A **Naval** torpedo. (Army and navy journal, New York, v. 26, 1888, p. 124.) **†† VWA**

Invention of George E. Haight and William H. Wood.

506a. Newton, J. T. Torpedoes. (In: United States.—Naval Intelligence Office. General information series no. 7: Naval reserves, training, and matériel, Washington, 1888, p. 391–397.) **VYEB**

Notes on the Brennan, Patrick, Nordenfelt, Whitehead, Schwartzkopff, Howell, and Hall torpedoes.

507. Nordenfeldt electric torpedo. (Army and navy journal, New York, v. 25, 1888, p. 685, 1020.) **†† VWA**

508. The **Nordenfelt** torpedo. (Marine engineer, London, v. 10, 1888, p. 137.) **VXA**

509. Position of the torpedo in naval warfare. (Engineer, London, v. 65, 1888, p. 367.) **VA**

510. Ramos Azcárraga, Enrique de. Los torpedos, su material y su valor militar como arma de guerra. (Revista general de marina, Madrid, tomo 23, 1888, p. 9–29, 171–185.) **VXA**

511. Reisinger, W. W. Torpedoes. (United States Naval Institute, Proceedings, Annapolis, v. 14, 1888, p. 483–538.) **VXA**

Abstracted in *Army and navy journal,* New York, v. 25, 1888, p. 880, †† *VWA,* and in *Mittheilungen aus dem Gebiete des Seewesens,* Pola, Bd. 17, 1889, p. 11–18, *VXA.*

Description of various types of torpedoes and their place in naval warfare.

512. Solomiac torpedo net. illus. (Scientific American supplement, New York, v. 26, 1888, p. 10700.) **VA**

513. Torpedo defence. (Army and navy journal, New York, v. 26, 1888, p. 519, 787.) **†† VWA**

514. Torpedo school at Willet's Point. (Army and navy journal, New York, v. 26, 1888, p. 82.) **†† VWA**

515. Torpedoes vs. guns. (Army and navy journal, New York, v. 25, 1888, p. 839.) **†† VWA**

Editorial.

516. Torpedos Brennan. (Revista general de marina, Madrid, tomo 22, 1888, p. 575–590.) **VXA**

517. Yarrow's diverging torpedo guns. illus. (Engineering, London, v. 46, 1888, p. 476, 479–480.) **VDA**

518. Zalinski, E. L. The naval uses of the pneumatic torpedo gun. illus. (United States Naval Institute, Proceedings, Annapolis, v. 14, 1888, p. 9–55.) **VXA**

Translated in *Revista general de marina,* Madrid, tomo 23, 1888, p. 186–203, *VXA.*

1889

519. B., F. J. Fire-ships, powder-vessels, and obstructions during the Civil war. (United service, Philadelphia, new series, v. 2, 1889, p. 142–149.) **VWA**

Notes on use of torpedoes.

520. Buchard, H. Torpilles et torpilleurs des nations étrangères; suivi d'un atlas des flottes cuirassées étrangères. Paris: Berger-Levrault et Cie., 1889. xv, 222 p., 11., 114 pl. 8°. (Bibliothèque du marin.) **VXR**

521. Clark's gyroscopic torpedoes. illus. (Scientific American supplement, New York, v. 28, 1889, p. 11353.) **VA**

Abstracted from *Revue industrielle.*

522. Donaldson, John. The more recent improvements on the Thornycroft torpedo-boats. illus. (Royal United Service Institution, Journal, London, v. 33, 1889, p. 121–148.) **VWA**

523. Espitallier, G. Tubes lance-torpilles Canet. illus. (Le génie civil, Paris, tome 15, 1889, p. 214–219.) **VA**

Also printed in *Scientific American supplement,* v. 28, 1889, p. 11431–11433, *VA.*

1889, continued.

524. The **Evolution** of the torpedo boat. (United service, Philadelphia, new series, v. 2, 1889, p. 549–572.)   **VWA**
From the *Revue du cercle militaire.*

525. The **Graydon** torpedo projector. (Marine engineer, London, v. 11, 1889, p. 11.)   **VXA**

526. **Holman,** George F. W.   The torpedo boat Stiletto.   (Scientific American, New York, v. 60, 1889, p. 276–277.)   **VA**

527. **Hovgaard,** George William.   The seaworthiness of torpedo boats. illus. (Engineering, London, v. 48, 1889, p. 101–103, 128–132.)   **VDA**
Also printed in *Revista general de marina,* Madrid, 1889, tomo 25, p. 292–308, *VXA;* and in *Mittheilungen aus dem Gebiete des Seewesens,* Pola, Bd. 17, 1889, p. 305–318, *VXA.*

528. The **Lege** torpedo. illus. (Engineer, London, v. 67, 1889, p. 305.)   **VA**
A towing fish torpedo.

529. **Peter** Brotherhood's air compressors for torpedo service. illus. (Engineering, London, v. 35, 1883, p. 458–459; v. 47, 1889, p. 584–587; v. 48, 1889, p. 10.)   **VDA**

530. **R.,** E.   Torpille Sims Edison. (La lumière électrique, Paris, tome 34, 1889. p. 583–584.)   **VGA**

531. **Rigging** torpedo net defense.   illus. (Scientific American supplement, New York, v. 28, 1889, p. 11580.)   **VA**
Brief note.

532. **Schwickert,** Friedrich. Über die Pulverlancierung der Torpedos in der französischen Kriegsmarine. (Mittheilungen aus dem Gebiete des Seewesens, Pola, Bd. 17, 1889, p. 406–417.)   **VXA**

533. **Sims-Edison** torpedo.   (Scientific American, New York, v. 61, 1889, p. 21.)   **VA**
Invention of W. Scott Sims and Thomas A. Edison.

534. **Sleeman,** Charles William.   Torpedoes and torpedo warfare: containing a complete account of the progress of submarine warfare; also a detailed description of matters appertaining thereto, including the latest improvements.   Portsmouth, Eng.: Griffin & Co., 1889. viii p., 1 l., 354 p., 82 diagr., 1 pl. 8°.   **VXV**

535. **Spanish** torpedo boats.   (Scientific American, New York, v. 60, 1889, p. 197.)   **VA**

536. **Torpedo** boats of the British navy. (Engineering, London, v. 48, 1889, p. 709.)   **VDA**
With illustration on p. 707.
Also in *Revista general de marina,* Madrid, tomo 25, 1889, p. 626–630, *VXA.*

537. **Torpedo** impulse tubes manufactured by the General Engine and Boiler Co. illus.   (Engineer, London, v. 67, 1889. p. 181.)   **VA**

538. **Torpille** en papier comprimé.   (Le génie civil, Paris, tome 15, 1889, p. 480.) **VA**
Brief description of a German invention.

539. **Trial** of the Brennan torpedo.   (Engineer, London, v. 68, 1889, p. 45.)   **VA**
Abstracted in *Army and navy journal,* New York, v. 26, 1889, p. 1031, †† *VWA.*

540. The **True** use of torpedoes.   (Army and navy journal, New York, v. 36, 1889, p. 516.)   †† **VWA**

541. **Wainwright,** R.   Graydon torpedo thrower.   (United States Naval Institute, Proceedings, Annapolis, v. 15, 1889, p. 385–386.)   **VXA**

542. **Zalinski,** E. L.   The pneumatic torpedo-gun, its use ashore and afloat. (Royal United Service Institution, Journal, London, v. 33, 1889, p. 991–1023.)   **VWA**

1890

543. **Bucknill,** J. T.   The Victoria torpedo. (Engineering, London, v. 50, 1890, p. 280.)   **VDA**

544. **Clowes,** William Laird.   Naval warfare, 1860–1889, and some of its lessons. (Royal United Service Institution, Journal, London,   v. 34,   1890,   p. 719–728.)   **VWA**
Notes on torpedoes.

545. **Combe,** Jules.   Torpilles automobiles et dirigeables.   Torpille Whitehead — torpille Victoria. illus. (Le génie civil, Paris, tome 18,   1890,   p. 133–136; tome 19,   1891, p. 303–306.)   **VA**

546. **Drake,** F. J.   Sea-going torpedo boat no. 1, United States Navy.   illus. (Scientific American, New York, v. 62, 1890, p. 65, 71–72.)   **VA**

547. **Ellicott,** John M.   Automatic torpedoes.   illus.   (Engineering, London, v. 50, 1890, p. 573–574, 628–633, 737, 740–742, 772.)   **VDA**
Description of the Whitehead and Howell torpedoes.

548. **English** and German torpedo boats. (Scientific American, New York, v. 62, 1890, p. 99.)   **VA**

549. **Experiments** with the Sims-Edison torpedo. illus. (Scientific American, New York, v. 63, 1890, p. 47–48.)   **VA**

550. **Field,** Edward.   Our coast defences. (United Service, Philadelphia, new series, v. 3, 1890, p. 1–10, 164–178.)   **VWA**
Valuable notes on torpedoes and mines.

1890, continued.

551. Figuier, Louis. Les torpilles… illus.
(In his: Les merveilles de la science, Paris,
1890, Supplément 2, p. 321–352.) **V**

Gives valuable historical data; notes on the inventions of Bushnell and Fulton; the Whitehead, Jacobi, Baril and Bouée torpedoes.

552. Fiske, Bradley Allen. Electricity in
warfare. (Franklin Institute, Journal,
Philadelphia, v. 130, 1890, p. 183–203.) **VA**

Abstracted in *Scientific American supplement,* New York, v. 30, 1890, p. 12272–12273, *VA.*

Notes on various types of torpedoes.

553. H., G. Les torpilles dans la défense
de Canton pendant la guerre franco-chi-
noise (1884–1885). (La lumière électrique,
Paris, tome 36, 1890, p. 242–246.) **VGA**

554. Heinz, Julius. Über die Unterwasser-
Lancierungen des automobilen Torpedos
in der Kielrichtung und über einige schwe-
bende torpedistische Fragen. illus. (Mittheilungen aus dem Gebiete des Seewesens,
Pola, Bd. 18, 1890, p. 537–552.) **VXA**

Abstracted in *Journal* of the Royal United Service Institution, London, v. 37, 1893, p. 910–914, *VWA.*

555. The **Holmes** torpedo-finder. illus.
(Marine engineer, London, v. 12, 1890,
p. 289–290.) **VXA**

Invention of Joseph R. Holmes.

556. Leavitt, F. M. The Whitehead torpedo. (Stevens indicator, Hoboken, N. J.,
v. 10, 1890, p. 2–8.) **VDA**

557. Lisbonne, E. Torpedo con caldera
par petróleo. (Revista general de marina,
Madrid, tomo 26, 1890, p. 360–364.) **VXA**

558. —— Torpedos y artillería en el
Ministerio de Marina. (Revista general de
marina, Madrid, tomo 26, 1890, p. 505–511.)
VXA

Translated from *Le Yacht.*

559. Murphy, G. Read. The Victoria torpedo. (Engineering, London, v. 50, 1890,
p. 334.) **VDA**

560. Sánchez de León, Baldemero. Des-
cripción del nuevo taller de torpedos de
Cartagena. (Revista general de marina,
Madrid, tomo 27, 1890, p. 660–677.) **VXA**

561. The **Sims-Edison** mobile torpedo.
illus. (Army and navy journal, New York,
v. 27, 1890, p. 625–626.) **†† VWA**

Abstracted in *Scientific American supplement,* New York, v. 29, 1890, p. 11949–11950, *VA.*

562. Speed of torpedoes. (Army and navy
journal, New York, v. 27, 1890, p. 601.)
†† VWA

Brief note.

563. Torpederos en Alemania. (Revista
general de marina, Madrid, tomo 26, 1890,
p. 114–116.) **VXA**

Translated from the *Illustrated army and navy magazine.*

564. Torpedo target practice at Kiel. illus.
(Scientific American, New York, v. 63, 1890,
p. 102–103.) **VA**

565. United States torpedo boat "Cushing". (Scientific American, New York,
v. 62, 1890, p. 290.) **VA**

566. Very, E. W. The Howell automobile
torpedo. illus. (United States Naval
Institute, Proceedings, Annapolis, v. 16,
1890, p. 333–360.) **VXA**

Shows the differences between this torpedo and the Whitehead.

567. The **Victoria** torpedo. (Engineer,
London, v. 70, 1890, p. 172.) **VA**

The invention of G. Read Murphy.

568. The **Victoria** torpedo. illus. (Engineering, London, v. 50, 1890, p. 246–247.)
VDA

With illustrations on p. 237, 244, 245.

Also printed in *Scientific American supplement.* New York, v. 30, 1890, p. 12311–12313, *VA.*

Notes on the work of G. Read Murphy.

1891

569. Audra, R. La torpille dirigeable
Sims Edison. illus. (Le génie civil, Paris,
tome 19, 1891, p. 141–144.) **VA**

Abstracted in Institution of Civil Engineers, *Minutes of proceedings,* London, v. 106, 1891, p. 436, *VDA.*

570. Der **Automobile** Buonaccorsi-Tor-
pedo. illus. (Mittheilungen aus dem
Gebiete des Seewesens, Pola, Bd. 19, 1891,
p. 212–218.) **VXA**

Translated in the *Journal* of the Royal United Service Institution, London, v. 37, 1893, p. 271–276, *VWA,* and in the *Proceedings* of the United States Naval Institute, Annapolis, v. 19, 1893, p. 297–303, *VXA.*

571. Board of naval experts established by
the United States government. (Scientific
American, New York, v. 65, 1891, p. 33.)
VA

572. The **Brennan** torpedo. (Engineer,
London, v. 71, 1891, p. 303–304, 345.) **VA**

573. The **Canet** system of firing torpedoes.
illus. (Engineering, London, v. 51, 1891,
p. 4–7, 30–33.) **VDA**

Notes on the Canet apparatus.

574. The **Canet** system of firing torpedoes.
illus. (Scientific American, New York,
v. 64, 1891, p. 70–71.) **VA**

575. Cornejo Carvajal, Honorio. Los
torpederos. (Revista general de marina,
Madrid, tomo 29, 1891, p. 582–602.) **VXA**

576. Ellicott, John M. The Whitehead
torpedo. illus. (Engineer, London, v. 72,
1891, p. 110–111, 137–138, 156–157.) **VA**

A very complete article giving plans, equipment, etc.

1891, continued.

577. Die **Französischen** Torpedolancier-kanonen. System Canet. illus. (Mittheil-ungen aus dem Gebiete des Seewesens, Pola, Bd. 19, 1891, p. 87–95.)   **VXA**
From *Engineering.*

578. González Quintero, José. Experi-encias verificadas en el Havre el día 2 de mayo bajo los auspicios de la Sociedad forges et chantiers de la Mediterráneo con el torpedo eléctrico "Sims-Edison." (Re-vista general de marina, Madrid, tomo 28, 1891, p. 931–937.)   **VXA**

579. H., J. Der lenkbare Sims-Edison-Torpedo. illus. (Mittheilungen aus dem Gebiete des Seewesens, Pola, Bd. 19, 1891, p. 638–643.)   **VXA**

580. Heinz, Julius. Howells automobiler Torpedo. illus. (Mittheilungen aus dem Gebiete des Seewesens, Pola, Bd. 19, 1891, p. 158–174.)
A very complete article.

581. —— Über die Pulverlancierung des automobilen Torpedos. (Mittheilungen aus dem Gebiete des Seewesens, Pola, Bd. 19, 1891, p. 537–546, 604–616.)   **VXA**

582. Hunt, Ridgely. The torpedo vessel — a history of its development. (In: United States.—Naval Intelligence Office. Gen-eral information series, no. 10: The year's naval progress, 1891, Washington, 1891, p. 411–420.)   **VYEB**
Translated in *Mittheilungen aus dem Gebiete des Seewesens,* Pola, Bd. 20, 1892, p. 15–24, *VXA,* and *Revista general de marina,* Madrid, tomo 30, 1892, p. 548–556; tomo 31, 1892, p. 169–177, *VXA.*

583. Koudelka, Alfred, Freiherr von. Zur Torpedoboots-Taktik. (Mittheilungen aus dem Gebiete des Seewesens, Pola, Bd. 19, 1891, p. 691–697.)   **VXA**

584. Marcillac, P. Torpille électrique dirigeable, système D. Orecchioni. illus. (La lumière électrique, Paris, tome 39, 1891, p. 201–205.)   **VGA**

585. New torpedo protections. (Scien-tific American, New York, v. 64, 1891, p. 355.)   **VA**
Invention of Captain Wilson.

586. New trials of the Sims-Edison tor-pedo. (Scientific American, New York, v. 65, 1891, p. 113.)   **VA**

587. ¡Notes on the Whitehead torpedo.¡ (Engineer, London, v. 71, 1891, p. 401.) **VA**

588. Orecchoni electric dirigeable torpedo. (Army and navy journal, New York, v. 28, 1891, p. 602.)   †† **VWA**

589. Resultate einiger mit österreichisch-ungarischen Torpedobooten vorgenom-menen Neigungs- und Rollversuche. illus. (Mittheilungen aus dem Gebiete des See-wesens, Pola, Bd. 19, 1891, p. 201–212.)   **VXA**

590. Richard, Gustave. Applications mé-caniques de l'électricité. illus. (La lumière électrique, Paris, tome 43, 1892, p. 21–26.)   **VGA**
Account of invention of M. Hurrell.

591. Routledge, Robert. Torpedoes. illus. (In his: Discoveries and inventions of the nineteenth century, London, 1891, p. 161–175.)   **V**
Gives a very complete description of the various types of torpedoes.

592. The **Sims-Edison** electrical torpedo. (Engineer, London, v. 72, 1891, p. 519; v. 73, 1892, p. 91, 123, 150; v. 76, 1893, p. 104.) **VA**
Patented in England in 1883.

593. Sims-Edison torpedo. (Engineering, London, v. 51, 1891, p. 536.)   **VDA**

594. A **Steel** cruiser sunk by torpedo boats. illus. (Scientific American, New York, v. 64, 1891, p. 359–360.)   **VA**
Engagement in Caldera Bay near Valparaiso.

595. Torpederos franceses. (Revista gen-eral de marina, Madrid, tomo 28, 1891, p. 382–390.)   **VXA**

596. Torpedo net protection. (Marine engineer, London, v. 13, 1891, p. 346, 404.)   **VXA**

597. Torpedo netting of domestic manu-facture. (Army and navy journal, New York, v. 29, 1891, p. 66.)   †† **VWA**
Brief note.

598. Torpille Edison Sims (1891). illus. (La lumière électrique, Paris, tome 40, 1891, p. 478–480.)   **VGA**

599. ¡Use of the torpedo in Chilian war.¡ illus. (Engineering, London, v. 51, 1891, p. 652–653, 677, 705, 741; v. 52, 1891, p. 190.)   **VDA**

Sinking of the "Blanco Encalada."

600. Whitehead torpedo. (Engineering, London, v. 51, 1891, p. 536, 652.)   **VDA**

1892

601. An **Aerial** and sub-aquatic torpedo. illus. (Scientific American, New York, v. 67, 1892, p. 329.)   **VA**
The Gathmann torpedo and torpedo gun.

602. British torpedo depot ship "Vulcan". illus. (Scientific American supplement, New York, v. 34, 1892, p. 14058–14059.) **VA**

603. Clowes, William Laird. The place and uses of torpedo-boats in war. (Royal United Service Institution, Journal, Lon-don, v. 36, 1892, p. 667–698.)   **VWA**

604. —— Torpedo-boats; their organiza-tion and conduct. (United States Naval Institute, Proceedings, Annapolis, v. 18, 1892, p. 181–219.)   **VXA**

1892, continued.

605. Considerations on the employment of torpedo boats. (Royal United Service Institution, Journal, London, v. 35, 1891, p. 59–69.) **VWA**

From *Internationale Revue über die gesammten Armeen und Flotten*, translated by Capt. J. F. Daniell.

606. Controlled torpedoes. (Engineer, London, v. 73, 1892, p. 323–324.) **VA**

Also in *Scientific American*, New York, v. 66, 1892, p. 309, *VA*.

Notes on the Brennan and the Sims-Edison torpedoes.

607. Cornejo Carvajal, Honorio. Táctica de torpederos. (Revista general de marina, Madrid, tomo 31, 1892, p. 3–58.) **VXA**

608. Explosion of dry torpedoes. illus. (Scientific American supplement, New York, v. 33, 1892, p. 13546.) **VA**

Abstracted from *La nature*.

609. Hamilton, E. T. Electricity as applied to the torpedo and other naval uses. illus. (Royal United Service Institution, Journal, London, v. 36, 1892, p. 617–634.) **VWA**

610. McEvoy's torpedo detector. illus. (Scientific American supplement, New York, v. 33, 1892, p. 13659.) **VA**

611. Précis of the instructions for gunnery and torpedo school-ships of the Italian navy. (Royal United Service Institution, Journal, London, v. 36, 1892, p. 810–818.) **VWA**

Translated by H. Garbett from the *Giornale militare per la marina*.

612. Sea rocket torpedo invented by Commander T. W. Aylesbury, late of the Indian navy. illus. (Scientific American supplement, New York, v. 33, 1892, p. 13550.) **VA**

613. Sims-Edison torpedo. (Naval annual, Portsmouth, 1892, p. 4–6.) **VXA**

614. Sims-Edison torpedo. illus. (Scientific American supplement, New York, v. 33, 1892, p. 13479–13480.) **VA**

615. A Study of the effects of the German torpedo shell. illus. (Military Service Institution of the United States, Journal, New York, v. 13, 1892, p. 391–394.) **VWA**

Translated by T. C. Patterson from the *Rivista di artiglieria e genio*.

616. ₁Torpedo boat attack.₁ (Engineering, London, v. 54, 1892, p. 86–87, 266, 300–301, 331–332.) **VDA**

Problems in naval manoeuvres.

617. Torpedo-net defences. (Royal United Service Institution, Journal, London, v. 36, 1892, p. 1024–1032.) **VWA**

Translated by T. J. Haddy from the *Rivista marittima*, June, 1892.

618. Torpedoes. (Iron age, New York, v. 49, 1892, p. 758–759.) **VDA**

Brief note on the various types of torpedoes.

619. Winn, Frank L. Torpedoes and submarine mines. (United service, Philadelphia, new series, v. 8, 1892, p. 464–475.) **VWA**

620. Zalinski, E. L. "The German torpedo shell." (Military Service Institution of the United States, Journal, New York, v. 13, 1892, p. 756–757.) **VWA**

1893

621. Astuto, G. Submerged discharge for Whitehead torpedoes. illus. (Royal United Service Institution, Journal, London, v. 37, 1893, p. 903–909.) **VWA**

Translated from the *Rivista marittima* of May, 1893 by T. J. Haddy.

622. Attlmayr, F. Der Torpedo und die Schnellfeuergeschütze grossen Kalibers. (Mittheilungen aus dem Gebiete des Seewesens, Pola, Bd. 21, 1893, p. 409–434, 537–553.) **VXA**

623. Bolton, Reginald. The submarine torpedo. (Engineer, London, v. 75, 1893, p. 208.) **VA**

Contains an extract from the work of James Kelly, published in 1818, giving an account of the attempt to blow up H. M. S. Ramilies by a "gentleman at Norwich, U. S."

624. Dary, Georges. Chargement et vérification des torpilles coulées. illus. (Le génie civil, Paris, tome 22, 1893, p. 238–240, p. 306–308, 404.) **VA**

625. Drake, Franklin J. Automobile torpedoes. (United States Naval Institute, Proceedings, Annapolis, v. 19, 1893, p. 1–53.) **VXA**

A very complete article. General description of the Howell torpedo.

626. Escribano, Gabriel. Modificaciones más importantes que se han introducido en el torpedo Whithead Schwartzkopff. (Revista general de marina, Madrid, tomo 32, 1893, p. 741–745.) **VXA**

627. Howell torpedo. (Scientific American, New York, v. 69, 1893, p. 378.) **VA**

Abstracted from the *Army and navy journal*.

628. Knapp, H. S. Results of some special researches at the torpedo station. (United States Naval Institute, Proceedings, Annapolis, v. 19, 1893, p. 249–266.) **VXA**

629. Nasmyth's torpedo boat of 1853. illus. (Scientific American, New York, v. 69, 1893, p. 135.) **VA**

Invention of James Nasmyth.

1893, continued.

630. Naval torpedoes. (Scientific American, New York, v. 69, 1893, p. 66.) **VA**
Notes on the Whitehead, Cunningham, Howell, and Sims-Edison torpedoes.

631. Protection against torpedo-boats. (United States Naval Institute, Proceedings, Annapolis, v. 19, 1893, p. 489–490.) **VXA**
Conclusions deduced from the Italian naval manœuvres.

632. Torpedo net tests. (Scientific American, New York, v. 69, 1893, p. 331, 402.) **VA**
Tests made at Newport, R. I.

633. Tullinger, Karl. Studie über die Stabilität der Rotationsachse mit besonderer Rücksicht auf den Howell-Torpedo. (Mittheilungen aus dem Gebiete des Seewesens, Pola, Bd. 21, 1893, p. 113–132.) **VXA**

634. The United States torpedo cruiser "Vesuvius." illus. (Scientific American, New York, v. 68, 1893, p. 88–89.) **VA**
Notes on the Zalinski guns.

635. Vogt, H. C. The Simplex and Huge torpedoes. illus. (Scientific American supplement, New York, v. 35, 1893, p. 14362–14363.) **VA**

1894

636. Again a torpedo sinks a war vessel. (Scientific American, New York, v. 71, 1894, p. 18.) **VA**
Engagement in the Brazilian revolt.

637. An Aluminum torpedo boat. illus. (Scientific American, New York, v. 71, 1894, p. 261; v. 72, 1895, p. 283.) **VA**

638. Borja y Goyeneche, Joaquin de. El marinero torpedista. Resumen de las principales ideas sobre torpedos, puesto al alcance de los marineros. Barcelona: Heinrich y Ca., 1894. 241 p., 1 l. 3. ed. 8°. **VXV**

639. British torpedo boat destroyer the "Hornet." illus. (Scientific American, New York, v. 70, 1894, p. 313.) **VA**

640. Calthorpe, A. G. The tactics best adapted for developing the power of existing ships and weapons (gun, ram, and torpedo) which should regulate fleets, groups, and single vessels in action. (Royal United Service Institution, Journal, London, v. 38, 1894, p. 481–509.) **VWA**

641. Cipriani, M. Torpedo-boats in fleet actions. (Royal United Service Institution, Journal, London, v. 38, 1894, p. 762–767.) **VWA**
Translated from *Marittima* by T. J. Haddy.

642. A Dirigible torpedo. (Engineering news, New York, v. 32, 1894, p. 496.) **VDA**
Brief note on the invention of Lieut. N. J. L. T. Halpine, U. S. N.

643. E., J. C. Nuevo torpedo terrestre. illus. (Memorial de ingenieros, Madrid, año 49, 1894, p. 378–384.) **VWA**

644. Fulton's torpedo. illus. (Scientific American, New York, v. 70, 1894, p. 104–105.) **VA**

645. Jaques, William Henry. The detachable ram, or the submarine gun as a substitute for the ram. (Institution of Naval Architects, Transactions, London, v. 35, 1894, p. 242–261.) **VXA**
With discussion, p. 261–270.

646. Marvá, José. El torpedo terrestre Pfund-Schmid. illus. (Memorial de ingenieros, Madrid, año 49, 1894, p. 173–179.) **VWA**

647. Radford, Cyrus S. The Halpine dirigible torpedo. (United States Naval Institute, Proceedings, Annapolis, v. 20, 1894, p. 606–609.) **VXA**
Notes on its use in the Brazilian navy.

648. Richard, Gustave. Torpille auto-directrice Ayton. illus. (La lumière électrique, Paris, tome 51, 1894, p. 166–167.) **VGA**

649. Robinson, Eugene. The evolution of the torpedo. (United service, Philadelphia, new series, v. 11, 1894, p. 1–7.) **VWA**

650. Some remarks on modern naval tactics. (Engineering, London, v. 58, 1894, p. 479–482, 512–513, 539–542, 585–586.) **VDA**
Notes on torpedoes and torpedo boats.

651. Sturdee, Sir Frederick Charles Doveton. The tactics best adapted for developing the power of existing ships and weapons (gun, ram, and torpedo) which should regulate fleets, groups, and single vessels in action. (Royal United Service Institution, Journal, London, v. 38, 1894, p. 365–418.) **VWA**

652. Submarine torpedo. (Scientific American, New York, v. 71, 1894, p. 339.) **VA**
Brief note on the invention of Seymour Allan.

653. Torpedo boat destroyer "Ferret." illus. (Scientific American, New York, v. 71, 1894, p. 201.) **VA**

654. Torpedo net cutters. (Engineer, London, v. 78, 1894, p. 233.) **VA**
Brief note.

655. Torpilleur en aluminium construit par MM. Yarrow et Cie. (L'Éclairage électrique, Paris, tome 1, 1894, p. 429–430.) **VGA**

656. Visibility of torpedo boats. (Scientific American, New York, v. 71, 1894, p. 258.) **VA**

1895

657. Clergeau, Manuel. Guide pratique du chauffeur et du mécanicien sur les bateaux-torpilleurs. Paris: L. Baudouin, 1895. x, 239 p., 39 pl. illus. 2. ed. 8°.
VXV

658. Cost of the new American torpedo boats. (Scientific American, New York, v. 73, 1895, p. 344.) **VA**

659. Defences against torpedoes. (Scientific American supplement, New York, v. 40, 1895, p. 16268.) **VA**
Brief note.

660. Gleaves, Albert. The Howell torpedo. illus. (United States Naval Institute, Proceedings, Annapolis, v. 21, 1895, p. 125–129.) **VXA**
An elementary description.

661. —— Problem of torpedo discharge. illus. (United States Naval Institute, Proceedings, Annapolis, v. 21, 1895, p. 339–348.) **VXA**
Abstracted in Institution of Civil Engineers, *Minutes of proceedings,* London, v. 124, 1895–96, p. 493–495, *VDA.*
Compiled from the report of Lieut. Frank F. Fletcher, U. S. N., commanding U. S. torpedo boat Cushing.

662. Instrument for placing torpedoes. illus. (Scientific American, New York, v. 72, 1895, p. 295.) **VA**
Invention of James D. Seamands.

663. Marvá, José. Experiencias con el torpedo terrestre Pfund-Schmid. (Memorial de ingenieros, Madrid, año 50, 1895, p. 292–295.) **VWA**

664. Romocki, S. J. von. Geschichte der Explosivstoffe. Berlin: R. Oppenheim, 1895. 2 v. in 1. illus. 8°. **VOG**
Die Anfänge des Sprengminen-Wesens, [Teil] 1, p. 241–253.
Die Sprengschiffe vor Antwerpen im Jahre 1585, [Teil] 1, p. 300–322.
Ansetz-Torpedos und Seeminen, [Teil] 1, p. 323–337.
Wurf- und Fallgeschosse mit Zündung durch Stahl und Stein, [Teil] 1, p. 338–351.
Spieren- und treibende Torpedos vor La Rochelle im Jahre 1628, [Teil] 1, p. 352–363.
Weitere Erfindungen Cornelius Drebbels, [Teil] 1, p. 364–376.
Raketen- und Fisch-Torpedos, [Teil] 1, p. 377–386.

665. The **Russian** torpedo boat destroyer "Sokol." illus. (Scientific American, New York, v. 73, 1895, p. 313.) **VA**

666. Thornycroft, John I. On torpedo boat destroyers. (Royal United Service Institution, London, Journal, v. 39, 1895, p. 871–885.) **VWA**

667. Torpedo boats for the cruiser Maine. illus. (Scientific American, New York, v. 72, 1895, p. 1–2, 376–377.) **VA**

668. Wilson, J. E. Howell automobile torpedo. illus. (Army and navy journal, New York, v. 33, 1895, p. 124.) **†† VWA**
Abstract of paper read before Providence, R. I., Association of Mechanical Engineers, Sept. 10, 1895.

669. Yarrow, A. F. Description of an aluminum torpedo-boat built for the French government. (Institution of Naval Architects, Transactions, London, v. 36, 1895, p. 269–286.) **VXA**
Notes on torpedoes.

1896

670. L'Application du magnétisme à la direction des torpilles. (L'Éclairage électrique, Paris, tome 8, 1896, p. 94–95.) **VGA**

671. Armored torpedo boats. (Scientific American, New York, v. 75, 1896, p. 439.) **VA**

672. Armstrong, G. E. Torpedoes and torpedo-vessels. London: George Bell and Sons, 1896. xvi, 287 p., 4 diagr., 1 pl. 12°. (Royal Navy handbooks. [no.] 3.) **VXV**
The 2. ed., 1901, is reviewed in *Arms and explosives,* London, v. 9, 1901, p. 139. † *VOG.*

673. Bacon, R. H. The value of torpedo boats in war time. (In: The naval annual, 1896. Portsmouth [Eng.], 1896. 4°. p. 156–166.) **VXA**
Translated in *Mittheilungen aus dem Gebiete des Seewesens,* Pola, Bd. 24, 1896, p. 822–836, *VXA.*

674. Battello sottomarino Le Goubet. (Rivista di artiglieria e genio, Roma, anno 13, v. 1, 1896, p. 168–171.) **VWW**

675. Die Englischen Torpedobootszerstörer. illus. (Mittheilungen aus dem Gebiete des Seewesens, Pola, Bd. 24, 1896, p. 91–102.) **VXA**

676. Heinz, Julius. Eine neue Erfindung im Torpedowesen. (Mittheilungen aus dem Gebiete des Seewesens, Pola, Bd. 24, 1896, p. 948–954.) **VXA**

677. Howell torpedo tests. (Engineer, London, v. 82, 1896, p. 365.) **VA**

678. An **Improved** Howell torpedo. (Engineering news, New York, v. 36, 1896, p. 204.) **VDA**
Brief note.

679. Lassoc, V. F. Battleships and torpedo defence. illus. (Engineering, London, v. 62, 1896, p. 565–566.) **VDA**

680. Mier, Eduardo. Torpedos automóviles. (Memorial de ingenieros, Madrid, año 51, 1896, p. 171–175, 211–216.) **VWA**

681. A **New** torpedo. illus. (Scientific American, New York, v. 74, 1896, p. 33, 39.) **VA**

682. Sears, W. J. A general description of the Whitehead torpedo. illus. (United

1896, continued.

States Naval Institute, Proceedings, Annapolis, v. 22, 1896, p. 803–808; v. 24, 1898, p. 89–110.)   **VXA**
A very comprehensive article.

683. ₁Target steering device for torpedoes.₁ (Scientific American supplement, New York, v. 41, 1896, p. 16973.)   **VA**
Brief note.

684. Torpedoes in flight. illus. (Engineer, London, v. 81, 1896, p. 524.)   **VA**
Also in *Scientific American supplement*, New York, v. 41, 1896, p. 17086, *VA*.

1897

685. A propos des connaisances en électricité des officiers torpilleurs. (Journal de la marine, le yacht, Paris, année 20, 1897, p. 501, 585.)   †† **VXF**

686. Aerial torpedoes. (Engineering, London, v. 64, 1897, p. 235–236.)   **VDA**
Invention of Hiram Maxim.

687. Carden, G. L. Thirty knot torpedo boat catcher "Bailey." illus. (Scientific American, New York, v. 77, 1897, p. 394–395.)   **VA**

688. Colomb, Philip Howard. The future of the torpedo. (Royal United Service Institution, Journal, London, v. 41, 1897, p. 1465–1489.)   **VWA**
Translated in *Revista general de marina*, Madrid, tomo 43, 1898, p. 774–798; tomo 44, 1899, p. 96–110, *VXA*.

689. D., P. Torpilleurs et défenses mobiles. (Journal de la marine, le yacht, Paris, année 20, p. 491–493, 535.)   ††**VXF**

690. The Defenceless navies of the world. illus. (Marine engineer, London, v. 18, 1897, p. 480–482.)   **VXA**
A scheme for protecting ships against torpedo attack.

691. Duboc, Émile. La torpille aérienne et les obus perforants. (Journal de la marine, le yacht, Paris, année 20, p. 487–488, 573–575.)   †† **VXF**
Invention of Hudson Maxim.

692. Ellicott, J. M. Torpedoes in exercise and battle. (United States Naval Institute, Proceedings, Annapolis, v. 23, 1897, p. 413–445, 563–566.)   **VXA**
Data on the Whitehead and Howell torpedoes.

693. Firing a torpedo. illus. (Scientific American, New York, v. 77, 1897, p. 155.)   **VA**

694. The Future of the torpedo. (Engineer, London, v. 83, 1897, p. 589, 595.)   **VA**
Editorials on the relative value of battleship and torpedo boat.

695. Gillmor, H. G. Torpedo-boat design. (Society of Naval Architects and Marine Engineers, Transactions, New York, v. 5, 1897, p. 51–65.)   **VXA**
With discussion, p. 66–79.
Notes on torpedo armament and equipment.

696. Howell torpedo. (Engineer, London, v. 83, 1897, p. 71–72.)   **VA**

697. Jane, Frederick T. The torpedo book. A series of sketches with torpedo craft in fair weather and foul. London: N. Beeman, 1897. 2 p.l., 1 l., 20 pl. 8°.   **VYA**

698. Maxim, Hudson. Aerial torpedoes. (Engineer, London, v. 84, 1897, p. 57–58.)   **VA**

699. A New torpedo. (Marine engineer, London, v. 19, 1897, p. 331.)   **VXA**
Invention of Admiral Wilson.

700. New torpedo tube for the Japanese battleship "Fuji." (Iron age, New York, v. 60, 1897, p. 12.)   **VDA**
From the London *Times*; also printed in United States Naval Institute, *Proceedings*, v. 23, 1897, p. 576–577, *VXA*.

701. Notes on torpedoes. (Journal of the United States artillery, Fort Monroe, v. 8, 1897, p. 220–224.)   **VWA**

702. Protection against torpedoes. (Army and navy journal, New York, v. 34, 1897, p. 419.)   †† **VWA**

703. Smith, R. C. Torpedo boat policy. (United States Naval Institute, Proceedings, Annapolis, v. 23, 1897, p. 1–67, 360–364.)   **VXA**
Valuable data on torpedoes.

704. Sypher, J. H. Notes on the Obry device for torpedoes. (United States Naval Institute, Proceedings, Annapolis, v. 23, 1897, p. 655–661.)   **VXA**

705. Torpedo boat "Porter." illus. (Scientific American, New York, v. 76, 1897, p. 328, 392.)   **VA**

706. Torpille à direction magnétique de Haskins. (L'Éclairage électrique, Paris, tome 10, 1897, p. 236.)   **VGA**

707. Trial of the W. T. Carter torpedo. (Engineer, London, v. 83, 1897, p. 584.) **VA**

708. U. S. torpedo boat no. 6. illus. (Scientific American, New York, v. 76, 1897, p. 155.)   **VA**

1898

709. Bara, E., and H. NOALHAT. Les torpilles automobiles. Paris: J. Fritsch, 1898. 2 p.l., xv, 189 p., 11 pl. 8°.   **VXV**

710. Brillié, H. Torpilles et torpilleurs. Paris: G. Carré & C. Naud, 1898. 2 p.l., 204 p., 11 pl. 8°.   **VXV**

1898, continued.

711. Capehart, E. E. The mine defense of Santiago harbor. illus. (United States Naval Institute, Proceedings, Annapolis, v. 24, 1898, p. 585–604.) **VXA**

712. Dangers from torpedo tubes to the ship itself. (Engineer, London, v. 86, 1898, p. 121.) **VA**

Lesson learned in the destruction of the "Vizcaya."

713. El Desarrollo del torpedero. (Revista general de marina, Madrid, tomo 42, 1898, p. 45–49.) **VXA**

Translated from the *United service gazette.*

714. Dickie, G. W. Torpedo-boat destroyers for sea service. (Society of Naval Architects and Marine Engineers, Transactions, New York, v. 6, 1898, p. 43–74.) **VXA**

Valuable data on torpedoes.

715. Fairburn, William A. Discussion of the merits of torpedo craft and some of the features of design and construction. (Marine engineering, New York, v. 4, Sept., 1898, p. 10–14, Oct., 1898, p. 4–9.) †**VXA**

A resumé and analysis of this article by M. d'Auriac is given in *Revue maritime,* Paris, v. 140, 1899, p. 340–346, *VXA.*

716. Gercke, Hermann. Die Torpedowaffe, ihre Geschichte, Eigenart, Verwendung und Abwehr. Mit einem Anhange "Ueber den Untergang des Panzerschiffes 'Maine' der Flotte der Vereinigten Staaten von Amerika." Berlin: E. S. Mittler & Sohn, 1898. vi, 115(1) p., 8 pl. illus. 8°. **VXV**

717. Guierre, A. L'avenir de la torpille et la guerre future. Avec une préface de M. le lieutenant de vaisseau Duboc. Paris: Berger-Levrault & Cie., 1898. xv, 279 p. 12°. **VXV**

718. H., J. Neuerungen im Torpedowesen. illus. (Mittheilungen aus dem Gebiete des Seewesens, Pola, Bd. 26, 1898, p. 1010–1018.) **VXA**

719. ——— Obrys Richtungsregulator für den automobilen Torpedo. illus. (Mittheilungen aus dem Gebiete des Seewesens, Pola, Bd. 26, 1898, p. 1086–1093.) **VXA**

720. ——— Über Breitseit-Unterwasser-Lancierapparate. (Mittheilungen aus dem Gebiete des Seewesens, Bd. 26, 1898, p. 22–32.) **VXA**

Reprinted in *Journal* of the Royal United Service Institution, London, v. 42, 1898, p. 184–189, *VWA.*

721. Hollands neues unterseeisches Torpedoboot. illus. (Mittheilungen aus dem Gebiete des Seewesens, Pola, Bd. 26, 1898, p. 1033–1038.) **VXA**

722. Jane, Frederick T. The torpedo in peace and war. London: W. Thacker & Co., 1898. 164 p. illus. 4°. **VXV**

723. Lakin-Smith, C. Torpedoes. (Engineer, London, v. 85, 1898, p. 448.) **VA**

Abstract of an address delivered before the Mason University College Engineering Society, May 5, 1898.

724. Limitations of the torpedo boat. (Scientific American, New York, v. 79, 1898, p. 226–227.) **VA**

725. Maxim, Hudson. Aerial torpedoes. illus. (Cassier's magazine, New York, v. 14, 1898, p. 250–254.) **VDA**

726. May, J. H. Le canon, la torpille et l'éperon; essai de tactique moderne. Traduit de l'anglais par G. de Saint-Pair. (Revue maritime, Paris, v. 136, 1898, p. 523–578; v. 137, 1898, p. 77–114.) **VXA**

727. Messrs. Schneider & Co.'s works at Creusot. illus. (Engineering, London, v. 66, 1898, p. 692–694.) **VDA**

Notes on torpedoes and torpedo boats.

728. Mine subacquee. loro importanza, modo di impiegarle e di combatterle. (Rivista di artiglieria e genio, Roma, anno 15, v. 4, 1898, p. 143–147.) **VWW**

729. Noalhat, H. Nouvelle torpille automobile. illus. (Le génie civil, Paris, tome 32, 1898, p. 347–351.) **VA**

Description of the Howell torpedo manufactured by the French Hotchkiss Co.

730. ₁**Notes** on torpedoes.₎ (Scientific American supplement, New York, v. 45, 1898, Navy edition, p. 36–39.) **VA**

731. Proyectil-torpedo Maxim. illus. (Revista general de marina, Madrid, tomo 42, 1898, p. 894–900.) **VXA**

Translated from *Rivista di artiglieria e genio.*

732. Riera y Alemañy, José. Torpedos mecánicos. (Revista general de marina, Madrid, tomo 42, 1898, p. 3–13, 168–179, 320–332.) **VXA**

The article commences in tomo 41, Dec., 1897, which the Library lacks.

733. Robert Fulton's torpedo. (Scientific American, New York, v. 78, 1898, p. 361.) **VA**

734. Sears, W. J. A general description of the Whitehead torpedo. (United States Naval Institute, Proceedings, Annapolis, v. 24, 1898, p. 89–110.) **VXA**

Abstracted in *Engineering,* London, v. 66, 1898, p. 89–91, *VDA;* and in *Scientific American supplement,* New York, v. 46, 1898, p. 18911–18914, *VA.*

735. Spanish destroyers and torpedo boats destined for Cuba. illus. (Scientific American, New York, v. 78, 1898, p. 184.) **VA**

736. Spanish torpedo boat destroyer "Terror." illus. (Scientific American, v. 78, 1898, p. 385, 391.) **VA**

737. Spears, John R. Torpedo boats in the war with Spain. (Scribner's magazine, New York, v. 24, 1898, p. 614–619.) ***DA**

1898, continued.

738. Submarine mining and torpedo warfare.   illus.   (Scientific American, New York, v. 78, 1898, p. 149–150.)   **VA**
Notes on the Sims-Edison, Victoria, Brennan, and Whitehead torpedoes.

739. The **Submarine** torpedo boat. (Scientific American, New York, v. 78, 1898, p. 227.)   **VA**
Notes on torpedoes.

740. The **Tesla** torpedo. illus. (Scientific American, New York, v. 79, 1898, p. 322, 326.)   **VA**
Invention of Nikola Tesla.

741. Torpedo defence. illus. (Army and navy journal, New York, v. 35, 1898, p. 612–613.)   †† **VWA**

742. Torpedo discharge tubes. illus. (Engineer, London, v. 85, 1898, p. 496–498.)   **VA**
Also in *Scientific American supplement*, New York, v. 46, 1898, p. 18866–18867, *VA*.

743. Torpedo work in the Civil war. (Scientific American supplement, New York, v. 45, 1898, no. 1167, p. 18678.)   **VA**
Brief note.

744. Torpedoes. illus. (Scientific American supplement, New York, v. 46, 1898, Coast defence supplement, p. 38–41.)   **VA**
A very complete article giving accounts of the Sims-Edison, Dirigible, Whitehead, and Howell torpedoes, and submarine mines.

745. Le **Torpilleur** de 1ʳᵉ classe 156. illus. (Journal de la marine, le yacht, Paris, année 21, 1898, p. 6.)   †† **VXF**

746. Le **Torpilleur** de 1ʳᵉ classe 216. illus. (Journal de la marine, le yacht, Paris, année 21, 1898, p. 534.)   †† **VXF**

747. Les **Torpilleurs** de haute-mer. (Journal de la marine, le yacht, Paris, année 21, 1898, p. 197–198.)   †† **VXF**

748. Wellman, H. Page.   Wellman's marine torpedo. illus. (Electrical review, New York, v. 32, 1898, p. 297.)   **VGA**

749. Whitehead torpedo. (Scientific American, New York, v. 78, 1898, p. 362.)   **VA**
Brief note.

1899

750. Les **Chaudières** des torpilleurs. (Journal de la marine, le yacht, Paris, année 22, 1899, p. 329–330.)   †† **VXF**

751. Del gobierno de los torpederos con mar cruesa. (Revista general de marina, Madrid, tomo 44, 1899, p. 145–160.) **VXA**
Translated from *Marine Rundschau.*

752. Die **Entwicklung** des technischen Wesens der k. u. k. Kriegs-Marine in den letzten 50 Jahren. illus. (Mittheilungen

aus dem Gebiete des Seewesens, Pola, Bd. 27, 1899, p. 1–14, 101–110, 205–219, 313–340, 405–413.)   **VXA**
On torpedoes, p. 313–340.

753. Japanese torpedo boat destroyer "Ikadsuchi." illus. (Scientific American, New York, v. 80, 1899, p. 85.)   **VA**

754. L., P. Les patrons-pilotes de torpilleurs. (Journal de la marine, le yacht, Paris, année 22, 1899, p. 401.)   †† **VXF**

755. Los **Lanzatorpedos** encima y debajo del agua. Extractado de la "Rivista marittima" por M. A. Bunel. (Revista general de marina, Madrid, tomo 44, 1899, p. 588–595.)   **VXA**

756. Lloyd, E. W. Discharge of torpedoes below water. (Engineering, London, v. 68, 1899, p. 386–387.)   **VDA**
Also in *Proceedings* of the United States Naval Institute, v. 25, 1899, p. 926–929, *VXA*. Abstracted in *Engineer*, London, v. 88, 1899, p. 292, *VA*, and in *Report* of the British Association for the Advancement of Science, Dover meeting, 1899, p. 855, * *EC.*
Paper read before the British Association for the Advancement of Science at the Dover meeting, 1899.

757. Niblack, Albert Parker.   Tactical considerations involved in the design of the torpedo-boat.   (Society of Naval Architects and Marine Engineers, Transactions, New York, v. 7, 1899, p. 245–255.)   **VXA**
With discussion, p. 255–266.
Also printed, without the discussion, in *Marine engineering*, New York, v. 5, 1900, p. 57–60, † *VXA*; United States Naval Institute, *Proceedings*, Annapolis, v. 26, 1900, p. 167–178, *VXA*; and in the *Revista general de marina*, Madrid, tomo 47, 1900, p. 542–550; tomo 48, 1901, p. 311–319, *VXA*.
Valuable data on torpedoes.

758. Noalhat, H. Art militaire; attaque et défense des côtes au moyen des torpilles. (Bulletin technique, Paris, année 1, tome 1, 1899, p. 111–131.)   **VDA**

759. Our new fleet of torpedo boat destroyers. illus. (Scientific American, New York, v. 81, 1899, p. 312.)   **VA**
Description of the "Bainbridge" class.

760. Parga, Luis F. de.   Cuatro palabras sobre el material de torpedos "Latimer Clark." (Revista general de marina, Madrid, tomo 44, 1899, p. 294–297.)   **VXA**

761. Preuschen, Franz, Freiherr von. Whitehead's neuer Breitseit-Unterwasserapparat für Torpedolancierung. illus. (Mittheilungen aus dem Gebiete des Seewesens, Pola, Bd. 27, 1899, p. 413–416.)   **VXA**

762. Richardson, J. B.   Coast defense against torpedo-boat attack. illus. (Journal of the United States Artillery, Fort Monroe, Va., v. 11, 1899, p. 65–83.) **VWA**
From the *Proceedings* of the Royal Artillery Institute.
Also printed in the *Journal* of the Military Service Institution of the United States, Governor's Island, N. Y., v. 24, 1899, p. 259–275, *VWA*.

1899, continued.

763. Roden, Ernest K. Submarine mines. illus. (Mechanic arts magazine, Scranton, Pa., v. 4, 1899, p. 118–122.)   **VA**

Why the submarine mine is a necessity in modern naval warfare; the camera obscura as an observation tower.

764. —— Torpedoes. illus. (Mechanic arts magazine, Scranton, Pa., v. 4, 1899, p. 167–171.)   **VA**

Data on the Whitehead and Howell torpedoes.

765. Somborn, Th. Rôle des torpilleurs en temps de guerre. (Revue maritime, Paris, v. 140, 1899, p. 559–565.)   **VXA**

Abstracted from *Harper's magazine* and *Scribner's magazine.*
Use of torpedoes in the Spanish-American war.

766. El **Torpedo**; su velocidad, su radio de acción y su eficacia destructiva. (Revista general de marina, Madrid, tomo 45, 1899, p. 748–757.)   **VXA**

Translated from the *Rivista marittima* by M. A. Bunel.

767. Torpedo boat practice. (Marine review, Cleveland, O., v. 19, March 2, 1899, p. 12–13.)   † **VXA**

Abstracted in *Revue maritime*, Paris, v. 144, 1900, p. 322–326, *VXA.*

768. Torpedo launching tubes. illus. (Engineering, London, v. 68, 1899, p. 261–264, 287–291.)   **VDA**

Schneider-Canet system.

769. Torpedo steering by ether waves. illus. (Electrician, London, v. 43, 1899, p. 112–114.)   **VGA**

Also printed in the *Electrical review,* New York, v. 34, 1899, p. 370–371, *VGA.* Abstracted in *Minutes of proceedings* of the Institution of Civil Engineers, London, v. 139, 1899, p. 469–470, *VDA.*
Invention of Walter Jamieson and John Trotter.

770. ¡Torpedoes controlled by invisible rays.¡ (Marine engineer, London, v. 21, 1899, p. 146.)   **VXA**

Editorial on the invention of Axel Orling and J. T. Armstrong.

771. Tube lance-torpilles immergé. illus. (Le génie civil, Paris, tome 35, 1899, p. 349.)   **VA**

1900

772. A., D. H. Aerial torpedoes. (Engineering, London, v. 69, 1900, p. 262.) **VDA**

773. Angier, R. H. Aerial torpedoes. (Engineering, London, v. 69, 1900, p. 230.)   **VDA**

774. Ballard, G. A. Considering the changes made in naval construction during the past twenty years, and in view of the experience gained during the China-Japanese and Spanish-American wars, what are the best types of war-vessels for the British navy, including armour, armament, and general equipment for ships of all types? (Royal United Service Institution, Journal, London, v. 44, 1900, p. 359–394.)   **VWA**

Torpedo craft and destroyers, p. 391–393.

775. Chandler, L. H. The automobile torpedo and its use. (United States Naval Institute. Proceedings, Annapolis, v. 26, 1900, p. 47–104.)   **VXA**

A discussion of the torpedo policy best adapted for the United States naval service.

776. —— Torpedo operations in naval warfare. (United States Naval Institute, Proceedings. Annapolis, v. 26, 1900, p. 417–440; Discussion, v. 27, 1901, p. 141–150.)   **VXA**

The automobile torpedo of to-day; the tactics and strategy of its use and the effect of its introduction upon old warfare in general.

777. Duranti, W. de. Les torpilleurs. (Journal de la marine, le yacht, Paris, année 23, 1900, p. 25–26.)   †† **VXF**

778. Engines of the torpedo boat destroyer "Viper." illus. (Scientific American, New York, v. 82, 1900, p. 248–249.)   **VA**

779. Forest, F., and H. Noalhat. Les bateaux sous-marins: technologie. Paris: Vᵛᵉ Dunod, 1900. 8°.   **VXV**

Chap. 11. Armement, p. 313–367.

780. G., A. J. Les torpilleurs "Audacieux" et "Trombe." (Journal de la marine, le yacht, Paris, année 23, 1900, p. 452–453.)   †† **VXF**

781. Gathmann, Emil. Torpedo safety devices. (United States Naval Institute, Proceedings, Annapolis, v. 26, 1900, p. 629–635.)   **VXA**

782. Gathmann aerial torpedo gun. (Engineer, London, v. 90, 1900, p. 191–192.) **VA**

Also in *Proceedings* of the United States Naval Institute, Annapolis, v. 26, 1900, p. 694–695, *VXA.*

783. Greenhill, A. G. The wind problem in gunnery. illus. (Journal of the United States artillery, Fort Monroe, Va., v. 13, 1900, p. 1–18.)   **VWA**

Notes on torpedo firing.

784. Interesting experiments with torpedoes. (Scientific American, New York, v. 83, 1900, p. 264.)   **VA**

Also published in United States Naval Institute, *Proceedings,* v. 26, 1900, p. 693–694, *VXA.*
Experiments with the whitehead torpedo in the gulf of Finland.

785. Jackson, R. H. Torpedo craft; type and employment. (United States Naval Institute, Proceedings, Annapolis, v. 26, 1900, p. 1–45.)   **VXA**

Valuable data on torpedoes.

786. L., P. L'emploi de la torpille à bord des navires de combat. (Journal de la marine, le yacht, Paris, année 23, 1900, p. 425–426, 533.)   †† **VXF**

1900, continued.

787. —— L'utilisation de nos torpilleurs et sous-marins. (Journal de la marine, le yacht, Paris, année 23, 1900, p. 205–206.) †† **VXF**

788. La Rouveraye, Paul de. Les torpilleurs et le pilotage. (Journal de la marine, le yacht, Paris, année 23, 1900, p. 97.) †† **VXF**

789. Laurenti, C. La navigazione subacquea a scopo di guerra. (Rivista marittima, Roma, anno 33, trimestre 2, 1900, p. 379–406.) **VXA**

790. —— La navigazione subacquea a scopo di guerra. (Rivista marittima, Roma, anno 33, trimestre 4, 1900, p. 114–116.) **VXA**
A reply to Giovanni Sechi's criticism of his article of the same title.

791. Noalhat, H. Le nouvel appareil directeur pour torpilles automobiles. illus. (La revue technique, Paris, tome 21, 1900, p. 364–367.) **VA**
Describes the Whitehead and Howell torpedoes and the Obry gyroscopic device.

792. The **Role** of the torpedo in war. (Marine review, Cleveland, O., v. 22, Sept. 6, 1900, p. 19.) † **VXA**
Abstracted from the *Admiralty and Horse Guards gazette.*

793. S. Les torpilleurs sous-marins, type "Holland." (Journal de la marine, le yacht, Paris, année 23, 1900, p. 265–266.) †† **VXF**

794. Sechi, Giovanni. La navigazione subacquea a scopo di guerra. (Rivista marittima, Roma, anno 33, trimestre 3, 1900, p. 277–282.) **VXA**
A criticism of Laurenti's article of the same title.

795. Talbot, F. A. A. Steering torpedoes by means of wireless telegraphy. (Scientific American, New York, v. 82, 1900, p. 291.) **VA**
Notes on the Sims-Edison, Brennan, Howell, and Whitehead torpedoes.

796. Torpedo practice at Newport, R. I. illus. (Scientific American, New York, v. 82, 1900, p. 152.) **VA**

797. Les **Torpilleurs** hollandais "Hydra et Scylla." illus. (Journal de la marine, le yacht, Paris, année 23, 1900, p. 406–407.) †† **VXF**

798. Wilmot, Sidney Eardley. Torpedo warfare. illus. (In his: Our fleet of to-day and its development during the last half century, London, 1900, p. 196–218.) **VYB**

1901

799. Above-water torpedo tubes. (Engineer, London, v. 92, 1901, p. 483–484.) **VA**

800. Die **Anwendung** des Torpedos auf Schlachtschiffen. (Mittheilungen aus dem Gebiete des Seewesens, Pola, Bd. 29, 1901, p. 83–87.) **VXA**
From *Le yacht.*

801. Arcangeli, Luigi. Torpediniere o caccia-torpediniere? (Rivista marittima, Roma, anno 34, trimestre 4, 1901, p. 61–66.) **VXA**

802. Carl E. Myer's electric aerial torpedo. illus. (Scientific American, New York, v. 84, 1901, p. 10.) **VA**

803. Ciano, Alessandro. Circa l'impiego delle controtorpediniere in tempo di pace. (Rivista marittima, Roma, anno 34, trimestre 4, 1901, p. 483–485.) **VXA**

804. Clowes, William Laird. A coming revolution in naval warfare. (The new liberal review, London, v. 1, 1901, p. 588–595.) ***DA**

805. Dentice, Edoardo. Le torpediniere — passato e futuro. (Rivista marittima, Roma, anno 34, trimestre 1, 1901, p. 281–282.) **VXA**
Comments on article of the same title by Gavotti in the *Lega navale* of Jan., 1901.

806. Discharging torpedoes by electricity. illus. (Electrical review, London, v. 49, 1901, p. 335–336.) **VGA**

807. Gaget, Maurice. La navigation sous-marine. Généralités et historique. Théorie du sous-marin. Bateaux sous-marins modernes. La guerre maritime. Paris: Ch. Beranger, 1901. 2 p.l., 472 p. illus. 12°. **VXV**
Un mot sur les torpilles automobiles, p. 62–90.

808. Garelli, A. Le torpediniere — passato e futuro. (Rivista marittima, Roma, anno 34, trimestre 1, 1901, p. 282–284.) **VXA**
Comments on article of the same title by Gavotti in the *Lega navale* of Jan., 1901.

809. Gathmann, Emil. Gathmann 18-inch torpedo gun. illus. (Scientific American, New York, v. 84, 1901, p. 313–314.) **VA**

810. Howell Torpedo Company, complainant, versus E. W. Bliss Company, defendant. Circuit Court of the United States, Eastern District of New York. The Whitehead torpedo suit. Decision of Judge Thomas, that the Whitehead torpedo does not infringe the Howell patent. Cooperstown, N. Y.: Crist, Scott and Parshall, 1901. 2 p.l., ii, 16, (i)xviii–xxi p. illus. 4°. †† **VXC p.v.8, no.5**

811. Jane, Fred T. The apotheosis of the torpedo. A brief for the new school. (Fortnightly review, London, v. 76 (new series, v. 70), 1901, p. 261–278.) ***DA**

1901, continued.

812. The **Jones** buoyant torpedo guard. illus. (Marine engineer, London, v. 23, 1901, p. 282–284.) **VXA**
Invention of Dr. G. Horatio Jones. · Protection of ships from torpedoes.

813. Kimball, William Wirt. Torpedo-boat organization and service: Atlantic coast of the United States. (United States Naval Institute. Proceedings, Annapolis, v. 27, 1901, p. 713–723.) **VXA**

814. Laurenti, C. L'antidoto dei sotto-marini. (Rivista marittima, Roma, anno 34, trimestre 3, 1901, p. 72–74.) **VXA**

815. —— La navigazione subacquea nel secolo XIX. (Rivista marittima, Roma, anno 34, trimestre 2, 1901, p. 457–494.) **VXA**

816. A **New** Swedish torpedo. (Engineering, London, v. 71, 1901, p. 184.) **VDA**
Invention of Major W. T. Unge.
Also in *Journal* of the American Society of Naval Engineers, Washington, D. C., v. 13, 1901, p. 465–467, *VXA.*

817. Orling-Armstrong torpedo. (United States Naval Institute, Proceedings, Annapolis, v. 27, 1901, p. 840.) **VXA**
Brief note.

818. The **Orling** torpedo. (Engineer, London, v. 92, 1901, p. 434.) **VA**
Also printed in *Scientific American supplement,* New York, v. 52, 1901, p. 21648–21649, *VA.*

819. Romero, Antonio, and JUAN CERVERA Y VALDERRAMA. Ejercicios de torpedos en la bahía de Cadiz. (Revista general de marina, Madrid, tomo 49, 1901, p. 165–177.) **VXA**

820. Rota, Giuseppe. Le chiglie laterali di rollio sulle controtorpediniere. (Rivista marittima, Roma, anno 34, trimestre 1, 1901, p. 467–469.) **VXA**

821. Die **Russischen** Torpedobootszerstörer in Kiel. illus. (Ueberall, Berlin, 1901, Bd. 1, p. 238–240.) **†† VXA**
Description of Russian torpedo boat destroyer.

822. Sechi, Giovanni. Il naviglio sottile. (Rivista marittima, Roma, anno 34, trimestre 4, 1901, p. 441–445.) **VXA**

823. Seeminen. (Ueberall, Berlin, 1901, Bd. 1, p. 408.) **†† VXA**
With illustration on p. 393.

824. Stabile, Giuseppe. "Torpediniere." (Rivista marittima, Roma, anno 34, trimestre 4, 1901, p. 479–483.) **VXA**

825. Steering torpedoes by wireless telegraphy. illus. (Scientific American, New York, v. 84, 1901, p. 101–102.) **VA**
Abstracted in United States Naval Institute, *Proceedings,* v. 27, 1901, p. 207–208, *VXA.*
Invention of Cecil Varicas.

826. Submarine mines. illus. (Scientific American supplement, New York, v. 52, 1901, p. 21386–21387.) **VA**
Valuable historical notes on the torpedo.

827. Torpedo boats and destroyers. illus. (Scientific American, New York, v. 85, 1901, p. 388.) **VA**
Description of the "Farragut."

828. Torpedoes and torpedo vessels. (Engineering, London, v. 72, 1901, p. 862–863.) **VDA**
Review of the second edition of Lieut. G. E. Armstrong's book of that title.

829. Torpedoes for the United States navy. (United States Naval Institute, Proceedings, Annapolis, v. 27, 1901, p. 839.) **VXA**
Abstract from report of the Chief of the Bureau of Ordnance.

830. Torpille autonome aérienne. (Journal de la marine, le yacht, Paris, année 24, 1901, p. 94–95.) **†† VXF**
Invention of Major W. T. Unge.

831. The **Whitehead** torpedo works at Fiume. illus. (Engineering, London, v. 72, 1901, p. 395, 398–401.) **VDA**
Biographical notes on Robert Whitehead.

1902

832. A, F. d'. Esploratori e cacciatorpediniere. (Rivista marittima, Roma, anno 35, trimestre 2, 1902, p. 79–81.) **VXA**

833. Arcangeli, Luigi. Esploratori e cacciatorpediniere. (Rivista marittima, Roma, anno 35, trimestre 2, 1902, p. 281–288.) **VXA**

834. Bonamico, D. La difesa mobile costiera. (Rivista marittima, Roma, anno 35, trimestre 3, 1902, p. 5–22.) **VXA**

835. Bonomo, Quintino. Le armi subaquee nel secolo XIX. (Rivista marittima, Roma, anno 35, trimestre 2, 1902, p. 437–477.) **VXA**

836. Bruzzone, Attilio. Torpediniere di 1ª classe. (Rivista marittima, Roma, anno 35, trimestre 4, 1902, p. 357–359.) **VXA**

837. Cloarec, P. Cuirassés, torpilleurs et sous-marins. (Journal de la marine, le yacht, Paris, année 25, 1902, p. 193–194.) **†† VXF**

838. Conti, Gerolamo. Torpediniere di 1ª classe. (Rivista marittima, Roma, anno 35, trimestre 4, 1902, p. 359–362.) **VXA**

839. Corsi, Cam. Sull' utilità dei cacciatorpediniere. (Rivista marittima, Roma, anno 35, trimestre 1, 1902, p. 307–311.) **VXA**

840. Cuniberti, Vittorio E. Scouts e destroyers. (Rivista marittima, Roma, anno 35, trimestre 1, 1902, p. 536–544.) **VXA**

1902, continued.

841. Daniel, J.   Torpilles.   (In his: Poudres et explosifs: dictionnaire des matières explosives, Paris, 1902, p. 771–772.)   **VOG**

842. Delorenzi, Giuseppe. Tipi di torpediniera. (Rivista marittima, Roma, anno 35, trimestre 2, 1902, p. 479–483.) **VXA**

843. Fyfe, Herbert C.   The Whitehead torpedo. illus. (In his: Submarine warfare — past, present and future, London, 1902, p. 214–232.)   **VXV**

844. Heinz, J. Der Breitseit-Unterwasser-Lancierapparat, System Drzewiecki. illus. (Mittheilungen aus dem Gebiete des Seewesens, Pola, Bd. 30, 1902, p. 534–547.)
                                            VXA
Broadside submarine torpedo tubes.

845. Hurd, Archibald Spicer. The coming of the submarine. (United service, Philadelphia, series 3, v. 1, 1902, p. 390–403.)
                                            VWA
Notes on torpedoes.

846. Jacoucci, T.   Esploratori e cacciatorpediniere. (Rivista marittima, Roma, anno 35, trimestre 2, 1902, p. 75–79.) **VXA**

847. Le Roll, P.   Contre-torpilleurs d'escadre et torpilleurs de défense mobile. (Journal de la marine, le yacht, Paris, année 25, p. 613–614.)   **†† VXF**

848. M., E. Siluro dirigibile od "actinauta." illus. (Rivista marittima, Roma, anno 35, trimestre 1, 1902, p. 162–167.)   **VXA**

849. M., V.   Cacciatorpediniere e torpediniere degli Stati Uniti d'America. (Rivista marittima, Roma, anno 35, trimestre 1, 1902, p. 593–598.)   **VXA**

850. Malfatti, V.   Cacciatorpediniere inglesi e loro prove. (Rivista marittima, Roma, anno 35, trimestre 1, 1902, p. 172–177.)   **VXA**

851. The New torpedo. (Engineer, London, v. 94, 1902, p. 616; v. 95, 1903, p. 12.)
                                            VA
Has a range of 3,000 yards.

852. Perroni, L. Torpediniere di 1ª classe. (Rivista marittima, Roma, anno 35, trimestre 4, 1902, p. 79–81; anno 36, trimestre 1, 1903, p. 293–297.)   **VXA**

853. Plueddemann, M.   Modernes Seekriegswesen. Berlin: E. S. Mittler u. Sohn, 1902. vii, 298 p., 8 pl. 8°.   **VXM**
Die Torpedowaffe, p. 74–83; Torpedoschutznetze, p. 92–94.

854. Santoro, Cesare. Torpediniere di 1ª classe. (Rivista marittima, Roma, anno 35, trimestre 3, 1902, p. 333–339; anno 35, trimestre 4, 1902, p. 354–357.)   **VXA**

855. Schneider-Canet launching apparatus for submarine torpedoes. illus. (Scientific American, New York, v. 87, 1902, p. 151.)   **VA**

856. Schwarz, Tjard. Der Untergang der "Cobra" und seine Lehren für den Bau von Torpedofahrzeugen. (Marine Rundschau, Berlin, Jahrg. 13, 1902, p. 52–60.)   **VXA**

857. Sewell, John Stephen. Electricity in its application to submarine mines. (American Institute of Electrical Engineers, Transactions, New York, v. 19, 1902, p. 563–568.)   **VGA**

858. Spear, Lawrence. Submarine torpedo-boats, past, present, and future. (Society of Naval Architects and Marine Engineers, Transactions, Washington, v. 10, 1902, p. 323–350.)   **VXA**
Notes on inventions of Cornelius Von Drebbel, William Bourne, Bushnell, and Robert Fulton.

859. Submarines controlled by the Armol system. illus. (Scientific American, New York, v. 86, 1902, p. 40–41.)   **VA**
Invention of Messrs. Orling and Armstrong.

860. The Torpedo boat fiasco. (Scientific American, New York, v. 86, 1902, p. 102.)
                                            VA

861. Torpedo launching apparatus. (Army and navy journal, New York, v. 40. 1902, p. 69.)   **†† VWA**

862. Ueber die Moralität der submarinen Kriegführung. (Mittheilungen aus dem Gebiete des Seewesens, Pola, Bd. 30, 1902, p. 881–901.)   **VXA**
Translated from Herbert C. Fyfe's *Submarine warfare, past, present and future.*

863. Der Untergang des Torpedobootes "S 42." (Ueberall, Berlin, Jahrg. 4, 1902, p. 971–972.)   **VXA**

864. Walke, Willoughby. Lectures on explosives... New York: John Wiley & Sons, 1902. 4 p.l., vii–xvi, 435 p. 3. ed. rev. and enl. 8°.   **VOG**
Precautions to be observed in loading shell and torpedoes, p. 381–382.

1903

865. Beach, Edward L. Our torpedo-boat flotilla. (United States Naval Institute, Proceedings, Annapolis, v. 29, 1903, p. 117–159.)   **VXA**
Reprinted in *United service*, New York, series 3, v. 5, 1904, p. 443–482, *VWA.*

866. Börresen, Jacob. The torpedo-virator. illus. (Royal United Service Institution, Journal, London, v. 47, 1903, p. 67–74.)
                                            VWA

867. Bruzzone, Attilio. Caldaie a tubi d'acqua dei cacciatorpedinieri tipo Schichau. (Rivista marittima, Roma, anno 36, trimestre 1, 1903, p. 308–311.)   **VXA**

1903, continued.

868. Burgoyne, Alan H. Submarine navigation, past and present. New York: E. P. Dutton & Co., 1903. 2 v. 8°. **VXV**

For data on torpedoes see v. 2, p. 201–236.

869. Chandler, Lloyd H. Automobile torpedoes; their use and probable effectiveness. (United States Naval Institute, Proceedings, Annapolis, v. 29, 1903, p. 883–915.) **VXA**

Abstracted in *Journal of the United States artillery,* v. 22, 1904, p. 94–95. *VWA.*

870. Competitive trials of subsurface and submarine torpedo boats. (Scientific American, New York, v. 89, 1903, p. 327.) **VA**

871. Laurenti, C. Sull' impiego dei sottomarini. (Rivista marittima, Roma, anno 36, trimestre 2, 1903, p. 322–326.) **VXA**

872. Le Roll, P. Les nouveaux torpilleurs de 1ʳᵉ classe. (Journal de la marine, le yacht, Paris, année 26, 1903, p. 695–696.) **†† VXF**

873. Marulli, F. Sull' impiego dei sottomarini. (Rivista marittima, Roma, anno 36, trimestre 2, 1903, p. 5–15.) **VXA**

874. Morali, R. S. Torpediniere di 1ᵃ classe. (Rivista marittima, Roma, anno 36, trimestre 1, 1903, p. 78–84.) **VXA**

875. R. Die Torpedowaffe auf Schlachtschiffen. illus. (Ueberall, Berlin, Jahrg. 6, 1903, p. 228–231.) **†† VXA**

876. Ricart, Francisco. Submarinos. (Memorial de ingenieros, Madrid, año 58, 1903, p. 203–207, 236–240.) **VWA**

877. Rosendahl. Zur Wiedereinführung der Torpedoarmierung auf den Schlachtschiffen der Vereinigten Staaten. (Marine-Rundschau, Berlin, Jahrg. 14, 1903, p. 1344–1349.) **VXA**

Abstracted from the *Proceedings* of the United States Naval Institute.

878. Spear, Lawrence. Submarine torpedo boats. illus. (Scientific American supplement, New York, v. 55, 1903, p. 22653–22658.) **VA**

Notes on torpedoes.

879. Submarines and torpedoes. (Army and navy journal, New York, v. 41, 1903, p. 439.) **†† VWA**

Brief review of the report of Lieut. John Halligan, Jr., to the Navy Department.

880. Torpedo boat controlled by wireless transmission. illus. (Western electrician, Chicago, v. 32, 1903, p. 128.) **VGA**

881. The Torpedo boat destroyer Perry. (Scientific American, New York, v. 89, 1903, p. 308.) **VA**

882. Torpedo experiments with the "Belleisle" by the British admiralty. (Scientific American, New York, v. 89, 1903, p. 214–215.) **VA**

883. Torpedo and submarine. (Army and navy gazette, London, v. 44, 1903, p. 1140–1141.) **VWA**

884. The Torpedo tube and our new battleships. (Scientific American, New York, v. 89, 1903, p. 78.) **VA**

885. Torpedo tubes. (Army and navy register, Washington, v. 34, 1903, p. 12–13.) **VWA**

886. Torpedo tubes in the war game. (Scientific American supplement, New York, v. 55, 1903, p. 22599.) **VA**

887. Torpedoing a battleship. (Marine engineer, London, v. 25, 1903, p. 261.) **VXA**

A brief note on the experiments on the battleship "Belleisle."

1904

888. Arthaud, d'. Torpilles et cuirassés. (Marine française, Paris, année 17, 1904, p. 118–124.) **VXA**

889. Battleship or torpedoes. (Scientific American, New York, v. 90, 1904, p. 358.) **VA**

Editorial.

890. The Belleisle torpedo experiments. (Journal of the United States artillery, Fort Monroe, v. 21, 1904, p. 220–221.) **VWA**

891. Börresens Torpedo-Virator. (Mitteilungen aus dem Gebiete des Seewesens, Pola, Bd. 32, 1904, p. 1051–1052.) **VXA**

892. Coast defense. (Journal of the United States artillery, Fort Monroe, v. 22, 1904, p. 215–261.) **VWA**

Valuable notes on torpedoes and mines.

893. Contract trial of torpedo boat no. 27, The Blakely. (American Society of Naval Engineers' Journal, Washington, v. 16, 1904, p. 1076–1094.) **VXA**

894. Cotter, E. W. Coast defence from an imperial standpoint. (Royal United Service Institution, Journal, London, v. 48, 1904, p. 510–532.) **VWA**

Notes on torpedo warfare.

895. Dahl, G. M. Blank torpedo shooting. illus. (United States Naval Institute, Proceedings, Annapolis, v. 30, 1904, p. 389–403.) **VXA**

896. La Défense navale de la France (1894–1904). Rapport du chef d'état-major général. (Marine française, Paris, année 17, 1904, p. 309–319, 392–394; année 18, 1905, p. 51–57.) **VXA**

Des progrès accomplis dans la défense mobile par torpilleurs, année 17, p. 309–315; Défense mobile par

1904, continued.

sous-marins, année 17, p. 316–319; Les torpilles et leurs progrès depuis 1894, année 17, p. 392–394; année 18, p. 51–57.

897. Dewar, A. C.   In the existing state of development of warships, and of torpedo and submarine vessels, in what manner can the strategical objects, formerly pursued by means of blockading an enemy in his own ports, be best attained? illus. (Royal United Service Institution, Journal, London, v. 48, 1904, p. 329–378, 457–509.) **VWA**

898. Dibos, M.   De la recherche et du dragage des torpilles vigilantes.   illus. (Société des ingénieurs civils de France, Mémoires et compte rendu des travaux, Paris, année 1904, v. 2, p. 501–514.)   **VDA**
Gives valuable data on the use of torpedoes in the Russo-Japanese war.

899.   The Effect of torpedo explosions. illus. (Engineering, London, v. 78, 1904, p. 468.)   **VDA**
With illustration on p. 472.
Also printed in *Proceedings* of the United States Naval Institute, Annapolis, v. 30, 1904, p. 883, *VXA.*
Loss of the "Hitachi Maru" and the "Sado Maru" in the Russo-Japanese war.

900. Fawcett, Waldon.   Electrically operated submarine mines. illus. (Electrical review, New York, v. 44, 1904, p. 906–908.)
VGA

901. Feldhaus, Franz Maria.   Lexikon der Erfindungen und Entdeckungen auf den Gebieten der Naturwissenschaften und Technik. Heidelberg: Carl Winter, 1904. viii, 144 p. 8°.   **V**
Gives the following dates in the invention of the torpedo and submarine:
1585. Federigo Gianibelli uses a torpedo in Antwerp.
1620. Cornelis Drebbel constructs the first submarine.
1797. Robert Fulton invents his submarine mine, which he calls the "Fish torpedo."
1860. Robert Whitehead invents the "Fish torpedo," the first automobile torpedo.

902. G., H. B.   Recent torpedo developments. (Nautical magazine, Glasgow, v. 73, 1904, p. 152–158.)   **VXA**
Also in *Mitteilungen aus dem Gebiete des Seewesens,* Pola, Bd. 32, 1904, p. 615–620, *VXA.*

903. Improvements needed in torpedoes. (Scientific American, New York, v. 91, 1904, p. 414.)   **VA**

904. Jane, Frederick T.   Defense of harbors against torpedo boat attack. (Journal of the United States artillery, Fort Monroe, v. 22, 1904, p. 187–191.)   **VWA**
Abstracted from the *Proceedings* of the Royal Artillery Institution.

905. Japan's use of torpedoes. (Army and navy journal, New York, v. 41, 1904, p. 657–658.)   †† **VWA**

906.   The Japanese destroyers. illus. (Scientific American, New York, v. 90, 1904, p. 209, 214, 383, 387.)   **VA**

907. Le Roll, P.   L'emploi de la torpille dans la guerre russo-japonaise. (Journal de la marine, le yacht, Paris, v. 27, 1904, p. 137–138.)   †† **VXF**

908. Maxim, Hudson.   Torpedoes and torpedo warfare. (American monthly Review of reviews, New York, v. 29, 1904, p. 558–564.)   * **DA**

909.   The Modern torpedo. illus. (Scientific American, New York, v. 90, p. 196.)
VA
Notes on the Whitehead and the Schwartzkopff torpedoes.

910. Monreal y Fernandez-Rodil, Federico, and F. MÚÑEZ QUIJANO. Torpedos automóviles. Obra declarada de texto para la Escuela de aplicación por real orden de 31 de diciembre de 1903. [With atlas.] Madrid: Imp. y lit. del Ministerio de Marina, 1904. 2 v. 8° and f°.   † **VXV**

911. Noalhat, H.   Attaque et défense des côtes au moyen des torpilles. illus. (Revue technique, Paris, tome 25, p. 7–11, 74–75, 123–128, 172–177, 223–227, 283–285, 337–342, 394–397, 460–464, 516–520, 566–570.)   **VA**

912. Paulus.   Versuche zur Ermittlung des Einflusses der Wassertiefe auf die Geschwindigkeit der Torpedoboote. (Verein deutscher Ingenieure, Zeitschrift, Berlin, Bd. 48, 1904, p. 1870–1878.)   **VDA**

913. Pouleur, Hector. Torpilleurs et sousmarins. illus. (Revue universelle des mines, Liége, série 4, tome 7, 1904, p. 131–198.)   **VA**

914. —— Torpilleurs & sous-marins. La tactique navale et les enseignements de la guerre russo-japonaise. Liége: C. Desoer, 1904. 74 p., 2 diagrs. illus. 8°.   **VXV**

915. Protection against the explosion of a torpedo. (Journal of the United States artillery, Fort Monroe, v. 22, 1904, p. 205–206.)   **VWA**
Abstracted from *Page's magazine,* Sept., 1904.

916. R.   Moderne   Torpedofahrzeuge. illus. (Ueberall, Berlin, Jahrg. 6, p. 321–324.)   †† **VXA**

917. R., G. E.   Der Minenkrieg in Ostasien. (Ueberall, Berlin, Jahrg. 6, 1904, p. 485–486.)   †† **VXA**

918. Reventlow, E., Graf.   Das Unterseeboot im Reichstage. illus. (Ueberall, Berlin, Jahrg. 6, 1904, p. 490–493.)   †† **VXA**

919. Saint-Requier. La défense contre les torpilleurs. (Journal de la marine, le yacht, Paris, v. 27, 1904, p. 449–450.)   †† **VXF**

920. "Sea-power," pseud. The torpedo in war. (United service magazine, London, v. 28, 1904, p. 437–443.)   * **DA**

921. Stansbury, Hubert. In the existing state of development of war-ships, and of torpedo and submarine vessels, in what

1904, continued.

manner can the strategical objects, formerly pursued by means of blockading an enemy in his own ports, be best attained? (Royal United Service Institution, Journal, London, v. 48, 1904, p. 599–630.) **VWA**

922. Suanzes, Victoriano. Los torpedos en la guerra. (La vida marítima, Madrid, año 3, 1904, p. 405–407.) **†† VXA**

923. The **Submarine** mine. illus. (Scientific American, New York, v. 90, 1904, p. 330.) **VA**

924. Submarines and torpedo warfare. illus. (In: The naval annual, edited by T. A. Brassey, London, 1904, p. 325–339.) **VXA**

Also in *Mitteilungen aus dem Gebiete des Seewesens,* Pola, Bd. 32, 1904, p. 1053–1066, *VXA.*

925. Tanif, Henri. Torpilles, torpilleurs et sous-marins. (Questions diplomatiques et coloniales, Paris, tome 17, 1904, p. 577–588.) **BAA**

926. Torpedo attack in the Russo-Japanese war. (Engineering, London, v. 78, 1904, p. 19–20.) **VDA**

Also printed in *Proceedings* of the United States Naval Institute, Annapolis, v. 30, 1904, p. 669–672, *VXA.*

927. The **Torpedo** boat in modern warfare. (Scientific American, New York, v. 90, 1904, p. 387.) **VA**

Notes on the Russo-Japanese war.

928. Torpedo harbor at Dover. (Scientific American supplement, New York, v. 58, 1904, p. 24123.) **VA**

929. Torpedo-Motorboote. illus. (Ueberall, Berlin, Jahrg. 7, Technisches Ueberall, Jahrg. 2, No. 7, 1904, p. 2–3.) **†† VXA**

930. Torpedo room of a modern battleship. illus. (Scientific American, New York, v. 91, 1904, p. 28.) **VA**

931. Torpedoes in action. (Army and navy gazette, London, v. 45, 1904, p. 156–157.) **† VWA**

932. Torpedoes in action. (Engineer, London, v. 98, 1904, p. 306–307.) **VA**

Letter signed Reflex, containing brief notes on the Russo-Japanese war.

933. United States. — Engineer School. Reprints of essays and lectures on coast defence. Washington Barracks, Washington, D. C.: Engineer School of Application, 1904. vi, 135 p. 8°. (Occasional papers. no. 11.) **VWI**

Contents. Vereker, C. G., Defence against torpedo-boat raids. Curteis, C. S. S., Defence against torpedo-boat raids. Saltmarshe, P., Defence against torpedo-boat raids. Hanna, J. C., Defence against torpedo-boat raids. Jane, Fred T., The defence of harbours against torpedo-boat attack. Cotter, E. W., Coast defence from an imperial standpoint.

The first five articles are reprinted from the

Proceedings of the Royal Artillery Institution for 1903 and 1904; the last from the *Journal* of the Royal United Service Institution, May, 1904.

934. Wie können Kriegsschiffe gegen die Wirkungen von Torpedos und Minen geschützt werden? illus. (Ueberall, Berlin, Jahrg. 7, Technisches Ueberall, Jahrg. 2, No. 10, 1904, p. 1–2.) **†† VXA**

935. Wisser, John Philip. War lessons for the coast artillery. (Journal of the United States artillery, Fort Monroe, v. 22, 1904, p. 262–279.) **VWA**

Torpedoes and submarine mines, p. 266–268.

1905

936. A. Torpedini terrestri automatiche. illus. (Rivista di artiglieria e genio, Roma, annata 22, v. 4, 1905, p. 89–101.) **VWW**

937. An Aerial torpedo. (Scientific American, New York, v. 92, 1905, p. 443.) **VA**

Invention of Joseph J. McIntyre.

938. B., L. Torpilles terrestres automatiques. (Revue du génie militaire, Paris, tome 30, 1905, p. 37–62.) **VWA**

939. Börresens Torpedo-Virator. illus. (Mitteilungen aus dem Gebiete des Seewesens, Pola, Bd. 33, 1905, p. 236–242.) **VXA**

940. Bridge, Sir Cyprian Arthur George. The Russo-Japanese naval campaign of 1904. (Naval annual, Portsmouth, 1905, p. 97–172.) **VXA**

Notes on the use of torpedoes.

941. Burr, S. D. V. The new Bliss-Leavitt torpedo. illus. (Iron age, New York, v. 76, 1905, p. 1594–1597.) **VDA**

Also gives brief description of the Howell and Russian torpedoes.

942. Davis, Henry C. Torpedo companies and company electricians. (Journal of the United States artillery, Fort Monroe, v. 24, 1905, p. 11–16.) **VWA**

943. Die durch Minen an den russischen Port Arthur-Schiffen verursachten Beschädigungen und die Reparaturen der verletzten Schiffe. illus. (Ueberall, Berlin, Jahrg. 7, Technisches Ueberall, Jahrg. 2, No. 8, 1905, p. 1–2.) **†† VXA**

Damage caused to the Russian battleship Port Arthur through mines.

944. E., G. Torpilles terrestres automatiques. illus. (Le génie civil, Paris, tome 47, 1905, p. 297–299.) **VA**

945. An Early submarine. (Army and navy journal, New York, v. 43, 1905, p. 193–194.) **†† VWA**

Account of the Confederate submarine "Handley."

1905, continued.

946. Ferragut y Sbert, Guillermo. Torpederos. illus. (La vida marítima, Madrid, año 4, 1905, p. 568–569.)   †† **VXA**

947. Gun-cotton for torpedoes. (Arms and explosives, London, v. 13, 1905, p. 14.)
          †† **VOG**

948. Incontri, Attilio. Circa un caso di attacco dei siluranti. (Rivista marittima, Roma, anno 38, trimestre 2, 1905, p. 153–159.)   **VXA**

949. Isham torpedo shell tests. illus. (Scientific American, New York, v. 93, 1905, p. 357–358.)   **VA**
Invention of W. S. Isham.

950. Kallenbach, Oscar G. H. Das Torpedowesen der deutschen Marine, mit Berücksichtigung der Erfolge der Torpedowaffe im russisch-japanischen Kriege. (Technologist, New York, Bd. 10, 1905, p. 57–66.)   **VDA**

951. L. Les mines sous-marines russes et japonaises. illus. (Journal de la marine, le yacht, Paris, v. 28, 1905, p. 404–405.)
          †† **VXF**

952. Laurenti, C. I disastri dei sottomarini. (Rivista marittima, Roma, anno 38, trimestre 3, 1905, p. 245–258.)   **VXA**

953. M. Einiges über Schiffsartillerie, Torpedos und Seeminen in der französischen Marine. (Marine Rundschau, Berlin, Jahrg. 16, 1905, p. 407–415.)   **VXA**

954. Max. La défense contre les sousmarins. (Journal de la marine, le yacht, Paris, année 28, 1905, p. 113–114.) †† **VXH**
Translated in *Revista general de marina*, Madrid, tomo 56, 1905, p. 427–432, *VXA.*

955. Mines and subterranean torpedoes at Port Arthur. illus. (Scientific American supplement, New York, v. 59, 1905, p. 24289.)   **VA**

956. The **Obry** apparatus. (Royal United Service Institution, Journal, London, v. 49, 1905, p. 1196.)   **VWA**
Also in the *Journal of the United States artillery,* Fort Monroe, v. 24, 1905, p. 179, *VWA.*

957. Rieva y Allemany, José. Mechanische torpedo's. (Marineblad, Den Helder, Jaarg. 20, 1905, p. 322–339.)   **VXA**

958. Robert Whitehead and his torpedo. (American machinist, New York, v. 28, 1905, p. 721–722.)   **VFA**
Obituary notice, p. 722.

959. Robert Whitehead and the torpedo. (Scientific American, New York, v. 93, 1905, p. 414.)   **VA**

960. The **Submarine** and torpedo and fixed defence local committees [France].

(Royal United Service Institution, Journal, London, v. 49, 1905, p. 1195–1196.)
          VWA
Also in *Journal of the United States artillery,* Fort Monroe, v. 24, 1905, p. 178–179, *VWA.*

961. Topham, James. Torpedoes. (Engineer, London, v. 99, 1905, p. 443.)   **VA**
Abstract of discussion before Leeds Association of Engineers, April 27, 1905.

962. Torpedo operations in the Russo-Japanese war. illus. (Engineering, London, v. 79, 1905, p. 19–20, 643, 709–710, 744–745, 808.)   **VDA**

963. Torpedo shells. (Engineer, London, v. 100, 1905, p. 519.)   **VA**

964. Les Torpilleurs. (Cosmos, Paris, nouv. série, tome 52, 1905, p. 618.)   **VA**

965. Torpilleurs à moteur tonnant. (Cosmos, Paris, nouv. série, tome 52, 1905, p. 617–618.)   **VA**

1906

966. B., L. Barche torpediniere automobili Yarrow. (Rivista marittima, Roma, anno 39, trimestre 4, 1906, p. 557–558.)
          VXA

967. Beasley, Walter L. The wonderful turbine torpedo. (Army and navy life and united service, New York, v. 8, 1906, p. 7–10.)   **VWA**

968. Die Bedeutung des Torpedos im modernen Seekriege. illus. (Ueberall, Berlin, Jahrg. 8, 1906, p. 444–446.)
          †† **VXA**
Importance of torpedoes in modern warfare.

969. Beith. Turbinenanlagen für Torpedoboote. illus. (Marine Rundschau, Berlin, Jahrg. 17, 1906, p. 581–593.)   **VXA**

970. The **Bliss-Leavitt** turbine torpedo. (Engineering, London, v. 82, 1906, p. 496–497.)   **VDA**

971. Blochmann, R. La protection des navires de guerre contre les mines et les torpilles. (Revue générale des sciences, Paris, tome 17, 1906, p. 80–83.)   **OA**
Notes lessons learned in the Russo-Japanese war.

972. Chandler, L. H. The bursting of metal chambers under internal air pressure. illus. (American Society of Naval Engineers, Journal, Washington, v. 18, 1906, p. 112–122.)   **VXA**
Results of experiments to determine the best kind of metal for torpedo flasks.

973. Commerce protection and submarine mines. (Army and navy gazette, London, v. 47, 1906, p. 276–277.)   † **VWA**

974. Detonation of submarine mines by means of sound waves. illus. (Scientific American, New York, v. 94, 1906, p. 170.)   **VA**

1906, continued.

975. Fernández, Gustavo. Los grandes desplazamientos y el torpedo. (Revista general de marina, Madrid, tomo 58, 1906, p. 999–1009.) **VXA**

976. Haenig, A. Der neue Bliss-Leavitt-Torpedo. (Zeitschrift für das gesamte Schiess- und Sprengstoffwesen, München, Jahrg. 1, 1906, p. 76–79.) **†VOA**

977. Hurd, Archibald Spicer. The future of torpedo craft. illus. (Cassier's magazine, New York, v. 29, 1906, p. 300–315.) **VDA**

978. L., P. L'action de la torpille automobile; importance de la charge. (Journal de la marine, le yacht, Paris, v. 29, 1906, p. 258–259.) **††VXF**

979. The **Lake** Torpedo Boat Co. Underwater torpedo-boats. The submarine versus the submersible. Their merits and their menace. [Bridgeport, cop.] 1906. 116 p. illus. 8°. **VXV**

980. Neudeck, G. Torpedo gegen Schiffsböden. illus. (Zeitschrift für das gesamte Schiess- und Sprengstoffwesen, München, Jahrg. 1, 1906, p. 96–98, 113–114, 133–134, 152–154.) **†VOA**

981. The **New** turbine torpedo of the United States navy. illus. (Scientific American, New York, v. 94, 1906, p. 7–8.) **VA**

Also in *Journal* of the Royal United Service Institution, London, v. 50, 1906, p. 241–243, *VWA;* and in *Journal* of the American Society of Naval Engineers, Washington, v. 18, 1906, p. 276–281, *VXA.* Translated in *Mitteilungen aus dem Gebiete des Seewesens,* Pola, Bd. 34, 1906, p. 479–480, *VXA.*

982. Noalhat, H. L'engin porte-torpille sous-marin et les expériences d'Antibes. (Cosmos, Paris, nouv. série, tome 54, 1906, p. 466–468.) **VA**

983. Noch einmal der Minenkrieg. (Ueberall, Berlin, Jahrg. 9, 1906, p. 23–24.) **††VXA**

General discussion of the use of mines in naval warfare.

984. Pesce, G. L. La navigation sous-marine. Paris: Vuibert & Nony, 1906. 2 p.l., 498 p. illus. f°. **†VXV**

Expérience de Fulton avec ses "torpedoes," p. 212–218. Fulton en Angleterre, p. 219–224. Torpilles et torpilleurs, p. 476–490.

This work also contains valuable biographical notes on the early inventors of the submarine and torpedo, including Drebbel, Mersenne, and Bushnell.

985. Reventlow, E., Graf. Die Entwickelung des Torpedofahrzeugs. (Ueberall, Berlin, Jahrg. 8, 1906, p. 222–223.) **††VXA**

986. Sechi, G. Naviglio torpediniero. (Rivista marittima, Roma, anno 39, trimestre 4, 1906, p. 283–286.) **VXA**

987. Self-directing torpedoes: mechanical and electrical control. illus. (Illustrated London news, London, v. 128, 1906, p. 410.) **•DA**

988. Torpedine a turbina, modello Bliss-Leavitt. illus. (Rivista di artiglieria e genio, Roma, annata 23, v. 2, 1906, p. 157–160.) **VWW**

989. Torpedo practice at Sandy Hook. (Army and navy journal, New York, v. 43, 1906, p. 1348.) **††VWA**

990. Un Torpilleur anglais à pétrole. (Journal de la marine, le yacht, Paris, v. 29, 1906, p. 69–70.) **††VXF**

991. A **Triple-screw** motor torpedo boat. (Scientific American, New York, v. 94, 1906, p. 190.) **VA**

992. White, Sir William H. The development of torpedoes and submarines. (Iron and coal trades review, London, v. 73, 1906, p. 663–664.) **VIA**

993. Wilcox, Frank A. The torpedo for coast defense. (Military Service Institution of the United States, Journal, Governor's Island, N. Y., v. 38, 1906, p. 279–288.) **VWA**

994. X. Der Minenkrieg. illus. (Ueberall, Berlin, Jahrg. 8, 1906, p. 380–381.) **††VXA**

1907

995. Bernay, Henri. La protection contre les torpilles. illus. (Journal de la marine, le yacht, Paris, v. 30, 1907, p. 595–596.) **††VXF**

996. —— Les torpilles de fond. (Journal de la marine, le yacht, Paris, v. 30, 1907, p. 241–242.) **††VXF**

997. British torpedo boat "Eden." illus. (Scientific American, New York, v. 97, 1907, p. 237.) **VA**

998. Control of torpedoes by Hertzian waves. illus. (Engineering, London, v. 83, 1907, p. 66.) **VDA**

999. Controlling torpedoes by wireless telegraphy. illus. (Scientific American, New York, v. 96, 1907, p. 250.) **VA**

Also printed in American Society of Naval Engineers, *Journal,* Washington, v. 19, 1907, p. 513–517, *VXA.*

1000. Erhitzer für Torpedos. (Mitteilungen aus dem Gebiete des Seewesens, Pola, Bd. 35, 1907, p. 716–717.) **VXA**

1001. Ferrand, Ch. Torpilles, torpilleurs et sous-marins. (Revue scientifique, Paris, série 5, tome 8, 1907, p. 385–391, 417–421.) **OA**

1002. Gody, Léon. Chargement des torpilles; mines électriques de contact. (In

1907, continued.

his: Traité théorique et pratique des matières explosives, Namur, 1907, p. 452–453.)
VOG

1003. Important torpedo trials. (United States Naval Institute, Proceedings, Annapolis, v. 33, 1907, p. 875–876.) **VXA**
Abstracted from the *London Times.*
Notes on the Whitehead and Bliss-Leavitt torpedoes.

1004. L., P. Au sujet du nombre de torpilleurs nécessaires à notre marine. (Journal de la marine, le yacht, Paris, v. 30, 1907, p. 1–2.) **†† VXF**

1005. Lindner, Kurt. Ueber elektrische Minenzündung, namentlich mit Bezug auf Seeminen. (Zeitschrift für das gesamte Schiess- und Sprengstoffwesen, München, Jahrg. 2, 1907, p. 348–350.) **† VOA**

1006. Loygorri, Joaquín de. Nuevos torpederos. illus. (La vida marítima, Madrid, año 6, 1907, p. 561–562.) **†† VXA**

1007. Max. Les nouveaux torpilleurs anglais. illus. (Journal de la marine, le yacht, Paris, v. 30, 1907, p. 539–541.) **†† VXF**

1008. Motor torpedo boat built by Messrs. Yarrow. (Scientific American, New York, v. 97, 1907, p. 406.) **VA**
Brief note.

1009. Myers, A. E. C. The needs of shore anti-torpedo defence are not necessarily the needs of naval anti-torpedo-boat defence; or, Why discard the 12-pr.? (Royal United Service Institution, Journal, London, v. 51, 1907, p. 496–500.) **VWA**
Valuable notes on defence from torpedoes.

1010. Die Neueste Entwickelung der Torpedowaffe. (Zeitschrift für das gesamte Schiess- und Sprengstoffwesen, München, Jahrg. 2, 1907, p. 474.) **† VOA**
From *Nauticus.*

1011. The New Bliss-Leavitt torpedo for the United States government. illus. (Compressed air, New York, v. 11, 1907, p. 4353–4356.) **VFM**

1012. A New method of reheating compressed air for use in torpedoes. illus. (Compressed air, New York, v. 11, 1907, p. 4339–4340.) **VFM**

1013. Noalhat, H. A propos d'un incident de lancement de torpilles automobiles. (Cosmos, Paris, nouv. série, tome 57, 1907, p. 328–329.) **VA**

1014. —— Contribution à l'étude des torpilles automobiles. (Journal de la marine, le yacht, Paris, v. 30, 1907, p. 284–285, 291–292, 318, 339–340.) **†† VXF**
Also in *Boletín del Centro naval,* Buenos Aires, tomo 25, 1907, p. 103–104, 522–530, 622–631, *VXA;* and in *Revista general de marina,* Madrid, tomo 61, 1907, p. 573–593, *VXA.*

1015. Ocean race of torpedo-boat destroyers. illus. (Scientific American, New York, v. 96, 1907, p. 493–494.) **VA**
Account of race from Sandy Hook to Cape Charles.

1016. Parisi, Raffaele. Esploditore meccanico per torpedini terrestri in uso nell' esercito austro-ungarico. (Rivista di artiglieria e genio, Roma, annata 24, v. 3, 1907, p. 123–126.) **VWW**

1017. ₁Range of torpedoes.₁ (Scientific American, New York, v. 84, 1907, p. 207–208.) **VA**
Editorial.

1018. Reventlow, E., Graf. Minenkrieg. illus. (Ueberall, Berlin, Jahrg. 10, 1907, p. 162–167.) **†† VXA**
Discussion of the legality of the use of mines in naval warfare.

1019. Sueter, Murray Fraser. The evolution of the submarine boat, mine and torpedo, from the sixteenth century to the present time. Portsmouth, England: J. Griffin & Co., 1907. xxiv, 384 p., 22 diagr., 103 pl. 8°. **VXV**
The evolution of the submarine mine, p. 262–292; The evolution of the locomotive torpedo, p. 293–330; Protection of warships against submarine explosives, p. 331–340.

1020. La Telegrafía sin hilos aplicada á la dirección de los torpedos. illus. (La vida marítima, Madrid, año 6, 1907, p. 185.) **†† VXA**

1021. Torpedo guided by electric waves. illus. (Scientific American supplement, New York, v. 64, 1907, p. 100.) **VA**

1022. Torpedo planter. (Army and navy journal, New York, v. 44, 1906, p. 479, 864, 867, 1115, 1268.) **†† VWA**
Brief notes.

1023. The Torpedo situation. (Army and navy journal, New York, v. 44, 1907, p. 653.) **†† VWA**

1024. ₁Torpedo trial at Weymouth.₁ (Naval annual, Portsmouth, 1907, p. 12.) **VXA**

1025. Ueber die Armierung von Torpedobooten auf Grund taktischer Erwägungen. (Mitteilungen aus dem Gebiete des Seewesens, Pola, Bd. 35, 1907, p. 356–370.) **VXA**

1026. V. La construction des torpilleurs en Allemagne. illus. (Journal de la marine, le yacht, Paris, v. 30, 1907, p. 622.) **†† VXF**

1908

1027. Anti-torpedo armament. (Army and navy journal, New York, v. 45, 1908, p. 965.) **†† VWA**

1908, continued.

1028. B., F. Torpediniere e cacciatorpediniere moderne. (Rivista marittima, Roma, anno 41, trimestre 4, 1908, p. 159–169.) **VXA**

1029. Bernay, Henri. Torpilleurs et contre-torpilleurs. (Journal de la marine, le yacht, Paris, v. 31, 1908, p. 1–2, 49–50.) **†† VXF**

1030. Bocci, Carlo. Protezione delle navi da guerra contro l'offesa delle torpedini e dei siluri. (Rivista marittima, Roma, anno 41, trimestre 4, 1908, p. 471–483.) **VXA**

1031. Bonfiglietti, F. Torpediniere e cacciatorpediniere. (Rivista marittima, Roma, anno 41, trimestre 2, 1908, p. 67–78.) **VXA**

1032. Buckey, Mervyn C. Manual for the instruction of gunners of mine companies. ₁Ft. Worden, Wash.:₁ M. C. Buckey, 1908. 2 p.l., 53 p. 8°. **VXM p.v.4, no.3**

1033. Cardona, Pedro M. La prueba del elemento mar y otras pequeñeces de poca importancia en las instalaciones de torpedos eléctricos de observación. illus. (Revista general de marina, Madrid, tomo 62, 1908, p. 1134–1167.) **VXA**

1034. Chapuis. Tir des torpilles sur but mobile. Influence des erreurs commises dans l'appréciation de la vitesse et de la route du but. illus. (Association technique maritime, Bulletin, Paris, no. 19, 1908, p. 9–24.) **VXA**
Translated in *Proceedings* of the United States Naval Institute, Annapolis, v. 35, 1909, p. 153–183, *VXA.*

1035. Davis, Richmond P. Submarine mines and mining. illus. (Journal of the United States artillery, Fort Monroe, v. 29, 1908, p. 225–239.) **VWA**
Also in *Journal* of the American Society of Naval Engineers, Washington, v. 20, 1908, p. 674–691, *VXA.*

1036. Davis torpedo. (Army and navy journal, New York, v. 46, 1908–09, p. 45, 346, 376–377, 541, 1163; v. 47, 1909–10, p. 146, 200, 841, 843, 1248; v. 49, 1911, p. 255; v. 52, 1915, p. 694.) **†† VWA**
Invention of Lieut.-Commander Cleland Davis.

1037. A **Delayed-action** torpedo. (Scientific American, New York, v. 99, 1908, p. 150.) **VA**
Notes on the Russo-Japanese war.

1038. Destructive energy of torpedoes. (Army and navy journal, New York, v. 45, 1908, p. 530–531.) **†† VWA**

1039. La **Dirección** de los torpedos y la telegrafia sin hilos. (La vida marítima, Madrid, año 7, 1908, p. 89.) **†† VXA**

1040. Fernández, Gustavo. El problema de la protección de los acorazados contra

el torpedo automóvil. (Revista general de marina, Madrid, 1908, tomo 62, p. 526–544.) **VXA**

1041. G. Stand und Aussichten der Torpedowaffe in fremden Marinen. (Marine Rundschau, Berlin, Jahrg. 19, 1908, p. 1087–1099.) **VXA**

1042. Great Britain.—Admiralty. Courses of instruction of officers and seamen in torpedo. London: Eyre & Spottiswoode, 1908. 52 p. 8°. **VXV**

1043. The **Hardcastle** torpedo. (The navy, Washington, v. 2, Dec., 1908, p. 3, 9–10.) **† VYE**
Also in *Journal of the United States artillery,* Fort Monroe, v. 31, 1909, p. 214–215, 220–222, *VWA.*

1044. Hot-air-driven torpedoes. (Scientific American, New York, v. 99, 1908, p. 77.) **VA**
Experiments made by Sir William G. Armstrong, Whitworth & Co., and Messrs. Whitehead & Co.

1045. Increased range and speed of torpedoes. (Naval annual, Portsmouth, 1908, p. 284–286.) **VXA**

1046. Lalande, Louis. Contribution à l'étude des torpilles automobiles. (Marine française, Paris, année 21, 1908, p. 496–502, 573–591.) **VXA**

1047. ₁**Method** of recovering torpedoes.₁ (Engineer, London, v. 105, 1908, p. 397.) **VA**
Brief note.

1048. The **New** Davis projectile torpedo. illus. (Scientific American, New York, v. 99, 1908, p. 159.) **VA**
Abstracted in United States Naval Institute, *Proceedings,* Annapolis, v. 34, 1908, p. 1343–1344, *VXA.* Invention of Lieut.-Commander Cleland Davis, U. S. N.

1049. The **New** Greenock torpedo factory. (Engineer, London, v. 105, 1908, p. 529.) **VA**
Brief note.

1050. The **New** torpedo boat destroyers. (Engineer, London, v. 106, 1908, p. 326–327.) **VA**

1051. New type of torpedoes. (Engineering news, New York, v. 60, 1908, p. 235.) **VDA**
Brief note on invention of Lieut.-Commander Cleland Davis.

1052. Les **Nouveaux** torpilleurs de la marine bulgare. illus. (Journal de la marine, le yacht, Paris, v. 31, 1908, p. 646–648.) **†† VXF**

1053. P., L. Die Verwendung der Torpedowaffe in der Zukunft. (Schiffbau, Berlin, Jahrg. 9, 1908, p. 684–686.) **† VXA**

1054. Panzerbieter, W. Torpedos und Seeminen. illus. (Zeitschrift für das gesamte Schiess- und Sprengstoffwesen, München, Jahrg. 3, 1908, p. 185–189, 203–

1908, continued.

206, 227–230, 411–412, 446–450; Jahrg. 4, 1909, p. 48–51, 70–72, 90–92, 147–152; Jahrg. 6, 1911, p. 89–91.) † **VOA**

1055. Pedersen, B. La grenade Pedersen. illus. (Zeitschrift für das gesamte Schiess- und Sprengstoffwesen, München, Jahrg. 3, 1908, p. 81–82.) † **VOA**

1056. Phenomenal speed of latest torpedoes. (Scientific American, New York, v. 98, 1908, p. 326.) **VA**

1057. Podgurskiy, N. Empleo de las granadas de mano en Puerto Arturo. (Memorial de ingenieros, Madrid, año 63, 1908, p. 398–403.) **VWA**

1058. Los Progresos del "torpedo automóvil." (La vida marítima, Madrid, año 7, 1908, p. 103.) †† **VXA**

1059. The Progress of the torpedo. (Engineering, London, v. 85, 1908, p. 217–218.) **VDA**

Also printed in the *Proceedings* of the United States Naval Institute, Annapolis, v. 34, 1908, p. 730–733, *VXA*, and, in abbreviated form, in *The naval annual*, Portsmouth, 1908, p. 285–286, *VXA*.

1060. Ricart y Giralt, José. La protección de los fondos de los buques contra la explosión de los torpedos. (La vida marítima, Madrid, año 7, 1908, p. 216.) †† **VXA**

1061. Richter, Fritz. Eine neue militärische Waffe. illus. (Zeitschrift für das gesamte Schiess- und Sprengstoffwesen, München, Jahrg. 3, 1908, p. 288–291.) † **VOA**

1062. Senkowski, M. Ueber Torpedierung der Tiefbohrschächte. (Zeitschrift für das gesamte Schiess- und Sprengstoffwesen, München, Jahrg. 3, 1908, p. 169–171.) † **VOA**

1063. The Speed of torpedo-boat destroyers. (Engineer, London, v. 105, 1908, p. 37–38.) **VA**

1064. Stockton, Charles Herbert. The use of submarine mines and torpedoes in time of war. (American journal of international law, New York, v. 2, 1908, p. 276–284.) **XBA**

1065. Submarine mines. (Naval annual, Portsmouth, 1908, p. 286–287.) **VXA**
Brief note.

1066. Surface or submarine torpedo boats. (Engineer, London, v. 106, 1908, p. 503.) **VA**

1067. Tactical value of torpedo craft. (Scientific American, New York, v. 99, 1908, p. 330.) **VA**

1068. Thornycroft, J. E. Modern torpedo boats and destroyers. (Institution of

Naval Architects, Transactions, London, v. 50, 1908, p. 59–68.) **VXA**
With discussion, p. 68–76.
Abstracted in *Engineer*, London, v. 105, 1908, p. 368–369, *VA*.
Translated in *Revista general de marina*, Madrid, tomo 62, p. 1020–1036, *VXA*.

1069. Torpedo and anti-torpedo armament. (Engineer, London, v. 105, 1908, p. 430.) **VA**

1070. Torpedo attack on the monitor "Florida." illus. (Scientific American, New York, v. 98, 1908, p. 456.) **VA**
Series of tests made near Sewell's Point, Va.

1071. Torpedo control by wireless. (Western electrician, Chicago, v. 43, 1908, p. 255.) **VGA**
Also printed in the *Journal of the United States artillery*, Fort Monroe, v. 30, 1908, p. 322–323, *VWA*.
Brief note on the invention of Charles A. Logue.

1072. Torpedo experiments at Cherbourg. (Engineer, London, v. 105, 1908, p. 182.) **VA**
Brief note.

1073. Torpedo experiments on the monitor Florida. (American Society of Naval Engineers, Journal, Washington, v. 20, 1908, p. 772–773.) **VXA**
Also in *Journal of the United States artillery*, Fort Monroe, Va., v. 29, 1908, p. 323–324, *VWA*.
Abstracted from the *New York Times*.

1074. Torpedos und Seeminen. (Schiffbau, Berlin, Jahrg. 10, 1908–09, p. 209–211, 251–253, 378–380, 573–575.) † **VXA**

1075. Torpedoschutznetze. (Mitteilungen aus dem Gebiete des Seewesens, Pola, Bd. 36, 1908, p. 325–335.) **VXA**

1076. Le **Torpilleur** allemand G. 137. illus. (Journal de la marine, le yacht, Paris, v. 31, 1908, p. 23.) †† **VXF**

1077. The **Unge** air torpedo. (Engineering, London, v. 86, 1908, p. 177.) **VDA**
Brief note.

1078. United States.—Chief of Staff. Questions and answers for use in the instruction of torpedo companies and detachments. (New system.) Washington: Gov. Prtg. Off., 1908. 30 p. 16°.
VWS

1909

1079. Aerial torpedoes. (Electrical review and western electrician, New York, v. 54, 1909, p. 920.) **VGA**

1080. Alex. Über Torpedoboot- und Unterseebootangriffe und deren Abwehr. (Mitteilungen aus dem Gebiete des Seewesens, Pola, Bd. 37, 1909, p. 232–243.) **VXA**
Translated in *Revista general de marina*, Madrid, tomo 64, 1909, p. 606–624, *VXA*.

1909, continued.

1081. Alger, Philip R. Torpedo firing at moving targets. illus. (United States Naval Institute, Proceedings, Annapolis, v. 35, 1909, p. 173–183.) **VXA**
Effect of errors in the estimation of the speed and course of the target.

1082. Aronson, Samuel. The torpedo a machine shop triumph. illus. (American machinist, New York, v. 32, 1909, p. 645–651.) **VFA**
Also note on p. 961.
Gives description of a Bliss-Leavitt torpedo.

1083. B., F. Nuovo siluripedio in cemento armato. illus. (Rivista marittima, Roma, anno 42, trimestre 1, 1909, p. 655–656.) **VXA**

1084. B., M. Lufttorpedos. illus. (Kriegstechnische Zeitschrift, Berlin, Bd. 12, 1909, p. 238–241.) **VWA**

1085. Bernay, Henri. Defense against submarine mines. illus. (Journal of the United States artillery, Fort Monroe, Va., v. 31, 1909, p. 192–194.) **VWA**
Translated from *Le Yacht.*

1086. —— La torpille automobile Gabet. illus. (Journal de la marine, le yacht, Paris, v. 32, 1909, p. 691.) **†† VXF**

1087. Brazilian torpedo-boat destroyers. (Engineer, London, v. 108, 1909, p. 4–6.) **VA**

1088. British and foreign torpedo-boat flotillas. (Naval annual, London, 1909, p. 226–243.) **VXA**

1089. Cavelier de Cuverville, Jules Marie Armand. Submarine mines and their effects in the Russo-Japanese war. (Journal of the United States artillery, Fort Monroe, v. 31, 1909, p. 176–179.) **VWA**
Translated from the author's *La leçon de la guerre.*

1090. Davis, Richmond P. The automobile torpedo in coast defense. illus. (Journal of the United States artillery, Fort Monroe, v. 31, 1909, p. 138–143.) **VWA**

1091. Effect of torpedoes on warships. (Marine review, Cleveland, O., v. 29, April 21, 1909, p. 36.) **† VXA**

1092. Einiges über die Entwickelung und den gegenwärtigen Stand des Unterseebootwesens in den verschiedenen Staaten. (Mitteilungen aus dem Gebiete des Seewesens, Pola, Bd. 37, 1909, p. 188–223.) **VXA**

1093. Folley, Paul. The torpedo service of to-day and of to-morrow. illus. (United States Naval Institute, Proceedings, Annapolis, v. 35, 1909, p. 513–532.) **VXA**

1094. The **Gabet** wireless controlled automobile torpedo. illus. (Scientific American, New York, v. 101, 1909, p. 241–242.) **VA**

1095. The **Hardcastle** torpedo. (Naval annual, Portsmouth, 1909, p. 250–251.) **VXA**
Brief description.

1096. Heinz, Julius. Ueber die Anwärmung der Betriebsluft des Torpedos. (Mitteilungen aus dem Gebiete des Seewesens, Pola, Bd. 37, 1909, p. 662–684.) **VXA**
Translated by Raoul Marsollet in *Revue maritime,* Paris, tome 188, 1911, p. 171–194, *VXA.*

1097. High-speed destroyers for the United States navy. illus. (Scientific American, New York, v. 101, 1909, p. 314.) **VA**

1098. Hoffmann, A. M. The automobile torpedo of to-day. illus. (International marine engineering, New York, v. 14, 1909, p. 57–59.) **VXA**
Reprinted in *Journal* of the American Society of Naval Engineers, Washington, v. 21, 1909, p. 629–636, *VXA.*

1099. Italian experiments on torpedo attack. illus. (Engineering, London, v. 88, 1909, p. 228.) **VDA**
Printed in slightly abbreviated form in *Journal of the United States artillery,* Fort Monroe, v. 32, 1909, p. 201–202, *VWA,* and in *Proceedings* of the United States Naval Institute, Annapolis, v. 35, 1909, p. 991–992, *VXA.*

1100. The **Latest** submarines of the United States. illus. (Scientific American, New York, v. 101, 1909, p. 296–297.) **VA**
Illustrations of torpedo tubes.

1101. Laurenti, C. Torpediniere "subaquee." (Rivista marittima, Roma, anno 42, trimestre 3, p. 459–466.) **VXA**

1102. Le Séven, E. Appareil moteur à turbines Parsons du torpilleur 293. (Revue maritime, Paris, tome 181, 1909, p. 361–394.) **VXA**

1103. Loygorri, Joaquín de. El acorazado-torpedero. illus. (La vida marítima, Madrid, año 8, 1909, p. 198–199.) **†† VXA**

1104. Michel-Schmidt, M. Batterie des maures. Ilot artificiel de lancement pour essais de torpilles automobiles. (Société des ingénieurs civils de France, Mémoires et travaux, Paris, année 1909, v. 1, p. 118–167.) **VDA**
Abstracted in *Engineering news,* New York, v. 62, 1909, p. 36–38, *VDA.*

1105. Montero, Enrique de. Submarinos y sumergibles. illus. (Memorial de ingenieros, Madrid, año 64, 1909, p. 469–479, 525–531, 549–564.) **VWA**

1106. Neudeck, G. Der Bau der Kriegschiffe und der Unterseeboote. illus. (In: Max Geitel, Der Siegeslauf der Technik, Berlin, 1909, Bd. 3, p. 387–416.) **V**

1909, continued.

1107. A **New** rifle-propelled grenade. illus. (Scientific American, New York, v. 100, 1909, p. 20.)   **VA**

Also printed in United States Naval Institute, *Proceedings*, Annapolis, v. 35, 1909, p. 310–313, *VXA*. Invention of F. T. Marten Hale.

1108. The **New** Schneider torpedo. (Journal of United States artillery, Fort Monroe, v. 32, 1909, p. 213–214.)   **VWA**

1109. The **New** torpedo battery at Léoube bay. (The Navy, Washington, v. 3, June, 1909, p. 37.)   **† VYE**

Also in *Journal of the United States artillery*, Fort Monroe, v. 32, 1909, p. 181–182, *VWA*.

1110. **New** type of sub-surface torpedo boat. (Scientific American, New York, v. 100, 1909, p. 280.)   **VA**

Invention of Clarence L. Berger.

1111. **Obus** de perforation et obus explosifs. (Revue de Paris, Paris, année 16, 1909, tome 5, p. 283–296.)   **• DM**

Translated in the *Journal of the United States artillery*, Fort Monroe, v. 33, 1910, p. 49–57, *VWA*.

1112. **Our** need of torpedoes. (Army and navy journal, New York, v. 46, 1909, p. 875.)   **†† VWA**

1113. A **Projectile** carrying a torpedo. (Army and navy journal, New York, v. 47, 1909, p. 146.)   **†† VWA**

Invention of Lieut.-Commander Cleland Davis.

1114. A **Radi-automatic** torpedo invented by M. Gustave Gabet. (Journal of United States artillery, Fort Monroe, v. 31, 1909, p. 213.)   **VWA**

Brief note.

1115. **S.**, E. D. Il siluro Hardcastle. (Rivista marittima, Roma, anno 42, trimestre 2, 1909, p. 350–352.)   **VXA**

1116. The **Schneider** torpedo-launching station. illus. (Scientific American, New York, v. 100, 1909, p. 222.)   **VA**

With illustration on p. 217.

1117. **Schneider** torpedo testing station. illus. (Engineering, London, v. 88, 1909, p. 170–173.)   **VDA**

Also printed in *Scientific American supplement*, New York, v. 68, 1909, p. 308–310, *VA*.

1118. **Spear**, Lawrence. Underwater torpedo boats. illus. (American Society of Naval Engineers, Journal, Washington, v. 21, 1909, p. 353–427.)   **VXA**

Notes on the Whitehead and other torpedoes and the Davis gun.

1119. **Sueter**, Murray F. Évolution de la mine sous-marine. illus. (Revue maritime, Paris, tome 180, 1909, p. 287–329.)   **VXA**

Translated by M. Bizot from the author's *The evolution of the submarine boat, mine and torpedo.*

1120. **Testing** a torpedo-boat defense. illus. (Scientific American, New York, v. 101, 1909, p. 124, 127.)   **VA**

Also printed in the *Proceedings* of the United States Naval Institute, v. 35, 1909, p. 970–971, *VXA*. Tests made in Portsmouth harbor by the British Admiralty.

1121. **Torpedo** battery in the Mediterranean. illus. (Engineer, London, v. 107, 1909, p. 412–413.)   **VA**

1122. **Torpedo-cañon** Davis. illus. (La vida maritima, Madrid, año 8, 1909, p. 264.)   **†† VXA**

1123. **Torpedo** defence. illus. (Marine engineer, London, v. 32, 1909, p. 28–29.)   **VXA**

Invention of Dr. G. Horatio Jones; method of protecting ships against torpedoes.

1124. El **Torpedo** proyectil "Davis." (Boletin del Centro naval, Buenos Aires, tomo 27, 1909, p. 83–86.)   **VXA**

1125. **Torpedoprojekte.** (Ueberall, Berlin, Jahrg. 11, 1909, p. 716–718.)   **†† VXA**

Development of the torpedo.

1126. **Torpedos** y minas. (Revista general de marina, Madrid, tomo 65, 1909, p. 337–348.)   **VXA**

1127. **Torpedoschlachtschiffe.** illus. (Mitteilungen aus dem Gebiete des Seewesens, Pola, Bd. 37, 1909, p. 243–247.)   **VXA**

1128. **Ueber** Torpedoboot- und Unterseebootangriffe und deren Abwehr. (Mitteilungen aus dem Gebiete des Seewesens, Pola, Bd. 37, 1909, p. 232–243.)   **VXA**

1129. **Unar**, Theodor. Lufttorpedos. illus. (Mitteilungen über Gegenstände des Artillerie- und Geniewesens, Wien, Jahrg. 40, 1909, p. 64–71.)   **VWI**

1130. **Vance**, Willis R. Observation firing of submarine mines. illus. (Journal of the United States artillery, Fort Monroe, v. 31, 1909, p. 144–149.)   **VWA**

1131. **Wagner**, Adolf. Von einem Schwimmer in bestimmter Wassertiefe gehaltener Torpedo. illus. (Zeitschrift für das gesamte Schiess- und Sprengstoffwesen, München, Jahrg. 4, 1909, p. 396.)   **† VOA**

1132. **Walther**, P. Die Minen und die Torpedos. illus. (In: Max Geitel, Der Siegeslauf der Technik, Berlin, 1909, Bd. 3, p. 371–387.)   **V**

1133. A **Warship** sunk by a torpedo as an experiment. (Scientific American supplement, New York, v. 68, 1909, p. 392.)   **VA**

1134. **Williams** torpedo. (Army and navy journal, New York, v. 46, 1909, p. 955.)   **†† VWA**

Brief note.

1909, continued.

1135. A Wirelessly-controlled torpedo. illus. (Scientific American, New York, v. 100, 1909, p. 206.) **VA**

Abstracted in the *Army and navy journal*, New York, v. 47, 1910, p. 122. †† *VWA.*

Notes on experiments by Tesla, Orling, Armstrong and Gabet.

1136. Wittmer, R. Die Torpedowaffe. Berlin: E. S. Mittler und Sohn. 1909. 33(1) p., 1 diagr. illus. 8°. (Meereskunde. Jahrg. 3, Heft 4.) **PSRA**

1137. X. é Y. Necesidad de un poligono de torpedos. illus. (Boletin del Centro naval, Buenos Aires, tomo 27, p. 575–581.) **VXA**

1910

1138. Bernay, Henri. Les torpilles de blocus. (Journal de la marine, le yacht, Paris, v. 33, 1910, p. 33–34.) †† **VXF**

1139. Charmoille. La distance de lancement des torpilles automobiles. (Journal de la marine, le yacht, Paris, année 33, 1910, p. 369.) †† **VXF**

1140. Dary, Georges. Torpilles dirigeables. (Cosmos, Paris, nouv. série, tome 62, 1910, p. 438–439.) **VA**

1141. Fournier, Lucien. Canots et torpilles dirigeables par les ondes électriques. illus. (Cosmos, Paris, nouv. série, tome 62, 1910, p. 286–287.) **VA**

1142. —— Télémécanique sans fil: la torpille dirigeable Gabet. illus. (Cosmos, Paris, nouv. série, tome 63, p. 37–40.) **VA**

1143. Le Franc, A. Nouvelles torpilles automobiles. (Moniteur de la flotte, Paris, année 57, no. 43, Oct. 23, 1910, p. 3.) †† **VYH**

1144. Material de torpedos y minas para el Brasil. illus. (Boletin del Centro naval, Buenos Aires, tomo 27, 1910, p. 632–638.) **VXA**

1145. A New type of torpedo boat: a double-hulled boat with its engines entirely below the waterline. illus. (Scientific American, New York, v. 102, 1910, p. 276.) **VA**

1146. Noalhat, H. Un nouvel engin porte-torpille. illus. (Cosmos, Paris, nouv. série, tome 63, 1910, p. 329–331.) **VA**

1147. Ryan, L. S. Mine commander's board. illus. (Journal of the United States artillery, Fort Monroe, v. 33, 1910, p. 33–37.) **VWA**

Method adopted for checking the firing of submarine mines.

1148. Sueter, Murray Fraser. Protection des navires contre les explosifs sous-marins. (Revue maritime, Paris, tome 184, 1910, p. 281–292.) **VXA**

Extracted from his *Evolution of the submarine boat, mine and torpedo.* Translated by M. Bizot.

1911

1149. Chalon, Paul F. Effets produits par les explosions sous-marines; Explosions sous-marines; Application des explosifs aux travaux sous-marins. (In his: Les explosifs modernes, Paris, 1911, p. 607–670.) **VOG**

Valuable data on torpedoes and submarine mines. Also consult the index.

1150. Charmoille. Les barrages. (Journal de la marine, le yacht, Paris, année 34, 1911, p. 737–738.) †† **VXF**

1151. La Défense contre les mines flottantes. illus. (Armée et marine, Paris, année 12, 1911, p. 444–445.) †† **VWA**

1152. Efficiency of torpedoes. (Army and navy journal, New York, v. 48, 1911, p. 1579.) †† **VWA**

Details of tests made on various types of torpedoes by the United States government.

1153. Filets pare-torpilles. (Moniteur de la flotte, Paris, année 58, no. 13, April 1, 1911, p. 3.) †† **VYH**

1154. Fletcher, R. A. Warships and their story, with coloured frontispiece by Charles Dixon. London: Cassell & Company, Ltd., 1911. xxii, 348 p., 81 pl. illus. 8°. **VXR**

See index under torpedoes, torpedo boats, torpedo gunboats, torpedo nets, and torpedo tubes.

1155. ₁Der **Kleine** Kreuzer "Cassini," Minenleger.₁ (Schiffbau, Berlin, Jahrg. 13, 1911, p. 21.) † **VXA**

Notes on the French mine layer "Cassini."

1156. Le Franc, A. La défense contre les sous-marins. (Moniteur de la flotte, Paris, année 58, no. 17, April 29, 1911, p. 3.) †† **VYH**

1157. —— Les mines sous-marines. (Moniteur de la flotte, Paris, année 58, no. 41, Oct. 14, 1911, p. 3.) †† **VYH**

1158. —— Le sous-marin mouilleur de mines. (Moniteur de la flotte, Paris, tome 58, no. 6, Feb. 11, 1911, p. 3.) †† **VYH**

1159. —— Les torpilles à réchauffeur d'air. (Moniteur de la flotte, Paris, année 58, no. 15, April 15, 1911, p. 3.) †† **VYH**

1160. Naval officer invents aerial torpedo. (Aeronautics, New York, v. 9, 1911, p. 141–142.) **VDS**

Invention of Paul E. Chamberlin, U. S. M. C.

1161. Nouveaux essais sur la commande à distance des bateaux et torpilles auto-

1911, continued.

mobiles. illus. (Journal de la marine, le yacht, Paris, année 34, 1911, p. 716–717.) †† **VXF**
From *Cosmos.*

1162. Der **Stand** der Torpedowaffe im Jahre 1911. illus. (Jahrbuch für Deutschlands Seeinteressen, Berlin, Jahrg. 1911, p. 167–188.) **VYL**
Also printed in *Revue maritime,* Paris, tome 192, 1912, p. 149–175, *VXA.*

1163. Stenzel, Alfred. Seekriegsgeschichte in ihren wichtigsten Abschnitten mit Berücksichtigung der Seetaktik. Hannover and Leipzig: Hahn'sche Buchhandlung, 1907–11. 5 v. 8°. **VXP**
See index to Teil 5, p. 426, under Minen- und Torpedowesen.

1164. Test of the Davis torpedo. (Army and navy journal, New York, v. 49, 1911, p. 255–256.) †† **VWA**
First United States government test of the torpedo invented by Cleland Davis, U. S. N.

1165. La Torpille de 533. (Moniteur de la flotte, Paris, année 58, no. 51, Dec. 23, 1911, p. 3.) †† **VYH**

1912

1166. Automatic submarine mines. illus. (Engineering, London, v. 93, 1912, p. 520–524, 584–587.) **VDA**
Also printed in the *Journal of the United States artillery,* Fort Monroe, v. 38, 1912, p. 70–84, 232–240, *VWA.*
A very comprehensive article giving a description of Elia's automatic system and the twin mines of the Vickers-Bréquet system; also tests and apparatus for laying mines.

1167. Beck, Z. Rechnerische Untersuchung über die Gefährlichkeit von Kontaktminen. (Mitteilungen aus dem Gebiete des Seewesens, Pola, Bd. 40, 1912, p. 1–11.) **VXA**

1168. Charmoille. Les lancements à cône de choc. (Journal de la marine, le yacht, Paris, année 35, 1912, p. 401.) †† **VXF**

1169. The **Davis** gun-torpedo. illus. (Engineer, London, v. 113, 1912, p. 205–206.) **VA**
Translated in *Mitteilungen aus dem Gebiete des Seewesens,* Pola, Bd. 40, p. 939–944, *VXA;* and in *Marine-Rundschau,* Berlin, Bd. 23, 1912, p. 529–532, *VXA.*

1170. Ferragut y Sbert, Guillermo. Torpedos automóviles; estudios de punteria. (Revista general de marina, Madrid, tomo 70, 1912, p. 681–745.) **VXA**

1171. Filets pare-torpilles. illus. (Moniteur de la flotte, Paris, année 59, 1912, no. 6, Feb. 10, 1912, p. 3.) †† **VYH**

1172. Firing submarine mines by wireless telegraphy. illus. (Scientific American, New York, v. 107, 1912, p. 101.) **VA**
Invention of Dr. Branly, the French scientist.

1173. Die **Lancierungen** mit Manöversprengpatronen. (Mitteilungen aus dem Gebiete des Seewesens, Pola, Bd. 40, 1912, p. 1410–1413.) **VXA**

1174. Le Franc, A. Les mines sous-marines. (Moniteur de la flotte, Paris, année 59, no. 20, May 18, 1912, p. 3.) ††**VYH**

1175. —— Nouvelles torpilles automobiles. (Moniteur de la flotte, Paris, année 59, no. 25, June 22, 1912, p. 3.) †† **VYH**

1176. M., L. Mines et poseurs de mines de blocus. (Journal de la marine, le yacht, Paris, année 35, 1912, p. 289–290.) †† **VXF**
Description of three types of automatic torpedoes.

1177. A **Mine-laying** squadron. (Journal of the United States artillery, Fort Monroe, Va., v. 38, 1912, p. 115–116.) **VWA**
From *United service gazette,* May 30, 1912.

1178. Seeminen. illus. (Ueberall, Berlin, Jahrg. 14, 1912, p. 322–327, 475–480.) †† **VXA**

1179. Skerrett, Robert G. A new form of attack; a torpedo that carries a gun. illus. (Scientific American, New York, v. 107, 1912, p. 89, 94.) **VA**
Description of the Davis gun torpedo.

1180. Ueber die Möglichkeit, Torpedoboote zu panzern. illus. (Ueberall, Berlin, Jahrg. 15, 1912, p. 57–61.) †† **VXA**
Translated by J. Kreil from *Morskoi Sbornik* (*Russische Marine-Rundschau*) of Nov., 1911.

1181. The **Whitehead** torpedo. (Army and navy journal, New York, v. 49, 1912, p. 1235.) †† **VWA**
Abstracted from *United service gazette.*

1913

1182. Algo sobre nuestros destróyers. (Boletín del Centro naval, Buenos Aires, tomo 31, p. 583–587.) **VXA**
Account of new Chilian destroyers.

1183. Antona, A. Cannone antisilurante. (Rivista marittima, Roma, anno 46, trimestre 2, 1913, p. 53–57.) **VXA**

1184. L'Augmentation du calibre des torpilles automobiles. (Cosmos, Paris, nouv. série, tome 69, 1913, p. 145.) **VA**

1185. Bannerman-Phillips, H. Mining the air with balloon torpedoes. illus. (Scientific American, New York, v. 108, 1913, p. 538.) **VA**
Illustration on p. 533.

1913, continued.

1186. Bernotti, Romeo. Il siluro sulle navi di linea. (Rivista marittima, Roma, anno 46, trimestre 3, 1913, p. 211–224.) **VXA**

Translated by Thomas Withers, Jr., in *Proceedings* of the United States Naval Institute, Annapolis, v. 40, 1914, p. 1775–1786, *VXA*.
The torpedo on capital ships.

1187. Bohn & Kähler. Auf Zeit einstellbare Vorrichtung zum Versenken von Seeminen. illus. (Zeitschrift für das gesamte Schiess- und Sprengstoffwesen, München, Jahrg. 8, 1913, p. 475–476.) **† VOA**

Patent granted Aug. 6, 1912, for a time device for the sinking of submarine mines.

1188. Ceppi, Guillermo. Algunas consideraciones sobre la importancia del torpedo. (Boletín del Centro naval, Buenos Aires, tomo 31, 1913, p. 173–204.) **VXA**

1189. Charmoille. Le calibre de la torpille automobile. (Journal de la marine, le yacht, Paris, année 36, 1913, p. 433–434.) **†† VXF**

1190. —— Torpilleurs d'escadre. (Journal de la marine, le yacht, Paris, année 36, 1913, p. 509–510.) **†† VXF**

1191. Cirinei, Egisto. Lancio di siluri dall' aeroplano. (Rivista marittima, Roma, anno 46, trimestre 4, 1913, p. 306.) **VXA**

1192. Cuniberti, Vittorio. Tutti siluri. (Rivista marittima, Roma, anno 46, trimestre 2, 1913, p. 199–203.) **VXA**

Translated by Thomas Withers, Jr., in *Proceedings* of the United States Naval Institute, Annapolis, v. 40, 1913, p. 27–31, *VXA*.
A general article on torpedoes.

1193. Davis, Richmond P. Development of the submarine mine in the United States service. illus. (Journal of the United States artillery, Fort Monroe, v. 39, 1913, p. 15–32.) **VWA**

Notes on the use of mines in the Russo-Japanese war.

1194. El Destróyer "Commandant Rivieri." (Revista general de marina, Madrid, tomo 73, 1913, p. 600–604.) **VXA**

Also printed in *Boletín del Centro naval, Buenos Aires,* tomo 31, 1913, p. 587–593, *VXA*.

1195. Elia, Giovanni Emanuele. Selbsttätige Ankervorrichtung für Seeminen mit Lot zur Regelung der Tauchtiefe. illus. (Zeitschrift für das gesamte Schiess- und Sprengstoffwesen, München, Jahrg. 8, 1913, p. 236–237.) **† VOA**

Patent for a device to haul in a mine independent of its anchor.

1196. French destroyer "Commandant Rivière." illus. (Engineer, London, v. 116, 1913, p. 178–179.) **VA**

1197. The French mine layers Cerbere and Pluton. illus. (Engineer, London, v. 116, 1913, p. 515.) **VA**

With illustration on p. 516.
Also printed in *Journal of the United States artillery,* Fort Monroe, v. 41, 1914, p. 361–363, *VWA*.

1198. French torpedo boat destroyer "Magon." illus. (Engineer, London, v. 115, 1913, p. 658, 663–664.) **VA**

1199. Frost, H. H. The problem of firing at a fleet under way with long-range torpedoes. illus. (United States Naval Institute, Proceedings, Annapolis, v. 39, 1913, p. 681–698.) **VXA**

1200. Giraldi, A. Pecori. Velocità dei siluri in uso presso la marina inglese. (Rivista marittima, Roma, anno 46, trimestre 4, 1913, p. 65.) **VXA**

1201. Gray, James G. The properties and methods of operation of gyroscopes. illus. (Institution of Engineers and Shipbuilders in Scotland. Transactions, Glasgow, v. 57, 1913, p. 121–146.) **VDA**

Use on torpedoes.

1202. The Greek torpedo-boat destroyers of the "Lion" class. illus. (Engineer, London, v. 116, 1913, p. 59–60.) **VA**

With large illustration facing p. 70.

1203. Guidoni, Alessandro. Lancio di grossi pesi dall' aeroplano. (Rivista marittima, Roma, anno 46, trimestre 4, 1913, p. 15–20.) **VXA**

1204. H., F. La construction et la pose des mines sous-marines, système Elia. illus. (Le génie civil, Paris, tome 62, 1913, p. 189–192.) **VA**

1205. Hellweg, J. F. Emergency repairs to a destroyer. illus. (Scientific American, New York, v. 109, 1913, p. 175, 180.) **VA**

Notes on repairs on the "Burrows."

1206. Hintze. Die Treffaussichten des Torpedos. (Marine-Rundschau, Berlin, Jahrg. 24, 1913, p. 415–429.) **VXA**

1207. Iachino, A. Impiego del siluro nel combattimento fra navi. (Rivista marittima, Roma, anno 46, trimestre 2, 1913, p. 219–242, 453–455.) **VXA**

1208. Jane, Frederick T. Recognition book of German torpedo crafts. No. 1. Adapted from "Fighting ships." London: S. Low, Marston & Co., Ltd., 1913. 3 folded l. obl. 24°. **VXV**

1209. Kerc'hoat, L. de. La protection intérieure contre les torpilles et les mines. illus. (Journal de la marine, le yacht, Paris, année 36, 1913, p. 653–654.) **†† VXF**

1210. —— La torpille automobile. (Journal de la marine, le yacht, Paris, année 36, 1913, p. 472–473.) **†† VXF**

1913, continued.

1211. Kretschmer, O. Torpedos und Torpedoboote. (In: Technik des Kriegswesens, Berlin, 1913, p. 693–705.) **VWC**

1212. —— Die Unterseeminen. (In: Technik des Kriegswesens, Berlin, 1913, p. 686–693.) **VWC**

1213. Le Franc, A. Les mines-ludions. (Moniteur de la flotte, Paris, année 60, no. 18, May 3, 1913, p. 3.) **†† VYH**

1214. Lernet, Alexander. Seemine mit mechanischer Stosszündung. illus. (Zeitschrift für das gesamte Schiess- und Sprengstoffwesen, München, Jahrg. 8, 1913, p. 356.) **† VOA**
Patent granted for a submarine mine with mechanical percussion fuse, April 9, 1911.

1215. Livramento, A. O papel dos torpedeiros na guerra russo-japoneza. (Revista maritima brazileira, Rio de Janeiro, v. 62, 1913, p. 527–548.) **VXA**

1216. The **Marten-Hale** aeroplane bomb. illus. (Engineering, London, v. 96, 1913, p. 536.) **VDA**
Also printed in the *Proceedings* of the United States Naval Institute, Annapolis, v. 39, 1913, p. 1766–1767, *VXA.*

1217. Mewes, Rudolf. Ueber Lufttorpedos. (Zeitschrift für Sauerstoff- und Stickstoff-Industrie, Leipzig, Jahrg. 5, 1913, p. 31–35, 82–85, 272–273.) **† VOA**

1218. Michelsen, S. Die Entwicklung der Torpedowaffe. illus. (Schiffbautechnische Gesellschaft, Jahrbuch, Berlin, Bd. 14, 1913, p. 192–206.) **† VXA**
Discussion, p. 207–208.

1219. Ocenásek, Ludvig. Von der Sendestelle aus gesteuerter Torpedo. illus. (Zeitschrift für das gesamte Schiess- und Sprengstoffwesen, München, Jahrg. 8, 1913, p. 475.) **† VOA**
Patent granted Oct. 3, 1911, for a torpedo steered from the place of starting.

1220. Operating a torpedo from a land station. (Wireless age, New York, v. 1, 1913, p. 97.) **VGA**
Also printed in *Proceedings* of the United States Naval Institute, Annapolis, v. 40, 1914, p. 257–258, *VXA.*
A mechanism for operating a torpedo by non-interferable radio impulses, invented by John Hays Hammond, Jr.

1221. Peltier, J. Les torpilleurs d'escadre "Fourche" et "Faulx." illus. (Journal de la marine, le yacht, Paris, année 36, 1913, p. 406–410.) **†† VXH**
Translated in *Boletín del Centro naval,* Buenos Aires, tomo 31, 1913, p. 463–469, *VXA.*

1222. Pierreval, C. La torpille automobile. (Moniteur de la flotte, Paris, année 60, no. 43, Oct. 25, 1913, p. 3.) **†† VYH**

1223. Pirajá, Mauricio. Instructoria de torpedos e minas. (Revista · maritima brazileira, Rio de Janeiro, v. 63, 1913, p. 315–328. 649–659; v. 64, 1914, p. 1695–1706; v. 65, 1914, p. 499–504; v. 68, 1916, p. 95–100; v. 69, 1916, p. 45–49.) **VXA**

1224. Les **Porteurs** de mines "Cerbère et Pluton." illus. (Journal de la marine, le yacht, Paris, année 36, 1913, p. 837–838.) **†† VXF**

1225. Reymond, P. Les nouvelles fusées. illus. (Moniteur de la flotte, Paris, tome 60, no. 25, June 21, 1913, p. 3.) **†† VYH**

1226. —— Le sous-marin mouilleur de mines. (Moniteur de la flotte, Paris, année 60, no. 1, Jan. 4, 1913, p. 3.) **†† VYH**

1227. Sechi, Giovanni. Armamento anti-silurante. (Rivista marittima, Roma, anno 46, trimestre 2, 1913, p. 455–460.) **VXA**

1228. Skerrett, Robert G. The modern automobile torpedo. illus. (Scientific American, New York, v. 108, 1913, p. 18–19.) **VA**
Notes on the Whitehead and the Bliss-Leavitt torpedoes.

1229. Smith, Émile. Sonde à signal et appareil suédois pour découvrir les bas-fonds et les mines sous-marines. illus. (Le génie civil, Paris, tome 63, 1913, p. 50–52.) **VA**

1230. Torpedo boats and mines. (Army and navy journal, New York, v. 50, 1913, p. 381.) **†† VWA**

1231. Torpedo tubes but not torpedoes. (Scientific American, New York, v. 109, 1913, p. 82.) **VA**
Editorial on torpedo shortage.

1232. Whitehead & Co. A.-G., Fiume. Vorrichtung zum Ausstossen von Torpedos aus einem an der Breitseite des Schiffes unter Wasser schwenkbar angelenkten Führungsrahmen. illus. (Zeitschrift für das gesamte Schiess- und Sprengstoffwesen, München, Jahrg. 8, 1913, p. 237–238.) **†† VOA**
Patent granted March 15, 1911.

1914

1233. Andler, S. Der Torpedoweitschuss. illus. (Marine-Rundschau, Berlin, Jahrg. 25, 1914, p. 512–525.) **VXA**
Translated in *Revista maritima brazileira,* Rio de Janeiro, v. 65, 1914, p. 659–675, *VXA.*

1234. Attack and defense by submarine mines. illus. (Scientific American, New York, v. 111, 1914, p. 270–271, 286.) **VA**

1914, continued.

1235. The **Automobile** torpedo. illus. (Scientific American supplement, New York, v. 78, 1914, p. 217–218.) **VA**

Also printed in *Journal of the United States artillery*, Fort Monroe, v. 42, 1914, p. 357–363, *VWA*. Compiled from *La nature* and *La science et la vie*. History of the Whitehead torpedo and notes on the Bliss-Leavitt torpedo.

1236. Avery, Ray L. The mine defense of harbors: its history, principles, relation to the other elements of defense, and tactical employment. (Journal of the United States artillery, Fort Monroe, v. 42, 1914, p. 1–17.) **VWA**

Notes on Bushnell's torpedo; use of torpedoes and mines during the Civil war; development of the submarine mine, 1585–1904.

1237. Barclay, Sir Thomas. The floating mines curse; an unsentimental study. (Nineteenth century, New York, v. 76, 1914, p. 745–752.) **•DA**

1238. Battleships and submarine attack. (Engineer, London, v. 118, 1914, p. 71–72.) **VA**

Also printed in *Journal* of the American Society of Naval Engineers, Washington, v. 26, 1914, p. 1401–1403, *VXA*.

1239. Benjamin, Park. The flying-fish torpedo. (Independent, New York, v. 80, 1914, p. 165–166.) **•DA**

Abstracted in *Army and navy journal*, New York, v. 52, 1914, p. 295, †† *VWA*.

1240. Bernay, Henri. L'utilisation de la torpille. (Journal de la marine, le yacht, Paris, année 37, 1914, p. 289–290.) †† **VXF**

1241. Bernotti, Romeo. L'attacco diurno torpediniero. (Rivista marittima, Roma, anno 47, trimestre 1, 1914, p. 225–233.) **VXA**

Translated by W. N. Jeffers in *Proceedings* of the United States Naval Institute, Annapolis, v. 40, 1914, p. 1155–1162, *VXA*. Valuable suggestions as to daylight torpedo-boat attack.

1242. Biles, Sir John Harvard. On the protection of battleships against submarine attack. illus. (Institution of Naval Architects, Transactions, London, v. 56, 1914, p. 257–262.) **VXA**

With discussion, p. 262–270. Also printed in *Engineering*, London, v. 98, 1914, p. 65–71, *VDA*; *Engineer*, London, v. 118, 1914, p. 33–35, *VA*. Abstracted in *Engineering magazine*, New York, v. 47, 1914, p. 909–911, *VDA*, and in *Marine engineer*, London, v. 37, 1915, p. 326–327, *VXA*.

1243. Bunker, Paul D. The mine defense of harbors: its history, principles, relation to the other elements of defense, and tactical employment. illus. (Journal of the United States artillery, Fort Monroe, v. 41, 1914, p. 129–170.) **VWA**

A very complete article, giving list of U. S. battleships torpedoed during the Civil war; an account of Elia's automatic mine; and the principles of mine laying.

1244. C., P. Les mines sous-marines pour la défense des ports. illus. (Le génie civil, Paris, tome 65, 1914, p. 360–362.) **VA**

1245. C., S. O torpedo moderno e as novas construcções navaes. (Revista maritima brazileira, Rio de Janeiro, v. 65, 1914, p. 505–524.) **VXA**

1246. Carteron, Charles Pierre Jules. Von einem Unterseeboot abzuwerfende, sich selbsttätig in bestimmter Tiefe verankernde, aus Schwimmer, Anker und Lot bestehende Seemine mit Auftrieb. (Zeitschrift für das gesamte Schiess- und Sprengstoffwesen, München, Jahrg. 9, 1914, p. 326.) † **VOA**

Patent for a submarine mine thrown out by a submarine and anchored at a certain depth.

1247. Curry, E. Hamilton. Menace of the torpedo. (Nineteenth century & after, New York, v. 76, 1914, p. 153–165.) **•DA**

1248. Defense against submarine mines. (Mechanical world, London, v. 56, 1914, p. 81.) **VFA**

Also printed in *Journal* of the American Society of Naval Engineers, Washington, v. 26, 1914, p. 1400–1401, *VXA*; and in *Journal* of the United States artillery, Fort Monroe, v. 44, 1915, p. 229–230, *VWA*.

1249. De Feo, V. Appunti sul lancio. (Rivista marittima, Roma, anno 47, trimestre 1, 1914, p. 449–470.) **VXA**

1250. Drop-hammers for Greenock torpedo factory. (Engineering, London, v. 98, 1914, p. 612.) **VDA**

1251. Elia, Giovanni Emanuele. Seemine. illus. (Zeitschrift für das gesamte Schiess- und Sprengstoffwesen, München, Jahrg. 9, 1914, p. 335–336.) † **VOA**

1252. —— Selbsttätige Zündvorrichtung für Seeminen. illus. (Zeitschrift für das gesamte Schiess- und Sprengstoffwesen, München, Jahrg. 9, 1914, p. 15, 94.) † **VOA**

Patents granted April 9, 1911 and March 19, 1911.

1253. —— Vorrichtung zur Sicherung der Zündvorrichtung von Seeminen. illus. (Zeitschrift für das gesamte Schiess- und Sprengstoffwesen, München, Jahrg. 9, 1914, p. 264–265.) † **VOA**

Patent granted Jan. 24, 1912, for safety device when igniting submarine mines.

1254. —— Zündvorrichtung für Seeminen. illus. (Zeitschrift für das gesamte Schiess- und Sprengstoffwesen, München, Jahrg. 9, 1914, p. 133.) † **VOA**

Patent granted July 30, 1912.

1255. Feldhaus, Franz Maria. Torpedo. (In his: Die Technik der Vorzeit, der geschichtlichen Zeit und der Naturvölker, Leipzig, 1914, col. 1181–1182.) **V**

Gives valuable bibliographical notes.

1914, continued.

1256. Ferguson, J. N. The submarine mine. (United States Naval Institute, Proceedings, Annapolis, v. 40, 1914, p. 1697–1706.) **VXA**

Notes on use of rams during the Civil war and the Russo-Japanese war.

1257. Fiske, Bradley Allen. Wireless controlled torpedoes. (Army and navy journal, New York, v. 51, 1914, p. 940.) **†† VWA**

A communication claiming priority in the invention of wireless-controlled torpedoes.

1258. Floating and anchored mines. (Marine review, Cleveland, v. 44, 1914, p. 402–403.) **† VXA**

Describes how they are laid and how removed.

1259. Four German destroyers sunk. (Engineer, London, v. 118, 1914, p. 396.) **VA**

1260. Fournier, A. L'état actuel du type contre-torpilleur. illus. (Le génie civil, Paris, tome 64, 1914, p. 314–316.) **VA**

1261. The **French** destroyers Bisson and Renaudin. illus. (Engineer, London, v. 117, 1914, p. 615–616.) **VA**

With illustration facing p. 636.

1262. Gosse, Joseph. Les mines sous-marines. Paris: Librairie générale de droit & de jurisprudence, 1914. 2 p.l. 185 p., 1 l. 8°. **XD**

1263. Gray, James G. On experiments leading up to new gyrostatic controls for torpedoes, submarines, airships, and aeroplanes. illus. (Institution of Engineers and Shipbuilders in Scotland, Transactions, Glasgow, v. 58, 1914, p. 87–106.) **VDA**

Also printed in *Scientific American supplement,* New York, v. 79, 1915, p. 172–173, 188–189, *VA.* Abstracted in *Proceedings* of the United States Naval Institute, Annapolis, v. 41, 1915, p. 1324–1326, *VXA.*

1264. H. M. torpedo boat destroyer Laverock aground. illus. (Engineer, London, v. 117, 1914, p. 286.) **VA**

1265. Interior protection against torpedoes and mines. illus. (Journal of the United States artillery, Fort Monroe, v. 42, 1914, p. 358–361.) **VWA**

Abstracted from *Le Yacht,* 1914.

1266. Jaeger, Christian. Einrichtung zum Zünden der Minen von Minensperren mittels des elektrischen Stromes von einer Landstation aus, bei der das Bild der Wasseroberfläche auf der Tafel einer Dunkelkammer wiedergegeben wird, auf der die Lage der Minen angemerkt ist. (Zeitschrift für das Schiess- und Sprengstoffwesen, München, Jahrg. 9, 1914, p. 112.) **† VOA**

Patent granted May 25, 1912.

1267. Jourdan, Sauvaire. La torpille automobile. illus. (La nature, Paris, année 42, semestre 1, 1914, p. 264–267.) **OA**

1268. L., P. Mines sous-marines et mouilleurs de mines. (Journal de la marine, le yacht, Paris, tome 37, 1914, p. 305–306, 322.) **†† VXF**

1269. Laghezza, G. L'uso delle mine nella guerra marittima, secondo l'VIII convenzione dell' Aja. (Rivista marittima, Roma, anno 47, trimestre 1, 1914, p. 234–252.) **VXA**

Translated by Piers K. Kekewich in the *Journal* of the Royal United Service Institution, London, v. 59, 1914, p. 455–468, *VWA.*

1270. Lanchester, Frederick William. Aircraft in war. (Engineering, London, v. 98, 1914, p. 568–569, 597–598.) **VDA**

Notes on the aerial torpedo.

1271. Le Franc, A. Le service central des torpilles. (Moniteur de la flotte, Paris, année 61, no. 20, May 16, 1914, p. 3.) **†† VYH**

1272. Lissak, Ormond Mitchell. Ordnance and gunnery; a text-book prepared for the cadets of the United States Military Academy, West Point. New York: J. Wiley & Sons. 1914. 1 p.l., v–xiv p., 1 l., 604 p. illus. 8°. **VWW**

Submarine mines and torpedoes. Submarine torpedo boats, p. 576–594.

1273. M. de T., E. de. Necesidad de los barcos sumergibles en España. (Memorial de ingenieros, Madrid, año 69, 1914, p. 86–102, 107–123.) **VWA**

1274. McElgin, Hugh J. B. Suggestions for the organization of work on a large mine command. (Journal of the United States artillery, Fort Monroe, v. 42, 1914, p. 301–311.) **VWA**

1275. Machado de Castro e Silva, J. Uma visita ás officinas Schneider, secção de torpedos. (Revista maritima brazileira, Rio de Janeiro, v. 64, 1914, p. 1217–1231.) **VXA**

1276. Machado de Castro e Silva, J., and M. ROCHA DE AZAMBUJA. Nova pistola ou percutor universal. (Revista maritima brazileira, Rio de Janeiro, v. 64, 1914, p. 1201–1215.) **VXA**

1277. The **Marten-Hall;** an aeroplane bomb that explodes only on striking the ground. illus. (United States Naval Institute, Proceedings, Annapolis, v. 40, 1914, p. 883–884.) **VXA**

1278. Mines in naval warfare. (Scientific American supplement, New York, v. 78, 1914, p. 198–199.) **VA**

Abstracted from *Navy and military record,* London, August 19, 1914.
Use of mines in the Russo-Japanese war.

1914, continued.

1279. Mr. Hammond's torpedo. illus. (Outlook, New York, v. 108, 1914, p. 802.)
•DA

Illustration on p. 826.
Also printed in the *Journal of the United States artillery*, Fort Monroe, v. 43, 1915, p. 141–142, *VWA*.
A radio-controlled torpedo, the invention of John Hays Hammond, Jr.

1280. Modern submarine warfare. illus. (Scientific American, New York, v. 111, 1914, p. 374, 376–377.) **VA**

Illustrations of a torpedo caught in a net, and of nets strung across harbor entrances.

1281. Moffett, Cleveland. Steered by wireless: the triumph of a man of twenty-five. illus. (McClure's magazine, New York, v. 42, March, 1914, p. 27–39.) **•DA**

1282. Muniz Barreto, Edmundo Williams. Elementos tacticos para o tiro de torpedos. (Revista maritima brazileira, Rio de Janeiro, v. 65, 1914, p. 235–323.) **VXA**

1283. —— Exercicios de tiro com torpedos. (Revista maritima brazileira, Rio de Janeiro, v. 65, 1914, p. 851–874.) **VXA**

1284. Neeser, Robert Wilden. The work of the torpedo flotillas. illus. (The navy, Washington, v. 8, 1914, p. 106–111.) † **VYE**

1285. Notes on torpedo work in H. M. ships, by R. P. Portsmouth: Gieve's [1914]. 2 p.l., 32 p., 1 l. 12°. **VXV**

1286. Ocenásek, Ludvik. Fernstromschlussvorrichtung, besonders zum Steuern und Beherrschen von elektrisch betriebenen Torpedos von der Ferne aus. illus. (Zeitschrift für das gesamte Schiess- und Sprengstoffwesen, München, Jahrg. 9, 1914, p. 75.) † **VOA**

Patent granted Oct. 3, 1911 for the steering and controlling of electrically driven torpedoes from a distance.

1287. Operating a torpedo from a land station. (Journal of the United States artillery, Fort Monroe, v. 42, 1914, p. 376.) **VWA**

1288. Owens, T. G. Battleship design. illus. (Engineering, London, v. 97, 1914, p. 449–452.) **VDA**

Notes on torpedoes.

1289. P., R. Notes on torpedo work in H. M. ships. Portsmouth: Gieve's [1914]. 2 p.l., 32 p., 1 l. 12°. **VXV**

1290. Persius, L. Die Entwicklung der Torpedowaffe. illus. (Technische Monatshefte, Stuttgart, Jahrg. 5, 1914, p. 68–70.) **VA**

1291. Pramer, Karl. Der Torpedo und seine Verwendung im Kriege. (Mitteilungen aus dem Gebiete des Seewesens, Pola, Bd. 42, 1914, p. 38–47, 226–248, 475–506, 580–596, 654–677, 765–800.) **VXA**

1292. Range of torpedoes. (Army and navy journal, New York, v. 52, 1914, p. 243.) †† **VWA**

1293. The Reckless strewing of mines. (Marine engineer, London, v. 37, 1914, p. 131, 148.) **VXA**

1294. Reymond, P. Contre les torpilles. (Moniteur de la flotte, Paris, année 61, no. 13, March 28, 1914, p. 3.) †† **VYH**

1295. Santini, Felice. L'uso delle mine nelle guerre marittima. (Rivista marittima, Roma, anno 47, trimestre 2, 1914, p. 65–66.) **VXA**

1296. Submarine mines and their place in naval warfare. (Scientific Australian, Melbourne, v. 20, 1914, p. 40–41.) **VA**

1297. Submarines in war. (Engineer, London, v. 118, 1914, p. 487.) **VA**

Editorial.

1298. Torpedo warfare. illus. (Scientific American, New York, v. 111, 1914, p. 374, 391.) **VA**

Description of the Bliss-Leavitt torpedo.

1299. Torpedorohre. (Schiffbau, Berlin, Jahrg. 15, 1914, p. 574, 625, 867.) † **VXA**

1300. United States.—Naval War College. International law topics and discussions, 1914. Washington, 1915. 169 p. 8°. **XBD**

Submarine mines, p. 100–138.

1301. Utley, S. W. Ten weeks with the battleship fleet. illus. (Marine review, Cleveland, v. 46, 1914, p. 207–210, 266–269, 290–293.) †† **VXA**

On p. 293 is an account of torpedo defence drill, which is quoted in *Army and navy journal*, New York, v. 51, 1914, p. 1528. †† *VWA*.

1302. Vannutelli, L. Sull' impiego delle torpediniere nella ricerca notturna. (Rivista marittima, Roma, anno 47, trimestre 3, 1914, p. 215–232.) **VXA**

1303. Vennin, L., and G. Chesneau. Les poudres et explosifs, et les mesures de sécurité dans les mines de houille... Paris: C. Béranger, 1914. xviii p., 1 l., 573 p., 1 l. illus. 8°. (Encyclopédie de science chimique appliquée. tome 6.) **VOG**

Chargement des torpilles, p. 452–454; Mines du génie militaire, p. 454–456.

1304. Walker, Sydney Ferris. Submarine engineering; all about work under water told in popular language. London: C. A. Pearson, Ltd., 1914. 126 p., 1 l., 8 pl. illus. 12°. ("How does it work" series. no. 8.) **VXV**

The torpedo, p. 37–47.

1305. Wilby, F. B. Tests of the Bangalore torpedo. (United States.—Engineer Bureau. Professional memoirs, Washington, D. C., v. 6, 1914, p. 102–110.) **VDA**

1915

1306. Abell, T. B. The submarine. (Marine engineer, London, v. 37, 1915, p. 264–269, 286.) **VXA**
Abstracted from his lecture before the Liverpool University Students' Engineering Society.

1307. Aerial torpedo controlled by wireless. (New York Times, Sept. 26, 1915, part 2, p. 12, col. 1.) ***D**
Invention of G. F. Russell.

1308. Aerial torpedo new weapon of offense. illus. (Popular mechanics, Chicago, v. 24, 1915, p. 354.) **VFA**

1309. Aerial torpedoes. (New York Times, Oct. 30, 1915, p. 3, col. 8.) ***D**
Hudson Maxim confers with Secretary Daniels on device for timing explosion of aerial torpedoes.

1310. American air compressors for testing torpedoes. illus. (Engineer, London, v. 119, 1915, p. 462.) **VA**

1311. An Automatic mine. illus. (Journal of the United States artillery, Fort Monroe, v. 44, 1915, p. 230–231.) **VWA**

1312. The Automobile torpedo. illus. (Engineer, London, v. 120, 1915, p. 77–78.) **VA**
A very complete article giving description of the Whitehead torpedo, largely based on data taken from *Le Génie civil*, v. 66, 1915, p. 401–403, *VDA*.

1313. The Automobile torpedo. illus. (Scientific American supplement, New York, v. 80, 1915, p. 152–154.) **VA**
Notes on the Whitehead, Spar, and Bliss-Leavitt torpedoes.

1314. Azevedo Milanez, João Francisco de. Notas sobre torpedos. (Revista maritima brazileira, Rio de Janeiro, v. 66, 1915, p. 1409–1416.) **VXA**

1315. Bache, Rene. Launching a torpedo on the wing. illus. (Technical world, Chicago, v. 22, 1915, p. 842–845.) **VDA**

1315a. —— Using a weapon twenty centuries old. illus. (Technical world magazine, Chicago, v. 23, 1915, p. 173–176.) **VDA**
Outlines the development of the grenade from ancient times to the revival of its use in the Russo-Japanese war and the present war in Europe.

1316. Baird, George Washington. Additional notes on submarines. (American Society of Naval Engineers, Journal, Washington, v. 27, 1915, p. 186–191.) **VXA**
Illustration of Bushnell's torpedo.

1317. Belloni, Angelo. L'immersione dei sommergibili. (Rivista marittima. Roma, anno 48, trimestre 2, 1915, p. 185–199.) **VXA**

1318. Benjamin, Park. The Fiske torpedo-launching seaplane. illus. (Flying. New York, v. 4, 1915, p. 540–541, 565–566.) **† VDS**
A new and terrible form of attack on the high seas or in harbors.

1319. Bertin, E. Le transport des mines par les courants sous l'action de la houle. (Le génie civil, Paris, tome 66, 1915, p. 138.) **VA**

1320. Blactot, René. La guerre navale et la torpille. illus. (La nature, Paris, année 43, semestre 2, 1915, p. 17–24.) **OA**

1321. Bravetta, Ettore. Sottomarini, sommergibili e torpedini. Con 78 incisioni intercalate nel testo. Milano: Fratelli Treves, 1915. 2 p.l., ₁vii–₁viii, 230 p. illus. 4°. **VXV**

1322. Bunker, Paul D. Forms for records of mine planting. (Journal of the United States artillery, Fort Monroe, v. 43, 1915, p. 331–335.) **VWA**

1323. Burberg, Gebrüder. Füllmaschine für Wurfminen, Granaten usw. illus. (Zeitschrift für das gesamte Schiess- und Sprengstoffwesen, München, Bd. 10, 1915, p. 200.) **† VOA**

1324. Campagna, Enzo. La nave subacquea; sottomarini e sommergibili. Milano: U. Hoepli, 1915. 4 p.l., ₁xi–₁xii, 346 p., 5 pl. illus. 16°. (Manuali Hoepli.) **VXV**
Armamento del sommergibile, p. 263–282.

1325. Chandler, Edward F. The modern automobile torpedo. How it is constructed, how it works and how it may be improved. illus. (Scientific American, New York, v. 113, 1915, p. 112–114, 128–130.) **VA**

1326. —— Providing a torpedo with ears. illus. (Popular science monthly, New York, v. 87, 1915, p. 489–496.) ***DA**

1327. ₁Checker-board system of microphone detectors.₁ (New York Times, Oct. 2, 1915, p. 3, col. 2.) ***D**
Described by E. F. Chandler and William Dubilier.

1328. Cohen, Samuel. Electricity and the modern automobile torpedo. illus. (Electrical experimenter, New York, v. 3, 1915, p. 266–267.) **VGA**

1329. Conness, Leland. Submarine mines. (Munsey's magazine, New York, v. 55, 1915, p. 257–265.) ***DA**

1330. Davis, Edmund J. Submarine attack. (Engineer, London, v. 119, 1915, p. 144.) **VA**

1331. Development of the science of mine-sweeping. (Royal United Service Institution, Journal, London, v. 60, 1915, p. 383–403.) **VWA**

1915, continued.

1332. Development of the torpedo. illus. (Arms and the man, Washington, v. 58, 1915, p. 145.) † **MYA**

1333. Device for steering torpedoes by wireless. (New York Times, July 24, 1915, p. 11, col. 3.) ● **D**
Invention of Admiral Fiske for his new aerial torpedo boat.

1334. Device to render battleships immune from attack. (New York Times, July 20, 1915, p. 2, col. 4.) ● **D**
Tried out in English waters and in the Dardanelles.

1335. Dropping bombs from aeroplanes. illus. (Scientific Australian, Melbourne, v. 20, 1915, p. 66.) **VA**

1336. Dumas, A. La torpille automobile. illus. (Le génie civil, Paris, tome 66, 1915, p. 401–408.) **VA**

1337. Duquet, Alfred. La torpille menaçante. (La revue, Paris, série 7, v. 110, 1915, p. 460–471.) ● **DM**

1338. Effect of German torpedo on merchantman. (Popular mechanics, Chicago, v. 24, 1915, p. 33.) **VFA**
Illustration.

1339. Electricity in submarine mining. illus. (The electrical review, London, v. 77, 1915, p. 454–455.) **VGA**

1340. English methods in combating submarine peril. (New York Times, Dec. 2, 1915, p. 1, col. 3.) ● **D**
Use of underwater telephones, motor boats, and aeroplanes.

1341. Explosionen unter Wasser. (Zeitschrift für das gesamte Schiess- und Sprengstoffwesen, München, Jahrg. 10, 1915, p. 116–118.) † **VOA**

1342. Gentsch, Wilhelm. Ueber den Antrieb selbstfahrender Torpedos im Auslande. (Verein zur Beförderung des Gewerbfleisses, Verhandlungen, Berlin, Jahrg. 94, 1915, p. 469–496.) **VA**

1343. German incendiary bombs. illus. (Engineering, London, v. 99, 1915, p. 609.) **VDA**

1344. Government torpedo secrets safe. (Army and navy journal, New York, v. 52, 1915, p. 1292, 1295.) †† **VWA**
Notes on Bliss-Leavitt torpedo.

1344a. Grenades. (Information annual, 1915, New York, 1916, p. 303.) **Information Div.**

1345. Guenther, Hanns. Torpedo-Flugzeuge. illus. (Technische Monatshefte: Technik für Alle, Stuttgart, Jahrg. 1915, Heft 10, p. 306–308.) **VA**

1346. La **Guerra** al commercio dal 1° agosto al 15 novembre 1915. (Rivista marittima, Roma, anno 48, trimestre 4, 1915, p. 217–232.) **VXA**

1347. La **Guerra** al commercio nei mari settentrionali d'Europa. Dall' inizio al 31 luglio 1915. (Rivista marittima, Roma, anno 48, trimestre 3, 1915, p. 104–120.) **VXA**

1348. Guidoni, Alessandro. Early experiments at launching torpedoes from an aeroplane. illus. (Flying, New York, v. 4, 1915, p. 539–540.) † **VDS**

1349. Hinkamp, C. N. Submarines and torpedoes. (American Society of Naval Engineers, Journal, Washington, v. 27, 1915, p. 438–453.) **VXA**
Also printed in *Journal of the United States artillery*, v. 44, 1915, p. 218–228, *VWA.*

1350. —— Torpedoes and submarines, how they are operated, maneuvered and navigated. illus. (Scientific American supplement, New York, v. 80, 1915, p. 136–138.) **VA**

1351. Horsnaill, W. O. War beneath the waves: submarine mines. (Chambers's journal, London, series 7, v. 5, 1915, p. 293–294.) ● **DA**

1352. —— War beneath the waves: torpedoes. (Chambers's journal, London, series 7, v. 5, 1915, p. 198–200.) ● **DA**

1353. Huber, James. Submarine mines; their design and their functioning. illus. (Engineering magazine, New York, v. 50, 1915, p. 120–121.) **VDA**
From *Journal* of the American Society of Marine Draftsmen.

1354. Inventions of Admiral Fiske. (Army and navy journal, New York, v. 52, 1915, p. 295, 1492, 1646.) †† **VWA**
Notes on his invention for control of torpedoes.

1355. Is there any defence against the submarine? (Scientific American, New York, v. 112, 1915, p. 152.) **VA**
Editorial.

1356. James, H. Protection from torpedoes. (New York Times, June 21, 1915, p. 8, col. 6.) ● **D**

1357. Kaempffert, Waldemar. Torpedoes. The Lusitania, and naval architecture. illus. (American review of reviews, New York, v. 51, 1915, p. 685–686.) ● **DA**

1358. Landminen. illus. (Schuss und Waffe, Neudamm, Bd. 8, 1915, p. 141–143.) † **VWA**
From *Die Umschau.*

1359. The Leon torpedo. illus. (Engineer, London, v. 120, 1915, p. 196–197.) **VA**

1915, continued.

1360. Leon torpedo. (New York Times, Oct. 2, 1915, p. 3, col. 1.) *** D**
United States Navy experiments.

1361. Leon torpedo and detectors. (New York Times, Oct. 3, 1915, part 1, p. 3, col. 3.) *** D**

1362. Loading and firing submarine torpedoes. illus. (Scientific American, New York, v. 112, 1915, p. 485, 493.) **VA**

1363. Machado, Orlando. Pro submarino. (Revista maritima brazileira, Rio de Janeiro, v. 67, 1915, p. 2499–2507; v. 68, 1916, p. 527–532.) **VXA**

1364. Magnetic steerage of torpedoes. (English mechanic and world of science, London, v. 101, 1915, p. 483–484.) **VA**

1365. Marine mines; their purpose: how they are planted and how destroyed. illus. (Scientific American supplement, New York, v. 80, 1915, p. 388–389.) **VA**
From *La nature.*

1366. Maury, Richard Lancelot. A brief sketch of the work of Matthew Fontaine Maury during the war, 1861–65. Richmond: Whittet & Shepperson, 1915. 36 p. 12°. **VXV**
Commander Maury's use of torpedoes in the Civil war.

1367. Miessner, B. F. A new solution for the problem of selectivity in torpedo control. illus. (Purdue engineering review, Lafayette, Ind., v. 15, 1915, p. 34–41.) **Tech. Div. — Vertical File**

1368. Moffett, Cleveland. A new defense against the submarine. illus. (American magazine, New York, v. 79, April, 1915, p. 11–15, 96–100.) *** DA**

1369. The "Nautilus." [Cleveland, O.: Cleveland Twist Drill Co., 1915.] broadside. diagr. f°. **† VXV**
"Robert Fulton...was designer of the first successful submarine...the Nautilus."

1370. Net used by British Admiralty. (New York Times, Aug. 27, 1915, p. 4, col. 6.) *** D**
Invention of H. J. Reinhardt.

1371. New torpedo boat for coast defense. (New York Times, Sept. 29, 1915, p. 8, col. 2.) *** D**
Invention of E. F. Chandler.

1372. New type of bomb, for use by aeroplanes, patented, May 13, 1914. illus. (Engineering, London, v. 100, 1915, p. 127.) **VDA**
Also in *Proceedings* of the United States Naval Institute, Annapolis, v. 41, 1915, p. 1656, *VXA.*

1373. Peculiarities of torpedoes. illus. (New York Times, May 10, 1915, p. 8, col. 3.) *** D**
Discussion by United States naval officers.

1374. Permanent Court of Arbitration. The Hague convention (VIII) of 1907 relative to the laying of automatic submarine contact mines. Washington: the endowment, 1915. iv, 6 p. 8°. (Carnegie Endowment for International Peace.—Division of International Law. Pamphlet 16.) **XBN**

1375. The Portuguese torpedo-boat destroyer Douro. illus. (Engineer, London, v. 119, 1915, p. 404.) **VA**
With illustration on p. 406.

1376. Possibilities of an aerial torpedo controlled by wireless. illus. (Sphere, London, v. 60, 1915, p. 286–287.) *** DA**

1377. Procacci, Gianni. Perigrafi e periscopi. illus. (Rivista marittima, Roma, anno 48, trimestre 2, 1915, p. 361–397.) **VXA**
Translated in *Revista general de marina,* Madrid, tomo 78, 1916, p. 306–338, *VXA,* and *Revista maritima brazileira,* Rio de Janeiro, v. 68, 1915, p. 663–676, *VXA.*

1378. Proença, Eduardo Justino de. Defesa contra submersiveis. (Revista maritima brazileira, Rio de Janeiro, v. 66, 1915, p. 1719–1723.) **VXA**

1379. Protection against torpedoes. (Engineer, London, v. 119, 1915, p. 41–42.) **VA**
Also printed in *Scientific American supplement,* New York, v. 79, 1915, p. 107, *VA.*
Notes on the torpedoing of ships in the European war.

1380. Repair of a torpedoed vessel, the "Gulflight." illus. (Marine engineer, London, v. 38, 1915, p. 97.) **VXA**

1381. Robert Fulton's experiments with submarines. (New York Times, Jan. 24, 1915, part 7, p. 3, col. 1.) *** D**

1382. Roji, Arsenio. Acorazados y sumergibles. (Revista general de marina, Madrid, tomo 76, 1915, p. 419–427.) **VXA**

1383. Root, E. N. Introduction of submarines as an instrument of war by Robert Fulton in 1807. (New York Times, Aug. 24, 1915, p. 10, col. 7.) *** D**

1384. Schmidt, Richard. Als Doppelmine wirkende Seemine. (Zeitschrift für das gesamte Schiess- und Sprengstoffwesen, München, Jahrg. 10, 1915, p. 185.) **† VOA**
Patent granted Nov. 29, 1913.

1385. Schromm, A. von. Einiges über Unterseeboote. illus. (Oesterreichische Wochenschrift für den öffentlichen Baudienst, Wien, Jahrg. 21, 1915, p. 270–278.) **3 – † VEA**

1386. Secor, H. Winfield. Combating the submarine by electrical means. illus. (Electrical experimenter, New York, v. 3, 1915, p. 184–185.) **VGA**

1915, continued.

1387. Seeminen. (Ueberall, Berlin, Jahrg. 17, 1915, p. 546–549.) † **VXA**

1388. Selter. Ueber Lufttorpedos. illus. (Zeitschrift für das gesamte Schiess- und Sprengstoffwesen, München, Jahrg. 10, 1915, p. 125–127, 142–144.) † **VOA**

1389. Spear, L. Y. The submarine of to-day and to-morrow. (Society of Naval Architects and Marine Engineers, Transactions, New York, v. 23, 1915, p. 201–216.) **VXA**

With discussion, p. 216–224.

1390. Special article on torpedoes. (New York Times, May 16, 1915, part 5, p. 4, col. 1.) *** D**

1391. Submarine attack swift and silent. (Marine review, Cleveland, v. 45, 1915, p. 328.) † **VXA**

An officer in the British marine service describes the torpedoing of a ship.

1392. Submarine torpedo that hunts its quarry. illus. (Popular mechanics, Chicago, v. 24, 1915, p. 11.) **VFA**

1393. Thomas, C. O. How a fast ocean liner can be torpedoed. (Canadian engineer, Toronto, v. 28, 1915, p. 696–697.) **VDA**

1394. The **Torpedo.** illus. (Marine engineer, London, v. 38, 1915, p. 7–10.) **VXA**

Outlines the development of the torpedo and gives valuable notes on the modern torpedo.

1395. The **Torpedo** damage to the steamship Gulflight. (Engineer, London, v. 120, 1915, p. 370.) **VA**

Torpedoed May 1, 1915.

1396. Torpedo fire directing. (Practical engineer, London, v. 52, 1915, p. 20–21.) **VDA**

1397. Torpedo guards. (United States Naval Institute, Proceedings, Annapolis, v. 41, 1915, p. 1339–1340, 1685–1687.) **VXA**

Professional notes.

1398. Torpedo that sank the Lusitania. (Army and navy journal, New York, v. 52, 1915, p. 1208.) †† **VWA**

Suggests that the Davis torpedo was used by the Germans.

1399. Torpedoes launched in mid-air. (Scientific Australian, Melbourne, v. 20, 1915, p. 67–68.) **VA**

Note on the invention of Admiral Bradley A. Fiske, U. S. N.

1400. La **Torpille-mine** Leon. illus. (Le génie civil, Paris, tome 67, 1915, p. 91–92.) **VA**

Abstracted in *Marine engineer*, London, v. 38, 1915, p. 115, *VXA*.

1401. Townsend, A. O. Fulton as inventor of torpedo. (New York Times, July 18, 1915, part 2, p. 14, col. 5.) *** D**

1402. Trebesius, Ernst. Torpedos, ihre Bauart und Wirkungsweise. illus. (Schuss und Waffe, Neudamm, Bd. 8, 1915, p. 163–168.) † **VWA**

1403. —— Treibende Seeminen und ihre Beseitigung. (Ueberall, Berlin, Jahrg. 17, 1915, p. 551–552.) † **VXA**

1404. Underground warfare; mine and countermine as they are used in the European war. (Illustrated London news, London, v. 147, 1915, p. 10–12.) *** DA**

1405. Uses and advantages of winged torpedoes. (New York Times, Sept. 1, 1915, p. 3, col. 3.) *** D**

1406. Warner, Oscar C. The German naval offensive and defensive mine. illus. (Journal of the United States artillery, Fort Monroe, v. 43, 1915, p. 336–339.) **VWA**

1406a. Where a Zeppelin is vulnerable: and where it is protected. illus. (Sphere, London, v. 61, 1915, p. 232.) *** DA**

Notes on incendiary bombs.

1407. Wireless controlled air torpedo. (Aeronautics, New York, v. 17, 1915, p. 21, 28.) **VDS**

Also printed in *Journal of the United States artillery*, Fort Monroe, v. 46, 1916, p. 122–123, *VWA*. Invention of George F. Russell of Hoboken, N. J.

1916

1408. Aerial torpedo torch lights battle field. illus. (Popular mechanics, Chicago, v. 26, 1916, p. 161–162.) **VFA**

1409. Aerial torpedoes. (New York Times, Feb. 24, 1916, p. 3, col. 5.) *** D**

Used by the Germans on the eastern front.

1410. Aerial torpedoes. Old devices that have been revived during the present war. illus. (Scientific American supplement, New York, v. 81, 1916, p. 132–133.) **VA**

1411. Aero wireless torpedo control. illus. (Wireless age, New York, v. 3, 1916, p. 364, 584–585, 774.) **VGA**

Invention of John Hays Hammond, Jr.

1412. Aeroplane guide for radio torpedo. (New York Times, Jan. 14, 1916, p. 1, col. 2.) *** D**

Invention of John Hays Hammond, Jr.

1413. Anti-submarine torpedo used from aeroplane. illus. (Popular mechanics, Chicago, v. 25, 1916, p. 338–339.) **VFA**

1414. Bannard, Walter. A torpedo with eyes. illus. (Popular science monthly, New York, v. 88, 1916, p. 424–425.) *** DA**

1916, continued.

1415. The **Barlow** aerial torpedo. illus. (Journal of the United States artillery, Fort Monroe, v. 46, 1916, p. 386–388.)
VWA

Also printed in *Aerial age weekly*, New York, v. 4, 1916, p. 385, † *VDS*.

1416. Barpi, A. I cacciatorpediniere germanici nella guerra attuale. (Rivista marittima, Roma, anno 49, trimestre 4, 1916, p. 397–407.)
VXA

1417. Belknap, Reginald R. The torpedo and submarine branches of the German navy. (United States Naval Institute, Proceedings, Annapolis, v. 42, 1916, p. 1485–1508.)
VXA

1418. Benjamin, Park. The Fiske torpedo launching seaplane. illus. (Flying, New York, v. 4, 1916, p. 540–542, 565–566.)
† VDS

1418a. Bomb throwing from aircraft. illus. (Aerial age weekly, New York, v. 4, 1916, p. 98, 106.)
† VDS
From *Technische Rundschau*.

1419. Bronze in torpedoes. (Metal industry, New York, v. 22 [new series, v. 14], 1916, p. 159.)
VIA

1420. Buck automatic aerial torpedo. illus. (Aerial age weekly, New York, v. 3, 1916, p. 445.)
† VDS

1421. Cardile, D. La questione del motore unico per i sommergibili. (Rivista marittima, Roma, anno 49, trimestre 4, 1916, p. 211–227.)
VXA

1422. Carvalho Santos, Firmino de. Torpedo moderno, seu emprego na guerra e sua adopção nos differentes typos de navios. (Revista maritima brazileira, Rio de Janeiro, v. 69, 1916, p. 27–43.)
VXA

1423. Cerio, Edwin. The rapid-fire, "revolver" principle applied to the submarine torpedo tube. illus. (Scientific American, New York, v. 114, 1916, p. 395, 409.)
VA

1424. —— Sull' armamento silurante dei sommergibili d'alto mare. illus. (Rivista marittima, Roma, anno 49, trimestre 1, 1916, p. 295–297.)
VXA

1425. Cooper, W. F. Hull protection against the torpedo. (Scientific American, New York, v. 115, 1916, p. 437.)
VA

1426. Craven, Francis S. Accurate measurement of torpedo ranges. illus. (United States Naval Institute, Proceedings, Annapolis, v. 42, 1916, p. 1225–1236.)
VXA

1427. A **Deadly** man-steered torpedo. (Popular science monthly, New York, v. 89, 1916, p. 694–695.)
* DA

1428. Detonation of submarine mines by electricity. illus. (Scientific American supplement, New York, v. 81, 1916, p. 253.)
VA
Abstracted from *Le Génie civil.*

1429. Dreadnought o sommergibile? (Rivista marittima. Roma, anno 49, trimestre 1, 1916, p. 587–601.)
VXA

1430. Fernández, Gustavo. Protección submarina de los acorazados. (Revista general de marina, Madrid, tomo 79, 1916, p. 5–15.)
VXA

1431. Flowers, John B. Torpedo screen for ships under way. Building up wall of whirling plates in the path of a submarine torpedo. illus. (Scientific American, New York, v. 115, 1916, p. 406, 421.)
VA

1432. The **German** submarine mine-layer U C 5. illus. (Illustrated London news, London, v. 149, 1916, p. 127–129.)
* DA
Abstracted in *Journal of the United States artillery,* Fort Monroe, v. 46, 1916, p. 227–228, *VWA.*

1433. Giacomuzzi, Virgilio. Torpediniere, cacciatorpediniere e derivati. (Rivista marittima, Roma, anno 49, trimestre 2, 1916, p. 477–503.)
VXA

1434. A **Giant** electric torpedo that eats thru the earth. illus. (Electrical experimenter, New York, v. 4, 1916, p. 551.)
VGA

1434a. Grenades, mortar shells and bombs. (Army and navy journal, New York, v. 54, 1916, p. 113.)
†† VWA
Editorial. Definition of these low velocity projectiles and description of their use.

1435. Hammond radio-controlled torpedo. (New York Times, Aug. 29, 1916, p. 9, col. 2.)
* D
Major General Leonard Wood, head of joint army and navy board to pass on Hammond torpedo.

1436. Hammond wireless torpedo. (New York Times, Feb. 3, 1916, p. 6, col. 4.)
* D
Discussion by Rear Admiral Strauss before the House Naval Committee.

1437. Hoar, Allen. The submarine torpedo boat; its characteristics and modern development. New York: D. Van Nostrand Co., 1916. xv, 211 p., 4 diagrs. illus. 8°.
VXV

1438. How mines are laid and fired. illus. (Popular mechanics, Chicago, v. 26, 1916, p. 68–69.)
VFA

1439. Lohr, Carl A. The principles involved in the mine defense of harbors. (Journal of the United States artillery, Fort Monroe, v. 45, 1916, p. 299–313.)
VWA

1440. López, Lutgardo. El torpedo "Bliss." Varias patentes de la casa Bliss para torpedos automóviles. illus. (Revista general de marina, Madrid, tomo 79, 1916, p. 697–716.)
VXA

1916, continued.

1441. Making the deadly trench torpedo. (Popular science monthly, New York, v. 8, 1916, p. 681.) ***DA**

1442. A Man-controlled torpedo. illus. (Scientific American, New York, v. 115, 1916, p. 393.) **VA**

1443. Mazzinghi, R. I sommergibili e i mezzi aerei nel blocco commerciale. (Rivista marittima, Roma, anno 49, trimestre 1, 1916, p. 445–462.) **VXA**

1444. Miessner, Benjamin Franklin. Radiodynamics, the wireless control of torpedoes and other mechanisms. New York: D. Van Nostrand Co., 1916. v, 206 p. illus. 8°. **PGO**

Ch. 11: The advent of wirelessly controlled torpedoes, p. 78–88. Ch. 12: Selectors, p. 89–91. Ch. 13: European control systems, p. 92–106. Ch. 14: Work of the Hammond radio research laboratory, p. 107–123. Ch. 15: The solution of the problems related to battle-range torpedo control, p. 124–136.

Also has notes on the inventions of Benjamin Franklin, Ernest Wilson, Nikola Tesla, J. Gordner, Devaux C. Wirth, E. Branley, and John Hays Hammond, Jr.

1445. Mine control protects neutral shipping. illus. (Popular mechanics, Chicago, v. 26, 1916, p. 481–482.) **VFA**

1446. Mines (at sea). (Information annual, 1915, New York, 1916, p. 389–390.) **Information Div.**

1447. Moore, Willard G. A time-controlled aerial torpedo. illus. (Aviation and aeronautical engineering, New York, v. 1, 1916, p. 322–323.) **†VDS**

1448. Muniz Barreto, Edmundo Williams. O contra-torpedeiro na esquadra moderna. (Revista maritima brazileira, Rio de Janeiro, v. 68, 1916, p. 201–220.) **VXA**

1449. Nets to protect warships from torpedoes. illus. (Popular mechanics, Chicago, v. 26, 1916, p. 830.) **VFA**

1450. Nordmann, Charles. La torpille et les immersibles. (Revue des deux mondes, Paris, période 6, tome 36, 1916, p. 217–228.) ***DM**

A very comprehensive article. The author states that the submarines of the Deutschland type are modifications of the inventions of French engineers.

1451. Procacci, Gianni. Impianto di bussola magnetica per sommergibile. illus. (Rivista marittima, Roma, anno 49, trimestre 2, 1916, p. 168–177.) **VXA**

1452. Proença, Nicanor J. de. Em torno do submarino. (Revista maritima brazileira, Rio de Janeiro, v. 68, 1916, p. 221–224.) **VXA**

1452a. —— Os submersiveis na presente guerra. (Revista maritima brazileira, Rio de Janeiro, v. 68, 1916, p. 677–682.) **VXA**

1453. Protecting a battleship against torpedoes. (Popular science monthly, New York, v. 90, 1916, p. 81.) ***DA**

1454. Protection against submarine torpedo attack. (New York Times, Feb. 6, 1916, part 5, p. 7, col. 1.) ***D**

Article on invention by M. Weil.

1455. Rosso, Alessandro Giovanni. I sommergibili nel diritto della guerra marittima. (Rivista marittima, Roma, anno 49, trimestre 4, 1916, p. 369–396; anno 50, trimestre 1, 1917, p. 27–44.) **VXA**

1456. S., E. D. Artiglieria per la difesa contro i sommergibili. (Rivista marittima, Roma, anno 49, trimestre 3, 1916, p. 323–326.) **VXA**

1457. Sea-going submarines and their torpedo armaments. (Scientific American, New York, v. 114, 1916, p. 396.) **VA**

Editorial.

1458. Ship's under-water eye sights hidden mines. illus. (Popular mechanics, Chicago, v. 25, 1916, p. 161.) **VFA**

1459. Ships proof against the torpedo. (Scientific American, New York, v. 115, 1916, p. 95.) **VA**

Also printed in the *Journal of the United States artillery*, Fort Monroe, v. 46, 1916, p. 253, *VWA.*

Brief note.

1460. Snow, Chester R., and Harold G. Douglas. Mine efficiency from storehouse to dock. illus. (Journal of the United States artillery, Fort Monroe, v. 46, 1916, p. 319–332.) **VWA**

1461. Sunderland, Archibald H. The S. S. "Noordam" and a mine. illus. (Journal of the United States artillery, Fort Monroe, v. 45, 1916, p. 314–316.) **VWA**

1462. Test of Hammond wireless control torpedo. (Army and navy journal, New York, v. 54, 1916, p. 338–339.) **††VWA**

Tests made at Gloucester, Mass.

1463. Torpedo catcher. (New York Times, Aug. 14, 1916, p. 4, col. 6.) ***D**

Invention of F. Lapan tried out at Newport.

1464. Torpedo nets. (Scientific American, New York, v. 114, 1916, p. 297.) **VA**

Brief note.

1465. Torpedo supply. (New York Times, May 1, 1916, p. 6, col. 5.) ***D**

Newport station turns out better variety than those purchased in Europe.

1466. Torpedo tubes. illus. (Marine engineer, London, v. 38, 1916, p. 124–125.) **VXA**

Also printed in *Scientific American supplement,* New York, v. 81, 1916, p. 149, *VA.*

1467. Torpedo tubes in large warships. (Engineer, London, v. 121, 1916, p. 441–442.) **VA**

Valuable historical notes on the evolution of the torpedo.

1916, continued.

1468. ₁United States torpedo.₁ (New York Times, Feb. 10, 1916, p. 3, col. 8.)   *** D**

1469. Vibrations of enemy ship steer new torpedo. illus. (Popular mechanics, Chicago, v. 26, 1916, p. 815.)   **VFA**

1469a. Wellenstein, A. Untersuchung einer feindlichen Flieger-Brandbombe. Welche Massnahmen sind bei feindlichen Fliegerangriffen mit Brandbomben zu beobachten? (Chemiker-Zeitung, Cöthen, Jahrg. 40, 1916, p. 9–10.)   **†† VOA**
Test of an incendiary bomb dropped in the city of Trier. Gives directions for extinguishing fires set by these bombs.

1470. Whitehead torpedo. (New York Times, March 10, 1916, p. 12, col. 3.)   *** D**
Placed on exhibition by American Defense Society.

1471. Wildrick, Meade. Effect upon measures for coast defense of the development of submarine and aerial attack. illus. (Journal of the United States artillery, Fort Monroe, v. 45, 1916, p. 145–180.)   **VWA**
Valuable notes on mines and torpedoes.

1472. Williamson, W. P. Some notes on torpedo gyroscopes and their adjustments in service. (United States Naval Institute, Proceedings, Annapolis, v. 42, 1916, p. 157–170.)   **VXA**

1917

1473. Admiral Fiske on sea blockades. (Army and navy journal, New York, v. 54, 1917, p. 763–764.)   **†† VWA**
Notes use of the torpedoplane at Gallipoli.

1474. An **Aerial** torpedo that makes bombardments from the air more effective. illus. (Scientific American, New York, v. 116, 1917, p. 156.)   **VA**

1474a. The **Barlow** aerial torpedo. (Scientific American, New York, v. 116, 1917, p. 57.)   **VA**
Brief description.

1475. Benjamin, Park. The Fiske torpedo-plane. illus. (Independent, New York, v. 90, 1917, p. 281–282.)   *** DA**

1476. Chandler, Edward F. The modern automobile torpedo. illus. (Scientific American, New York, v. 116, 1917, p. 548–549, 563–565.)   **VA**

1476a. Degouy, Jean Baptiste Charles Robert Mathieu. La guerre sous-marine de 1917. (Revue des deux mondes, Paris, période 6, tome 37, 1917, p. 443–456.)   *** DM**

1477. A **Dirigible** aero torpedo. illus. (Illustrated world, Chicago, v. 26, 1917, p. 903.)   **VDA**
Invention of George F. Russell of Hoboken, N. J.

1478. F., A. Torpilleurs allemands et destroyers anglais. illus. (Le génie civil, Paris, tome 60, 1917, p. 1–5.)   **VA**

1479. Fiske, Bradley Allen. Admiral Fiske tells of torpedoplane. (Army and navy journal, New York, v. 54, 1917, p. 780.)   **†† VWA**
Also in United States Naval Institute, *Proceedings,* Annapolis, v. 43, 1917, p. 855, *VXA.*

1479a. —— Defending America with torpedoplanes. illus. (Popular science monthly, New York, v. 90, 1917, p. 690–692.)   *** DA**

1480. —— ₁Urges adoption of the torpedoplane by the United States navy.₁ (New York Times, Feb. 13, 1917, p. 11, col. 3; March 26, 1917, p. 9, col. 2.)   *** D**
For comments by E. F. Chandler see issue for Feb. 18, 1917, part 1, p. 15, col. 3.

1481. Flowers, John B. Foiling torpedoes with whirling plates. illus. (Popular science monthly, New York, v. 90, 1917, p. 643–644.)   *** DA**

1482. French defence against submarines. (United States Naval Institute, Proceedings, Annapolis, v. 43, 1917, p. 1561–1562.)   **VXA**
Abstracted from the *New York Times.*

1483. Gautreau, J. B. Dewey and the offensive in warfare. (Army and navy journal, New York, v. 54, 1917, p. 1147.)   **†† VWA**

1484. Gernsback, H. Combating the torpedo. illus. (Electrical experimenter, New York, v. 5, May, 1917, p. 10–11, 68, 70.)   **VGA**

1484a. Gernsback, H., and H. W. SECOR. Electric "bloodhounds" to find and destroy U-boats. illus. (Electrical experimenter, New York, v. 5, 1917, p. 298, 347.)   **VGA**
Method intended to steer a torpedo by the sound of the submarine propellers.

1485. Gibson, Charles R. War inventions and how they were invented: an interestingly written description of the many appliances and weapons used in war, and how they work, told in simple language. London: Seeley, Service & Co., Ltd., 1917. 2 p.l., (1)10–255(1) p., 8 pl. 12°. (The science for children library.)   **V**
About the deadly torpedo, p. 155–167. How torpedoes and mines are exploded, p. 171–179.

1486. Joly, J. The origin of the submarine. (Blackwood's magazine, New York, v. 202, 1917, p. 106–117.)   *** DA**
Valuable biographical notes on Cornelius Drebbel and Marin Mersenne.

1486a. Kaiserov, B. Types of metal grenades and grenade guns. (International military digest, New York, v. 3, 1917, p. 335–336.)   **VWA**
Abstracted from *Voenny Sbornik,* December, 1916.

1917, continued.

1486b. Lestonnat, Raymond. La destruction des sous-marins ennemis. illus. (L'illustration, Paris, tome 149, 1917, p. 106–107.) **∗DM**

1487. Moltke, Helmuth Karl Bernhard, Graf von. Moltke on torpedo warfare. (Army and navy journal, New York, v. 54, 1917, p. 974–975.) **†† VWA**
Letter addressed to General McClellan, March 6, 1873.

1488. Nimitz, C. W. Valor militar e tactica do moderno submarino. (Revista maritima brazileira, Rio de Janeiro, v. 70, 1917, p. 493–510.) **VXA**

1489. Points on the torpedo. (Scientific American, New York, v. 117, 1917, p. 38.) **VA**

1490. Pollen, Arthur. Influence of the torpedo on ship construction. (United States Naval Institute, Proceedings, Annapolis, v. 43, 1917, p. 403–404.) **VXA**
Abstracted from *Land and water.*

1490a. A Submarine torpedo: what it is and how it works. illus. (Current history, New York, v. 6, 1917, p. 280–281.) **BTZE**

1491. Torpedo manufacturing project. (Army and navy register, Washington, v. 61, 1917, p. 194–195.) **†† VWA**

1492. Torpedo nets. (Army and navy register, Washington, v. 61, 1917, p. 419.) **†† VWA**
Also printed in *Proceedings* of the United States Naval Institute, Annapolis, v. 43, 1917, p. 1035–1036, *VXA.*

1493. Torpedo nets. (New York Times, Feb. 10, 1917, p. 1, col. 3, p. 8, col. 5; Feb. 17, 1917, p. 1, col. 2; Feb. 18, 1917, part 1, p. 13, col. 6; Feb. 28, 1917, p. 7, col. 4; March 31, 1917, p. 2, col. 6.) **∗D**
Nets used to protect New York harbor, Hampton Roads, Norfolk navy yard and Puget Sound.

1494. Torpedoes and torpedo craft. (Army and navy journal, New York, v. 54, 1917, p. 915.) **†† VWA**
Abstract of lecture delivered before the civilian volunteers' naval course of 1916 by Lieut. F. H. Roberts, U. S. N.

1495. Torpedoing the enemy's trenches as a preliminary to infantry attack. illus. (Scientific American, New York, v. 116, 1917, p. 463, 475.) **VA**
Account of a steam-propelled land torpedo.

1496. The Torpedoplane — an American invention — successfully used by Germans against British shipping. (Aerial age, New York, v. 5, 1917, p. 415–416.) **VDS**

1497. Torpedoplane invented by Rear-Admiral Fiske. illus. (United States Naval Institute, Proceedings, Annapolis, v. 43, 1917, p. 1524–1526.) **VXA**
Abstracted from the *New York Times.*

1498. United States. — Naval Intelligence Office. A brief description of submarine mines... Washington: Gov. Prtg. Off., 1917. 8 f. illus. 8°. **VXV**

1498a. United States. — Ordnance Office, War Department. Description and instructions for the use of rifle and hand grenades. Washington: Gov. Prtg. Off., 1917. 14 p., 3 pl. 8°. **VOD p. box**

1499. Walker, J. Bernard. The submarine problem: closing the North Sea with a bomb-curtain. illus. (Scientific American, v. 116, 1917, p. 616–617.) **VA**

1500. Weaver, Erasmus Morgan. Notes on military explosives. New York: John Wiley & Sons, Inc., 1917. viii, 382 p. 8°. **VOG**
Precautions to be observed in charging torpedoes and shell with high explosives, p. 241–242.

1501. Woodhouse, Henry. Textbook of naval aeronautics. With introduction by Rear Admiral Bradley A. Fiske. New York: The Century Co., 1917. 7 p.l., 3–288 p. illus. f°. **†VDY**
How the revolutionary Leavitt torpedo was developed, p. 14–15. The torpedoplane and its possibilities, Bradley A. Fiske, p. 16–19. Locating submerged mines with aircraft, p. 51–52.

SUPPLEMENT

1586

1502. Collado, Luys. Pratica manvale di arteglieria; nella quale si tratta della inuentione di essa, dell' ordine di condurla, & piantarla sotto à qualunque fortezza, fabricar mine da far volar in alto le fortezze, spianar le montagne, diuertir l'acque offensiue à i regni & prouincie, tirar co i pezzi in molti & diuersi modi, far fuochi artificiali; con altri bellissimi secreti all' essercitio dell' arteglieria appartenenti. Nuouamente composta & data in luce dal Mag. Signor Lvigi Collado. In Venetia, Presso Pietro Dusinelli, 1586. 6 p.l., 92 f., 1 diagr. illus. f°. **†VWW**

1775

1503. Gale, Benjamin. [The American Turtle, built at Saybrook by David Bushnell.] (Connecticut Historical Society, Collections, Hartford, v. 2, 1870, p. 315-318, 322-323, 333-335.) **IAA**

Letters to Silas Deane, written from Killingworth, Conn., Nov. 9, 22, and Dec. 7, 1775, in which he gives a report on the progress made on "our machine," the "American Turtle," invented by David Bushnell. Gale also states that Dr. Franklin was consulted in regard to its construction, and gives a description of the submarine and explains the method of using the explosive.

1778

1504. Symons, J. [Report on David Bushnell's attempt to blow up the Cerberus.] (The Remembrancer; or, Impartial repository of public events for the year 1778, London, 1778, p. 90-92.) **Reserve**

Letter written by the commander of the *Cerberus* to Rear Admiral Sir Peter Parker, giving an account of the attempted destruction of his ship by Bushnell's "infernal machine."

Symons reports that the torpedo was taken from the water by four men in a small boat and through their "fatal curiosity" the mechanism was examined with the result that "it blew the boat into pieces, and set her in a flame, killed the three men that were in the stern; the fourth, who was standing forward, was blown into the water." From this survivor the description of the torpedo was secured and a model made, which was forwarded to Admiral Parker. Symons remarks that the "ingenuity of these people is singular in their secret modes of mischief."

This letter is abstracted in Thomas Clark, *Naval history of the United States*, Philadelphia, 1814, v. 1, p. 72-74, *VYE.*

1813

1505. Clark, Thomas. Sketches of the naval history of the United States. Philadelphia, 1813. 12°. **VYE**

Chap. 5, p. 39-41. The torpedo, or American Turtle.

1814

1506. Clark, Thomas. Naval history of the United States, from the commencement of the Revolutionary war to the present time. Philadelphia, 1814. 2 v. 2. ed. 12°. **VYE**

v. 1, chap. 5, p. 63-74. D. Bushnell, inventor of the torpedo, &c.

Reprints letter written by Bushnell to Thomas Jefferson in October, 1787, giving a full account of his torpedo and submarine; also his experiments made with the design of firing shipping, and his attempt to destroy the *Cerberus.*

1815

1507. Notice sur les fusées incendiaires de Congrève; suivie de la description et de l'analyse qui en a été faite par M. d'Arcet. 1 pl. (Annales des arts et manufactures. Paris, 1815, tome 55, p. 52-76.) **VA**

Description and analysis of incendiary rockets. Notes their use at the battle of Leipzig.

1819

1508. Petitot, Claude Bernard. De la défaite et de la prise du Comte de Pembroc devant la Rochelle, par les flotes de France et d'Espagne dont la première étoit commandée par Ivain de Galles. (In his: Collection complète des mémoires... Paris, 1819. 8°. v. 5, p. 110-123.) **DBA**

Gives account of the use of fire ships at La Rochelle at the defeat of the Earl of Pembroke.

1845

1509. Reinaud, Joseph Toussaint, and ILDEPHONSE FAVÉ. Histoire de l'artillerie, 1ʳᵉ partie. Du feu grégeois, des feux de guerre et des origines de la poudre à canon d'après des textes nouveaux. Paris: J. Dumaine, 1845. 2 p.l., 285 p., 1 l., 8°, and atlas of 17 pl., 4°. **VWW**

No more published.

1861

1510. A **Rebel** torpedo. illus. (Frank Leslie's illustrated newspaper. New York, v. 13, 1861, p. 352.) ***DA**

1865

1511. Die **Hoellenmaschinen** oder Torpedo's des neueren amerikanischen Krieges. (Dingler's polytechnisches Journal, Augsburg, Bd. 176, 1865, p. 107-109.) **VA**

1865, continued.

1512. Sketch of a torpedo picked up in Morganza Bend, Mississippi river, by the crew of the U. S. S. Lafayette. (Frank Leslie's illustrated newspaper, New York, v. 20, 1865, p. 189.)   ***DA**

1868

1513. Figuier, Louis. Les poudres de guerre. (In his: Les merveilles de la science, Paris, tome 3, 1868, p. 209–308.) **V**

A very complete historical article, giving data on Greek fire, use of fire barrels on land and on ships, incendiary bombs, fire lances, and incendiary chariots. Greek fire used at the siege of Constantinople in 1453.

1870

1514. John Ericsson's neues System für den unterseeischen Angriff. (Dingler's polytechnisches Journal, Augsburg, Bd. 197, 1870, p. 120–127.)   **VA**

From *Militär-Wochenblatt* for May 11, 1870.

1515. Neuer Torpedo von John Ericsson. (Dingler's polytechnisches Journal, Augsburg, Bd. 196, 1870, p. 429–435.) **VA**

From *Militär-Wochenblatt* for April 23, 1870.

1516. Submarine warfare. illus. (Engineering, London, v. 9, 1870, p. 104–105.)   **VDA**

Review of work by J. S. Barnes entitled *Submarine warfare, offensive and defensive,* New York, 1870. Also reviewed in *Van Nostrand's eclectic engineering magazine,* New York, v. 2, 1870, p. 409–412, *VDA.*

1871

1517. The **Harvey** torpedo. illus. (Engineering, London, v. 11, 1871, p. 35–36.)   **VDA**

Translated in *Dingler's polytechnisches Journal,* Augsburg, Bd. 199, 1871, p. 460–463, *VA.*

1874

1518. Holmes, Nathaniel J. The application of electricity as a means of defence in naval and military warfare. (Society of Telegraph Engineers, Journal, London, v. 3, 1874, p. 32–45.)   **VGA**

Discussion, p. 46–51.
Abstracted in *Telegraphic journal and electrical review,* London, v. 2, 1874, p. 121–124, *VGA.*

1519. —— Military torpedo defences. (Society of Telegraph Engineers, Journal, London, v. 3, 1874, p. 54–60.)   **VGA**

Discussion, p. 60–79.
Abstracted in *Telegraphic journal and electrical review,* London, v. 2, 1874, p. 137–141, *VGA.* This

and the preceding article are abstracted in *Dingler's polytechnisches Journal,* Augsburg, Bd. 215, 1875, p. 259–270, *VA.*

1520. Unterwasserfahrten, Höllenmaschinen, &c. illus. (Das neue Buch der Erfindungen, Gewerbe und Industrien. Leipzig. 1875. 6. ed. 8°. Ergänzungs-Band, p. 357–364.)   **V**

1876

1521. Betts, J. A. Torpedoes and torpedo warfare. (Telegraphic journal and electrical review, London, v. 4, 1876, p. 293–295, 304–305.)   **VGA**

Lecture delivered at Foochow, China.

1522. Fluessige Kohlensäure al Motor. (Dingler's polytechnisches Journal, Augsburg, Bd. 219, 1876, p. 371–372.)   **VA**

On the use of liquid sulphid in torpedoes.

1523. Submarine gun. illus. (In: Knight's American mechanical dictionary, New York, 1876, v. 3, p. 2439.)   **VF**

Brief note on experiments made by Saint Cyr in 1797 and Fulton in 1814.

1524. A **Torpedo** college in China. (Telegraphic journal and electrical review, London, v. 4, 1876, p. 282.)   **VGA**

Imperial Torpedo College at Tientsin, Mr. J. A. Betts, director.

1877

1525. The **Eastern** war. Turkish divers removing Russian torpedoes [off Poti in the Black sea]. illus. (Frank Leslie's illustrated newspaper, New York, v. 44, 1877, p. 407.) ·   ***DA**

Full-page illustration on p. 408.

1526. Gakuma, G. Torpedoes, their history, construction and use. (Frank Leslie's illustrated newspaper, v. 44, 1877, p. 239.)   ***DA**

1527. Protection against torpedoes. (The manufacturer and builder, New York, v. 9, 1877, p. 232.)   **VA**

Brief note.

1528. A **Telescope** spar torpedo. (Telegraphic journal and electrical review, London, v. 5, 1877, p. 196.)   **VGA**

Brief note on experiment made at the Woolwich laboratory.

1529. Torpedoes. illus. (The manufacturer and builder, New York, v. 9, 1877, p. 181–182.)   **VA**

Historical notes.

1530. Whitehead torpedo. (Polytechnic review, Philadelphia, v. 4, 1877, p. 93, 105.)   **VA**

Brief notes.

1879

1531. Goodrich, Caspar Frederick. Torpedoes, their disposition and radius of destructive effect. (United States Naval Institute, Proceedings, Annapolis, v. 5, 1879, p. 479–491.) **VXA**

Reprinted by the Ordnance Office of the United States War Department as *Ordnance notes, no. 207,* † *VWS.*

1881

1532. The **Electric** light and the torpedo. (Telegraphic journal and electrical review, London, v. 9, 1881, p. 484.) **VGA**

Experiments made at Portsmouth in detecting the approach of a torpedo.

1533. The **Ericsson** torpedo. illus. (The manufacturer and builder, New York, v. 13, 1881, p. 35–36.) **VA**

1882

1534. Donaldson, John. Torpedo boats. illus. (Engineering, London, v. 34, 1882, p. 355–356, 375–378.) **VDA**

Reprinted by the Ordnance Office of the United States War Department as *Ordnance notes, no. 256,* † *VWS.*

Paper read before the Mechanical Science Section of the British Association at Southampton, 1882.

1883

1535. Lake's Boot, welches elektrisch vom Lande aus gelenkt wird. (Dingler's polytechnisches Journal, Augsburg, Bd. 248, 1883, p. 42.) **VA**

Note on torpedoes.

1536. Luft-Treibtorpedos. (Dingler's polytechnisches Journal, Augsburg, Bd. 250, 1883, p. 138.) **VA**

1537. Neuerungen an den in der Deutschen Marine gebräuchlichen Torpedos. (Dingler's polytechnisches Journal, Augsburg, Bd. 248, 1883, p. 362–363.) **VA**

1538. Ueber Neuerungen an Torpedobooten. (Dingler's polytechnisches Journal, Augsburg, Bd. 247, 1883, p. 56–64.) **VA**

Notes on Bushnell, Fulton, Harvey, Fish, Whitehead, and Nordenfeldt torpedoes.

1884

1539. Knight, Edward Henry. Knight's new mechanical dictionary. Boston: Houghton, Mifflin and Co., 1884. viii, 960 p., 56 pl. illus. 4°. **VF**

Torpedoes, p. 897–899.

1540. New torpedo boats. (Telegraphic journal and electrical review, London, v. 15, 1884, p. 176.) **VGA**

Notes on John Ericsson's boat and Professor Tuck's electric submarine torpedo boat.

1541. Scheel's Controlsteuer für Fischtorpedos. illus. (Dingler's polytechnisches Journal, Augsburg, Bd. 251, 1884, p. 27–28.) **VA**

1542. Th. Nordenfelt's Kartätschgeschütz. (Dingler's polytechnisches Journal, Augsburg, Bd. 254, 1884, p. 429–432.) **VA**

1885

1543. Canet's Geschütz zum Schleudern von Fischtorpedos. illus. (Dingler's polytechnisches Journal, Augsburg, Bd. 255, 1885, p. 21–23.) **VA**

1544. A **New** torpedo guide. (Telegraphic journal and electrical review, London, v. 16, 1885, p. 360.) **VGA**

Brief description of new method of controlling torpedoes.

1545. Paulson's self propelling and steering torpedo. illus. (Telegraphic journal and electrical review, London, v. 16, 1885, p. 213–215.) **VGA**

Invention of Richard Paulson.

1886

1546. Boyd, Robert. Report of torpedo attack and defenses of U. S. S. "Tennessee." (United States Naval Institute, Proceedings, Annapolis, v. 13, 1887, p. 266–268.) **VXA**

Experiments made in September, 1886.

1547. Torpedoes. (In: United States. — Office of Naval Intelligence. General information series no. 5, Washington, 1886, p. 246–254.) **VYEB**

Notes on the Whitehead, Howell, Sims-Edison, Patrick, Paulson, and Berdan torpedoes, on torpedo nets and on the torpedo experiments at Cherbourg.

1548. Torpedoes electrically steered. (Telegraphic journal and electrical review, London, v. 18, 1886, p. 237.) **VGA**

Brief note on invention of Thomas A. Edison.

1549. Value of torpedoes. (Telegraphic journal and electrical review, London, v. 19, 1886, p. 79.) **VGA**

Notes on the Whitehead torpedo and experiments made in Fareham creek.

1887

1550. Dynamite in war, the pneumatic torpedo gun. illus. (Manufacturer and builder, New York, v. 19, 1887, p. 128–129, 158–159, 182–184.) **VA**

Notes on the Lay, Patrick, and Sims torpedoes.

1887, continued.

1551. Kesselheizung mit flüssigen Kohlenwasserstoffen. (Dingler's polytechnisches Journal, Augsburg, Bd. 266, 1887, p. 202–208.) **VA**

1552. The **Lay** torpedo. (Telegraphic journal and electrical review, London, v. 20, 1887, p. 211, 217–218.) **VGA**
Notes on experiments.

1553. Ein **Neuer** Torpedo. (Mittheilungen aus dem Gebiete des Seewesens, Pola, Bd. 15, 1887, p. 390.) **VXA**
From the *United service gazette.* Reprinted in *Dingler's polytechnisches Journal,* Stuttgart, Bd. 267, 1888, p. 142, *VA.*
Notes on the torpedo invented by Edward C. Peck.

1554. The **New** submarine boat Nordenfelt. (Engineer, London, v. 63, 1887, p. 400.) **VA**
Reprinted in *Manufacturer and builder,* New York, v. 19, 1887, p. 223, *VA.*

1555. Schroeder, Seaton. The development of modern torpedoes. (In: United States. — Naval Intelligence Office. General information series no. 6: Recent naval progress, Washington, 1887, p. 1–44, 332–336.) **VYEB**
Notes on the following types of torpedoes: Berdan, Harvey, Barber, Burdett, Chambers, Whitehead, Rendel, Schwartzkopff, Howell, Mallory, Hall, Paulson, Callender, Lay, Patrick, Coda-Canati, Von Scheliha, Smith, Foster, Nordenfeldt, Nealy, Scott, Sims-Edison, and Brennan.

1556. Torpedo boats. (Telegraphic journal and electrical review, London, v. 21, 1887, p. 73, 297.) **VGA**
Brief description of the *Ariete* and *Benbow.*

1888

1557. Brialmont, Alexis Henri. Influence du tir plongeant et des obus-torpilles sur la fortification. Bruxelles: E. Guyot, 1888. 2 v. 4° and f°. **VWS** and † **VWS**
[v. 1.] Text.
[v. 2.] Atlas.

1558. Neuerungen im Schiffswesen. (Dingler's polytechnisches Journal, Augsburg, Bd. 270, 1888, p. 481–491, 540–551.) **VA**
Notes on torpedoes, p. 481, 488.

1559. New electrical torpedo. (Telegraphic journal and electrical review, London, v. 22, 1888, p. 682.) **VGA**
Brief note on the Nordenfeldt torpedo.

1560. Nordenfelt torpedo. (Engineering news, New York, v. 20, 1888, p. 61.) **VDA**
Brief note from Montreal *Star.*

1561. Torpedo service. (Western electrician, Chicago, v. 3, 1888, p. 204–205.) **VGA**
Torpedo experiments at College Point, with description of torpedo.

1889

1562. King, William R. Annual report, Willets Point, N. Y., Engineer School of Application. pl. (In: United States. — Engineer Department. Annual report of the chief of engineers, Washington, 1889, part 1, p. 467–502.) **VDDA**
Reports on torpedo experiments, p. 478–483, 489–490, 492; Report of a board of engineers on the Patrick "auto-mobile controllable torpedo," p. 497–502.

1563. Neues im Schiffswesen. (Dingler's polytechnisches Journal, Stuttgart, Bd. 272, p. 529–539.) **VA**
Descriptions of German patents granted to G. E. Haight, W. H. Wood, J. O. Kelly, B. A. Collins, H. S. Maxim, S. H. Nealy, L. Hutchins, T. Favarger, A. Corssen, and Graf Buonacorsi di Pistoja.

1564. Neues im Schiffswesen: Torpedoboote und Torpedos. (Dingler's polytechnisches Journal, Augsburg, Bd. 272, 1889, p. 486–500.) **VA**

1565. Newton, J. T. Fish-torpedo armament. 4 diagrs., 1 pl. (In: United States. — Office of Naval Intelligence, General information series no. 8, Washington, 1889, p. 185–198.) **VYEB**

1566. ⸺ Torpedoes. (In: United States. — Office of Naval Intelligence, General information series no. 8, Washington, 1889, p. 428–436.) **VYEB**
Notes on the Whitehead, Schwartzkopff, Howell, Brennan, Patrick, Sims-Edison, and Pietruski torpedoes.

1890

1567. Church, William Conant. John Ericsson, the engineer. illus. (Scribner's magazine, New York, 1890, v. 7, p. 169–185, 336–361.) ***DA**
Inventor of a torpedo boat destroyer and the famous *Monitor.*

1568. Ellicott, John M. Automobile torpedoes, the Whitehead and Howell with a detailed description of each. 12 diagrs. (In: United States. — Office of Naval Intelligence, General information series, no. 9, p. 381–408.) **VYEB**

1569. The **Gifford** liquid-gas gun. illus. (Engineering news, New York, v. 24, 1890, p. 121.) **VDA**

1570. Russische Kriegsschiffe. (Dingler's polytechnisches Journal, Stuttgart, Bd. 276, 1890, p. 597.) **VA**
Notes on torpedoes.

1571. Southerland, W. H. H. Torpedoes. (In: United States. — Naval Intelligence Office. General information series no. 9: A year's naval progress, Washington, 1890, p. 134–138.) **VYEB**
Notes on the Whitehead and Brennan torpedoes and the torpedo-director.

1891

1572. Sims-Edison automatic torpedo. illus. (Western electrician, Chicago, v. 8, 1891, p. 333.)   **VGA**

1573. Southerland, W. H. H.   Torpedoes. illus. (In: United States. — Naval Intelligence Office. General information series no. 10: The year's naval progress, Washington, 1891, p. 176–181.)   **VYEB**

1574. Trial of the Sims-Edison torpedo. (The manufacturer and builder, New York, v. 23, 1891, p. 186.)   **VA**

1892

1575. Submarine navigation. (The manufacturer and builder, New York, v. 23, 1892, p. 168.)   **VA**
Note on the early history of the submarine and torpedo.

1576. Torpedoboote und Torpedodepotschiffe. (Dingler's polytechnisches Journal, Stuttgart, Bd. 284, 1892, p. 22–23.) **VA**
Notes on various types of torpedoes.

1577. Torpedoes ₍and₎ Torpedo defense. 2 diagrs. (In: United States. — Office of Naval Intelligence, General information series no. 11: Notes on the year's naval progress, Washington, 1892, p. 128–135.) **VYEB**
Notes on the Sims-Edison and the Whitehead torpedoes, and the Ericsson submarine gun; also on torpedo-boom experiments, net-cutting attachments, and torpedo-discharging apparatus.

1578. Trials of the torpedo boat "Cushing." (Engineering news, New York, v. 27, 1892, p. 10.)   **VDA**

1893

1579. Robert Fulton. port. (In: National cyclopaedia of American biography, New York, v. 3, 1893, p. 104–105.)   *** R – AGZ**
Notes on his torpedo and submarine.

1580. Sears, James H., and B. W. WELLS, JR. The Chilean revolution of 1891. Washington: Gov. Prtg. Off., 1893. 66 p., 2 charts, 1 diagr., 4 maps, 3 pl., 1 table. 8°. (United States. — Office of Naval Intelligence. War series. no. 4.)   **VYEB**
The sinking of the *Blanco Encalada*, p. 18–24.
Official reports of the commanding officers on both sides are given in full, and extracts from the report of the commission appointed to examine into the possibility of raising the *Blanco Encalada*.

1581. Thomas Alva Edison. port. (In: National cyclopaedia of American biography, New York, v. 3, 1893, p. 441–444.)
* R – AGZ
Inventor of torpedo.

1894

1582. Torpedo launch for the U. S. battleship "Maine." illus. (Engineering news, New York, v. 32, 1894, p. 432–433.)   **VDA**

1896

1583. John Adams Howell. (In: National cyclopaedia of American biography, New York, v. 6, 1896, p. 44.)   *** R – AGZ**
Inventor of the Howell torpedo.

1584. Matthew Fontaine Maury. (In: National cyclopaedia of American biography, New York, v. 6, 1896, p. 35–36.)   *** R – AGZ**
Inventor of torpedo mines.

1585. Samuel Colt. (In: National cyclopaedia of American biography, New York, v. 6, 1896, p. 175–176.)   *** R – AGZ**
Inventor of submarine mines.

1586. William Henry Shock. (In: National cyclopaedia of American biography, New York, v. 6, 1896, p. 200.)   *** R – AGZ**
Inventor of torpedo devices.

1897

1587. Alexander Thompson Ballantine. port. (In: National cyclopaedia of American biography, New York, v. 7, 1897, p. 540.)
* R – AGZ
Inventor of oil-well torpedoes.

1588. Edmund Louis Gray Zalinski. port. (In: National cyclopaedia of American biography, New York, v. 7, 1897, p. 248.)
* R – AGZ
Inventor of the pneumatic torpedo-gun.

1589. George Bomford. (In: National cyclopaedia of American biography, New York, v. 7, 1897, p. 495.)   *** R – AGZ**
Inventor of a bomb cannon, known as the "columbiad."

1590. John Lewis Lay. (In: National cyclopaedia of American biography, New York, v. 7, 1897, p. 528–529.)   *** R – AGZ**
Inventor of the Lay torpedo.

1591. Thomas Oliver Selfridge. (In: National cyclopaedia of American biography, New York, v. 7, 1897, p. 552.)   *** R – AGZ**
Inventor of devices for protecting ships from torpedoes.

1898

1592. David Bushnell. (In: National cyclopaedia of American biography, New York, v. 9, 1898, p. 244.)   *** R – AGZ**
Notes on his torpedo and submarine.

1593. Davidson, Hunter. Torpedoes in our war. (United States Naval Institute, Proceedings, Annapolis, v. 24, 1898, p. 349–354.)
VXA
Valuable notes on the use of the torpedo during the Civil war.

1898, continued.

1594. A **Defence** of the torpedo-boat. (Iron age, New York, v. 62, Sept. 22, 1898, p. 2.) **VDA**

From the *New York Times.* Reprinted in the *Proceedings* of the United States Naval Institute, Annapolis, v. 24, 1898, p. 519–521, *VXA.*

1595. **Gentsch,** Wilhelm. Schiffstreiber. (Dingler's polytechnisches Journal, Stuttgart, 1898, Bd. 309, p. 240–246.) **VA**

Notes on torpedo invented by Louis Edmond Bolot of Paris, p. 246.

1596. **Trial** of new torpedo nets. (United States Naval Institute, Proceedings, v. 24, 1898, p. 385.) **VXA**

Trial of torpedo nets on H. M. S. "Hannibal."

1899

1597. **Koester,** O. W. The torpedo-boat, destroyer, and depot. (United States Naval Institute, Proceedings, v. 25, 1899, p. 851–855.) **VXA**

1901

1598. **Scott de Martinville.** Avant-propos d'un appareil de débarquement de torpilleurs embarqués sur le transport Mytho. (Mémorial du génie maritime, Paris, série 3, fasc. 2, 1901, p. 151–176.) **† VXA**

1905

1599. Les **Bombes** et le laboratoire municipal. illus. (Le monde illustre, Feb. 11, 1905, p. 88–89.) *** DM**

1600. **Torpedo-Motorboote.** (Dingler's polytechnisches Journal, Berlin, Bd. 320, 1905, p. 254–255.) **VA**

1906

1601. Die **Bedeutung** des Torpedos und Mittel zur Erhöhung seiner motorischen Leistungsfähigkeit. (Dingler's polytechnisches Journal, Berlin, Bd. 321, 1906, p. 535–537.) **VA**

1602. **Hudson** Maxim. port. (In: National cyclopaedia of American biography, New York, v. 13, 1906, p. 520–521.) *** R – AGZ**

Inventor of an automobile torpedo.

1603. **Infernal** machine discussed by great experts. illus. (Illustrated London news, London, v. 128, 1906, p. 836–837.) *** DA**

1604. **Lalande,** L. L'engin porte-torpilles sous-marin. (Bulletin technologique, Paris, année 1906, v. 2, p. 812–853.) **VA**

A very complete article giving mathematical formulae on the torpedo.

1907

1605. **Simon,** Alexander. Mittel zur Erhöhung der motorischen Leistungsfähigkeit von Torpedos. illus. (Dingler's polytechnisches Journal, Berlin, Bd. 322, 1907, p. 653.) **VA**

1908

1606. **Given,** E. C. Submarines and submersibles. (Liverpool Engineering Society, Transactions, Liverpool, v. 29, 1908, p. 129–196.) **VDA**

Outlines the history of the submarine and contains valuable data on the torpedo.

1909

1607. **Henry** Larcom Abbot. (In: National cyclopaedia of American biography, New York, v. 11, 1909, p. 194–195.) *** R – AGZ**

Inventor of a system of submarine mine defense.

1910

1608. **Bombenkanonen.** illus. (Illustrirte Zeitung, Leipzig, Bd. 135, 1910, p. 378.) *** DF**

1609. **Bortnovski,** A. Hand-grenades in the Russo-Japanese war. (United States. — Engineer Department, Professional memoirs, Washington, v. 7, 1915, p. 507–511.) **VDA**

From *Journal* of the United Service Institution of India, v. 39, 1910, p. 531–535. The original article was printed in the *Voyenny Sbornik* in January, 1910.

1610. **Sperry,** Elmer A. The gyroscope for marine purposes. (Society of Naval Architects and Marine Engineers, Transactions, New York, v. 18, 1910, p. 143–155.) **VXA**

1911

1611. **H.,** A. Les grenades à main. (Journal des sciences militaires, Paris, série 14, tome 11, 1911, p. 308–344.) **VWA**

1912

1612. **Neve,** C. J. J. de. Torpedotaktiek. (Marine-Vereeniging, Verslagen, Helder, Jaarg. 1911–12, p. 23–76.) **VXA**

Discussion, p. 76–95.

1613. Das **Projekt** eines Torpedobootzerstörers mit Diesel-Motorenantrieb. (Dingler's polytechnisches Journal, Bd. 327, 1912, p. 109–110.) **VA**

1614. **Seeminen** und Minenleger in der französischen Kriegsmarine. (Mitteilungen aus dem Gebiete des Seewesens, Pola, Bd. 40, p. 958–965.) **VXA**

Abstracted from *Le Yacht* and *Moniteur de la flotte.*

1913

1615. Cordeiro, Frederick Joaquin Barbosa. The gyroscope. New York: Spon & Chamberlain, 1913. vii p., 1 l., 3–105 p. illus. 12°. **PBK**

Howell torpedo, p. 72–73; The Obry device, p. 73–74.

1616. Die **Entwicklung** der Seemine und die Grundzüge ihrer Verwendung. illus. (Nauticus: Jahrbuch für Deutschlands Seeinteressen, Berlin, Jahrg. 15, 1913, p. 189–226.) **VYL**

Gives valuable historical notes and describes various types of mines and methods of using them.

1617. Gray, Andrew. Gyrostats and gyrostatic action. illus. (Royal Institution of Great Britain, Proceedings, London, v. 20, 1914, p. 631–645.) **∗EC**

Lecture delivered at the weekly evening meeting, Feb. 14, 1913.
Reprinted in the *Annual report for 1914* of the Smithsonian Institution, Washington, 1915, p. 193–208, *∗ EA.*
Valuable notes on the application of the gyroscope to the torpedo.

1618. Die **Halesche** Hand- und- Gewehr-granate. illus. (Kriegstechnische Zeitschrift, Berlin, Jahrg. 16, 1913, p. 108–111.) **VWA**

1619. Sperry, Elmer A. Engineering applications of the gyroscope. illus. (Franklin Institute, Journal, Philadelphia, v. 175, 1913, p. 447–482.) **VA**

First practical application made by Obry in the steering of a torpedo, p. 448.

1914

1620. Airey, John. The gyroscope — its principles and applications in practice. illus. (American machinist, New York, v. 40, 1914, p. 633–639.) **VFA**

Application to torpedoes, p. 636–637.

1621. Bomb-dropping from aeroplanes. (Flight, London, v. 6, 1914, p. 1213–1214.) **† VDS**

1622. Entwicklung und Stand des Minensuchwesens. illus. (Nauticus: Jahrbuch für Deutschlands Seeinteressen, Berlin, Jahrg. 16, 1914, p. 241–264.) **VYL**

A very complete article giving various methods of mine sweeping.

1623. Explosive bombs for use with aeroplanes. illus. (Popular mechanics magazine, New York, v. 21, 1914, p. 364.) **VFA**

1624. Ford, H. C. The electrically driven gyroscope in marine work. (American Institute of Electrical Engineers, Transactions, New York, v. 33, 1914, p. 857–871.) **VGA**

Discussion, p. 872.
Abstracted in *Electrician*, London, v. 74, 1914, p. 145–148, illus., *VGA.*
Notes on use in torpedoes.

1625. French build artificial island of concrete. illus. (Popular mechanics magazine, New York, v. 21, 1914, p. 773.) **VFA**

Torpedo experiment station near Toulon.

1626. Gardner's gyroscope. illus. (Engineering, London, v. 97, 1914, p. 229.) **VDA**

Invention of John Gardner. Notes on application to torpedoes.

1627. German warship in torpedo practice. illus. (Popular mechanics magazine, New York, v. 21, 1914, p. 729.) **VFA**

Illustration of discharge of torpedo.

1628. Grenade that is fired from a rifle. illus. (Popular mechanics magazine, New York, v. 21, 1914, p. 684–685.) **VFA**

1629. The **Menace** of the mine; how these death-dealing weapons are laid and how they may be removed. illus. (Navy and army illustrated, London, new series. v. 1, 1914, p. 14–16.) **† VWZH**

1630. Parrott, R. S. Smoke bomb practice. (Field artillery journal, Washington, v. 4, 1914, p. 519–525.) **VWA**

1631. The **"Roland"** bomb-dropping apparatus. illus. (Flight, London, v. 6, 1914, p. 1173.) **† VDS**

1632. Some more German anti-aircraft bombs. illus. (Flight, London, v. 6, 1914, p. 1196.) **† VDS**

1633. A **Torpedo** attack. illus. (Navy and army illustrated, London, new series. v. 1, 1914, p. 178–180.) **† VWZH**

1634. The **Torpedo** in war. illus. (Navy and army illustrated, London, new series, v. 1, 1914, p. 65–68.) **† VWZH**

Brief history of the development of the torpedo and methods of defense against it.

1635. Torpedo nets. (Shipbuilding and shipping record, London, v. 3, 1914, p. 410.) **† VXH**

Letter to the editor on the advisability of equipping ships with torpedo nets.

1636. Wood, Walter. Mine sweeping. illus. (Navy and army illustrated, London, new series. v. 1, 1914, p. 147–148.) **† VWZH**

1915

1637. Armstrong, James. The sweepers of the seas. illus. (Navy and army, London, new series, v. 4, 1915, p. 24–25.) **† VWZH**

1638. Aubigny, P. d'. Un nouvel explosif de guerre, la thermite. (La Revue, Paris, 1915, v. 111, p. 528–531.) **∗ DM**

Invention of John Hays Hammond, jr. Data on incendiary shell generating prussic acid gas.

1639. B., M. Eine behelfsmässig hergestellte Handgranathaubitze (Handgranat-schleuder). (Kriegstechnische Zeitschrift, Berlin, Jahrg. 17, 1914, p. 29–32.) **VWA**

1915, continued.

1640. Bennett, Arnold. In the fire-trenches. illus. (Illustrated London news, London, 1915, v. 147, p. 258–259.) • **DA**
Illustration of a bomb mortar, p. 259.

1641. Les Bombes incendiaires employées par les dirigeables et les avions allemands. illus. (Génie civil, Paris, tome 67, 1915, p. 11.) **VA**

1642. Bradwood, W. War missiles, ancient and otherwise. (The Field, London, v. 125, 1915, p. 525–527.) † **VPA**
A very complete article; gives history of the Greek fire and the use of petroleum in inflammable missiles.

1643. [British bomb-throwers in action at La Bassée.] illus. (Illustrated London news, v. 146, 1915, p. 490–491.) • **DA**

1644. The Business end of a submarine. illus. (Navy and army, London, new series, v. 4, 1915, p. 108–109.) † **VWZH**
Illustration of the breech blocks of a Holland submarine, showing four torpedo tubes arranged in pairs on each side of the central hand wheel.

1645. C., J. Air-torpedoes and air-mines, and the weapons that fire them. illus. (Illustrated London news, London, v. 147, 1915, p. 309.) • **DA**
Illustration of the firing of an air-mine weighing 236 pounds.

1646. —— French trench guns: crapouillot; taupia; and arbalist. illus. (Illustrated London news, London, v. 147, 1915, p. 308.) • **DA**
Fine illustrations showing use of these guns.

1647. Cossman, Edward C. Hand grenades. illus. (Scientific American, New York, 1915, v. 112, p. 427.) **VA**

1648. Fire warnings: how to deal with bombs. (Illustrated carpenter and builder, London, v. 77, 1915, p. 346.) † **3 – VEA**

1649. Flamel, Nicolas. Les torpilles aériennes. illus. (La nature, Paris, année 43, semestre 2, 1915, p. 263–266.) **OA**
Gives valuable historical notes on the bomb and several cuts of trench cannon.

1650. The Force of the torpedo of the kind which sunk the "Lusitania." illus. (Illustrated London news, London, v. 146, 1915, p. 613.) • **DA**
Illustration of damage done a ship by the explosion of a torpedo.

1651. German flame-projectors in use; French testing "Flammenwerfer" captured from the enemy. (Illustrated London news, London, v. 147, 1915, p. 330–331.) • **DA**

1652. German incendiary bombs. illus. (Applied science, Toronto, v. 27 [new series, v. 10], 1915, p. 50–51.) **VA**

1653. German Zeppelin raids over Great Britain. (Sphere, London, v. 62, 1915, p. 296–297, 334.) • **DA**

1654. Die **Gewehr-** und Handgranate der indischen Armee. illus. (Kriegstechnische Zeitschrift, Berlin, Jahrg. 18, 1915, p. 88–89.) **VWA**

1655. The Grasshopper and the torpedo of the air. illus. (Illustrated London news, London, v. 147, 1915, p. 144–145.) • **DA**
Illustration of crossbow for hurling bombs, etc., also the torpedo shell.

1656. The Greatest war. By Colonel "X." illus. (Navy and army, London, new series, v. 4, p. 158–161.) † **VWZH**
Part I. The war on land.
Gives illustrations of a German poisonous gas bomb mortar and French soldiers hurling grenades at the German trenches.

1657. Guenther, Hanns. Handgranaten. illus. (Schweizerische militärische Blätter: Schweizerische Monatschrift für Offiziere aller Waffen, Frauenfeld, Jahrg. 27, 1915, p. 192–196, 234–240.) **VWA**

1658. The "Gulflight" case. illus. (Literary digest, New York, v. 50, 1915, p. 1135.) • **DA**
Valuable notes on the torpedoing of this ship.

1659. Hand grenade. illus. (Engineer, London, v. 120, 1915, p. 566.) **VA**
Reprinted in *Génie civil*, Paris, tome 68, 1916, p. 141, *VA*.
Description of English patent issued Nov. 17, 1915, to F. E. Baker.

1660. [**Illustration** of bomb used by the Allies' airmen at Gallipoli.] (Illustrated London news, London, v. 147, 1915, p. 685.) • **DA**

1661. Lake, Simon. Submarines that are strictly invisible; a type that can pass through a mine field and attack a blockaded fleet. illus. (Scientific American, New York, v. 112, 1915, p. 68–69, 74–75.) **VA**
Abstracted in *Illustrated London news*, v. 146, 1915, p. 210–211, • *DA*, under title: A wheeled submarine designed to motor through mine fields, lay mines, and enter defended harbors.

1662. The Leon torpedo. (Royal Society of Arts, Journal, London, v. 63, 1915, p. 1031–1032.) **VA**
Invention of Carl Leon, a Swedish officer.

1663. Lewes, Vivian B. Modern munitions of war: poison gases and incendiary bombs. (Royal Society of Arts, Journal, London, v. 63, 1915, p. 827–831.) **VA**
Abstracted in *Engineer*, London, v. 120, 1915, p. 82–83, *VA*; *Nature*, London, v. 95, 1915, p. 608–609, *OA*; and in *Illustrated London news*, London, v. 147, 1915, p. 140, • *DA*.

1664. —— Modern munitions of war: shells and high explosives. (Royal Society of Arts, Journal, London, v. 63, 1915, p. 823–827.) **VA**
Abstracted in *Illustrated London news*, London, v. 147, 1915, p. 108, 98, • *DA*.
Valuable notes on bombs and grenades. The second of the Fothergill lectures for 1915.

1665. The "Lusitania" torpedoed. illus. (Literary digest, New York, v. 50, 1915, p. 1133–1134.) • **DA**

1915, continued.

1666. M., A. W. Mine-sweeping in the North sea. illus. (The Field, London, v. 125, 1915, p. 90.)   † **VPA**
Describes methods used.

1667. A **Master** of the torpedo. illus. (Navy and army, London, new series, v. 3, 1915, p. 367–370.)   † **VWZH**
Notes on the work of Sir Arthur Knivet Wilson, popularly known as "Tug Wilson," former commander of H. M. S. *Vernon*, the torpedo school at Portsmouth, Eng.

1668. Metallographische Untersuchung einiger Granatsplitter. illus. (Stahl und Eisen, Düsseldorf, Jahrg. 35, 1915, p. 170–171.)   **VIA**

1669. Mills, W. The Mills grenade. illus. (Arms and explosives, London, v. 23, 1915, p. 154.)   † **VOG**

1670. The **Mine** war in the trenches: explosion and crater. illus. (Illustrated London news, London, v. 60, 1915, p. 699.) * **DA**
Another illustration, p. 719.

1671. Modernizing the hand-grenade. illus. (Literary digest, New York, v. 50, 1915, p. 1015–1016.)   * **DA**
Compiled from *Technical world magazine*, April, 1915.

1672. Munitions of the present war. (Railway review, Chicago, v. 57, 1915, p. 373–376.)   † **TPB**
Poisonous gases and incendiary bombs, p. 375–376.

1673. Newton, W. Douglas. The bomber, a psychological study. (Illustrated London news, London, v. 147, 1915, p. 632.)   * **DA**
View of Germans throwing hand grenades from trenches.

1674. Oelker. Tabellarische Zusammenstellung in- und ausländischer Patente, betreffend Hand- und Gewehrgranaten und dgl. (Zeitschrift für das gesamte Schiess- und Sprengstoffwesen, München, Jahrg. 10, 1915, p. 87–89, 99–100, 112–113.)   **VOA**

1675. Pollen, A. H. The "L. S. D." of the submarine blockade. illus. (Illustrated London news, London, v. 146, 1915, p. 374.)   * **DA**
Illustration and description of the "Daylight torpedo-boat," a small automatic submarine torpedo.

1676. Polster. Hand- und Gewehrgranaten. illus. (Verein deutscher Ingenieure, Zeitschrift, Berlin, Bd. 59, 1915, p. 447–448.)   **VDA**

1677. —— Minen- und Bombenwerfer Frankreichs. illus. (Kriegstechnische Zeitschrift, Berlin, Jahrg. 18, 1915, p. 153–157.)   **VWA**

1678. Precautions against incendiary bombs. illus. (Oil and colour trades journal, London, v. 47, 1915, p. 1948.)   **VOP**

1679. Protection of battleships from submarine attack. illus. (Illustrated London news, London, v. 146, 1915, p. 34, 53.) * **DA**

1680. The **Recrudescence** of siege warfare. (Illustrated London news, London, v. 146, 1915, p. 204.)   * **DA**
Descriptions of various types of the German Minnenwerfer.

1681. The **Revival** of the hand-grenade in trench warfare: types and methods, French, British, and German. illus. (Illustrated London news, London, v. 146, 1915, p. 790–791.)   * **DA**

1682. Savorgnan di Brazzà, Francesco. Attacchi e battaglie aeree. (In his: La guerra nel cielo. Milano, 1915. 4°. p. 198–226.)   **VDY**

1683. Sinker of the "Bouvet," "Irresistible" and "Ocean." illus. (Illustrated London news, London, v. 146, 1915, p. 461.) * **DA**
Illustrations and description of the Leon torpedomine, invented by Capt. Karl Oskar Leon.

1684. Sinking of the "Lusitania." illus. (Illustrated London news, London, v. 146, 1915, p. 630–636.)   * **DA**
Valuable series of photographs and sketches.

1685. Sunk by an enemy's torpedo: a steamer going down. illus. (Illustrated London news, London, v. 147, 1915, p. 260–261.)   * **DA**
Account of the sinking of the *Carthage* and *Arabic*.

1686. Thomas, Tom R. Gyroscopic applications, with demonstrations. (Liverpool Engineering Society, Transactions, Liverpool, v. 36, 1915, p. 99–118.)   **VDA**
Discussion, p. 120–124.
The steering of torpedoes, p. 110–112.

1687. Throwing grenade bouquets to the enemy. (Literary digest, New York, v. 50, 1915, p. 1026–1028.)   * **DA**

1688. Torpedoes and torpedo craft, the development of a formidable naval arm. illus. (Navy and army, London, new series, v. 3, 1915, p. 100–102.)   † **VWZH**

1689. "The **Unworthy** method of making war"; German poison gas. illus. (Illustrated London news, London, v. 147, 1915, p. 77.)   * **DA**

1690. "**Weeping**" gas; poison gas and other enemy devices; trench warfare trophies. illus. (Illustrated London news, London, v. 147, 1915, n. 660–661.)   * **DA**
Interesting series of illustrations.

1691. What to do in the case of further air or sea raids. illus. (Sphere, London, v. 60, 1915, p. 162.)   * **DA**

1692. Zeppelin visit to London. illus. (Sphere, London, v. 61, 1915, p. 228–229, 232.)   * **DA**

1916

1693. Aerial torpedo is built by western inventor. illus. (Popular mechanics magazine, New York, v. 26, 1916, p. 207.) **VFA**

1694. Aerial torpedo of great power. illus. (Popular mechanics magazine, New York, v. 25, 1916, p. 25.) **VFA**
Wirelessly controlled.

1695. Automobile torpedo control. (Army and navy register, Washington, v. 60, 1916, p. 9, 73.) **† VWA**
Invention of John Hays Hammond, jr. Brief note on proposed congressional legislation. For an account of test see p. 316.

1696. Buttner, Alexander. Throwing bombs from airships. How to aim the projectile to hit a given object. illus. (Scientific American supplement, New York, v. 81, 1916, p. 85.) **VA**
Translated from *Die Umschau*. With a historical note on the attempt at the siege of Venice in 1849 to drop bombs from an unguided balloon.

1697. Dodge, William W. Liquid fire and asphyxiating gases. (Army and navy register, Washington, v. 60, 1916, p. 8.) **† VWA**
Gives history of the use of Greek fire.

1698. Dropping aerial bombs thru a cone of light. (Electrical experimenter, New York, v. 4, 1916, p. 86.) **VGA**

1699. Du Verseau, pseud. Un sous-marin allemand poseur de mines pêché par les Anglais. illus. (La nature, Paris, année 44, semestre 2, 1916, p. 169–172.) **OA**

1700. Eliphalet Bliss. (National cyclopaedia of American biography, New York, v. 15, 1916, p. 20.) *** R – AGZ**
Manufacturer of the Bliss-Leavitt torpedo.

1701. Fauntleroy, A. M. Grenades. (United States naval medical bulletin, Washington, v. 10, 1916, p. 46–48.) **WSR**

1702. Fighting with liquid fire. (Literary digest, New York, v. 52, 1916, p. 924–925.) *** DA**
Gives description of the effect of the "Flammenwerfer." Refers to the story by H. G. Wells giving "nightmarish" story of the Martians attacking England, which has become a fact.

1703. The Finned bomb of trench warfare: makers of air-torpedoes. illus. (Illustrated London news, London, v. 148, 1916, p. 404–406.) *** DA**

1704. Firing a torpedo from the deck of an American destroyer and loading a torpedo on the submarine "G-2." illus. (Popular mechanics magazine, New York, v. 25, 1916, p. 90–91.) **VFA**
Interesting illustrations.

1705. Frank McDowell. (National cyclopaedia of American biography, New York, v. 15, 1916, p. 20–21.) *** R – AGZ**
Notes on the Bliss-Leavitt torpedo.

1706. The Greek fire of the Germans. (Illustrated London news, London, v. 149, 1916, p. 168.) *** DA**
Notes on history.

1707. Grenades, rifle and hand. illus. (Scientific American supplement, New York, v. 81, 1916, p. 84.) **VA**
Illustrations of various grenades used at the front.

1708. Guns and flame projectors: battle spoil on the Somme front. illus. (Illustrated London news, London, v. 149, 1916, p. 795.) *** DA**
Description of a German Flammenwerfer.

1709. Hill, Allan. Molding hand grenades. illus. (Brass world, New York, v. 12, 1916, p. 167–168.) **VIA**
From *Foundry trade journal*, England.

1710. Hopkins, Albert Allis, compiler and editor. The Scientific American war book; the mechanism and technique of warfare, compiled and edited by Albert A. Hopkins ... Articles by Rear-Admiral Mahan, Major A. G. Piorkowski, Lieut.-Col. L. S. Roudiez...Fred C. Hild, the aviator, Major H. Bannerman-Phillips, Captain W. D. A. Anderson...and many others. New York: Munn & Co., Inc., 1916. 3 p.l., 338 p., 1 pl. illus. 8°. **BTZE**
Trench warfare, p. 107–116; Grenades in modern warfare, p. 156–164; The modern automobile torpedo, p. 283–286; Attack and defense by submarine mines, p. 287–291; Aerial torpedoes and torpedo mines, p. 298–301.

1711. Illustrations of German trench guns. illus. (Illustrated London news, London, v. 148, 1916, p. 96.) *** DA**

1712. Improvements in and connected with submarine mines. illus. (Engineer, London, v. 121, 1916, p. 50.) **VA**
Account of English patent, no. 2859, Feb. 22, 1915, issued to H. A. W. Middleditch. Also noted in *Le génie civil*, tome 68, 1916, p. 171, *VA*.

1713. John Hays Hammond, Jr. (National cyclopaedia of American biography, New York, v.15, 1916, p. 105–106.) *** R – AGZ**
Inventor of a radio-dynamic torpedo.

1714. Learning how to handle grenades and throw them to the best advantage: at a school of bombing. illus. (Illustrated London news, London, v. 148, 1916, p. 398–399.) *** DA**

1715. The "Mars" hand grenade. illus. (Arms and explosives, London, v. 24, 1916, p. 21.) **† VOG**

1716. A New aerial bomb. illus. (Popular mechanics magazine, New York, v. 26, 1916, p. 839.) **VFA**
Tested at Mineola, N. Y.

1717. Reginald Aubrey Fessenden. (National cyclopaedia of American biography, New York, v. 15, 1916, p. 21–22.) *** R – AGZ**
Inventor of a dirigible torpedo.

1916, continued.

1718. Scientific bomb dropping. Sighting devices for aircraft bombs. illus. (Scientific American supplement, New York, v. 81, 1916, p. 260.)   **VA**
From the *Illustrated war news.*

1719. Throwing liquid fire: one of the novel weapons brought forth by the war. illus. (Scientific American supplement, New York, v. 81, 1916, p. 405.)   **VA**

1720. Torpedoing of the "Sussex." (Illustrated London news, London, v. 146, 1916, p. 492–493.)   *** DA**
Illustrations showing explosive effect of a torpedo.

1721. Use of mines at sea. illus. (Illustrated London news, London, v. 148, 1916, p. 438.)   *** DA**

1722. Villard, Oswald Garrison. Submarine and the torpedo in the blockade of the Confederacy. (Harper's magazine, New York, v. 133, 1916, p. 131–137.)   *** DA**

1917

1723. Aerial bombardment. illus. (Engineering, London, v. 104, 1917, p. 198–200.)   **VDA**
Compiled chiefly from an article appearing in *La nature.* Gives valuable data on the German method of dropping bombs, and a description of the Goerz sighting apparatus.

1724. Ainslie, Graham Montgomery. Hand grenades; a handbook on rifle and hand grenades, compiled and illustrated by Major Graham M. Ainslie. New York: J. Wiley & Sons, Inc., 1917. v, 59 p. diagrs. 12°.   **VWS**

1725. Der Bombenwurf aus Flugzeugen und die Ballistik der Fliegerbombe. illus. (Schweizerische militärische Blätter: Schweizerische Zeitschrift für Artillerie und Genie, Frauenfeld, 1917, Jahrg. 53, p. 271–279.)   **VWA**

1726. Bravetta, Ettore. Macchine infernali, siluri e lanciasiluri, con un' appendice su gli esplosivi da guerra. Milano: Fratelli Treves, 1917. 2 p.l., 240 p. illus. 4°. **VXV**
Notes on torpedoes, torpedo boats, and explosives.

1727. Callan, John G. Submarines. illus. (Wisconsin engineer, Madison, v. 21, 1917, p. 295–303.)   **VDA**
Notes on the Whitehead and the Bliss-Leavitt torpedoes, p. 299–301.

1728. Campbell, Maurice Viele. Practical bombing as applied by the Canadian and British armies. Detroit, Mich.: Bartlett Publishing Co. [1917.] 127 p. 2. ed. 16°.   **VWS**

1729. Drag-bombing submarines from airplanes. illus. (Popular science monthly, New York, v. 91, 1917, p. 163.)   *** DA**

1730. Flexible steel curtain, new torpedo shield. illus. (Popular mechanics magazine, New York, v. 28, 1917, p. 182–183.)   **VFA**
Defense against torpedoes by the towing of steel plates.

1731. Floating bomb-laden net to foil submarines. illus. (Popular mechanics magazine, New York, v. 28, 1917, p. 321–322.)   **VFA**

1732. Freeman, Arnold. Liquid-fire and poison-gas. (Living age, Boston, series 8, v. 6, 1917, p. 496–498.)   *** DA**

1733. Freeman, Lewis R. Sailors' sensations in battle: being torpedoed; being mined; state of mind in a naval action. illus. (Popular mechanics magazine, New York, v. 27, 1917, p. 179–183.)   **VFA**

1734. French munitions output for the western front. illus. (Illustrated war news, London, new series, part 36, Feb. 14, 1917, p. 29.)   **† BTZE**
Illustrations of hand grenades and rockets.

1735. German bombs officially described. illus. (New York Tribune, Dec. 16, 1917, p. 15, col. 2–5.)   *** A**
Descriptions of German bombs seized in Norway; prepared by the Military Intelligence Section, War College Division, Washington.

1736. Gernsback, H. Firing bombs by electricity. illus. (Electrical experimenter, New York, v. 5, 1917, p. 370, 416.)   **VGA**

1737. Guenther, Hanns. Gewehrgranaten. illus. (Schweizerische militärische Blätter: Schweizerische Monatschrift für Offiziere aller Waffen, Frauenfeld, Jahrg. 29, 1917, p. 210–215, 237–241.)   **VWA**

1738. The Ideal aerial bomb. illus. (Popular science monthly, New York, v. 91, 1917, p. 386–387.)   *** DA**

1739. Incendiary bullets for air craft. (Scientific American, New York, v. 116, 1917, p. 148.)   **VA**
Brief note.

1740. Italian submarine mines. (Scientific Australian, Melbourne, 1917, v. 23, p. 13–14.)   **VA**
From the *Scientific American.*

1741. Kleinschmidt, F. E. A sea fight in the Adriatic; destroying a mine-field under the guns of the enemy. illus. (Scientific American, New York, v. 117, 1917, p. 24–25, 34.)   **VA**
Illustration of the hooking of the hoisting cable to a mine on the cover of the issue for July 14, 1917.

1742. Lathe for turning torpedo heads. illus. (Iron age, New York, v. 100, 1917, p. 432.)   **VDA**

1743. Lefranc, Jean Abel. Sur le bombardement aérien. illus. (La nature, Paris, année 45, semestre 1, p. 379–383.)   **OA**
Abstracted in *Scientific Australian,* Melbourne, v. 23, 1917, p. 17, *VA,* and in *Scientific American supplement,* New York, v. 84, 1917, p. 108–109, *VA.*

1917, continued.

1744. Maxim, Hudson. How to make ships torpedo-proof. illus. (Scientific American, New York, v. 116, 1917, p. 578–579.) **VA**

1745. Molding grenades for the French army. illus. (Iron trade review, Cleveland, v. 60, 1917, p. 828–829.) **VHA**
Also printed in *Foundry*, Cleveland, v. 45, 1917, p. 131–132, *VIA*.

1746. Moreno y Quesada, Manuel. Estaciones radiotelegráficas. Sistema "Marconi americano" — tipo "Submarinos y torpederos." illus. (Revista general de marina, Madrid, tomo 81, 1917, p. 5–34.) **VXA**

1747. Moss, James Alfred. Trench warfare; being a practical manual for training and instruction of officers and men... based on the latest information from the battle fronts of Europe... Menasha, Wis.: Geo. Banta Pub. Co. ₁1917.₁ 2 p.l., 7–274 p. illus. 12°. **VWK**
Grenades and grenadiers, p. 131–150; Gas warfare, p. 151–157; Bomb throwers, p. 209; Trench mortars, p. 210.

1748. The **Net** as a weapon of defense. illus. (Scientific American, New York, v. 117, 1917, p. 56.) **VA**
Illustration of a submarine-destroying net, which automatically lets fall torpedo bombs upon the deck of the submarine.

1749. Nets and steel plates as a defense against the torpedo. illus. (Scientific American, New York, v. 116, 1917, p. 596.) **VA**

1750. Poisoned arrows. (Illustrated London news, London, v. 150, 1917, p. 342.) **∗DA**

1751. Principles, promising and otherwise, which may be applied to detecting the U-boats. illus. (Scientific American, New York, v. 117, 1917, p. 10–11, 20.) **VA**
Notes use of nets.

1752. Protecting a convoy by overlapping lines of towed nets or plates. illus. (Scientific American, New York, v. 117, 1917, p. 97, 107.) **VA**

1753. ₁Protection against torpedoes.₁ illus. (Popular mechanics magazine, New York, v. 28, 1917, p. 206–207.) **VFA**
Illustration of use of nets on ships.

1754. Protection, internal to the ship, against the torpedo. illus. (Scientific American, New York, v. 117, 1917, p. 224–225, 233, 235.) **VA**

1755. Radio-controlled torpedo devised by California genius. illus. (Electrical experimenter, New York, v. 5, 1917, p. 387.) **VGA**
Invention of Henry H. Hyder of Los Angeles.

1756. Shells filled with liquid poison. (Field artillery journal, Washington, v. 7, 1917, p. 347–348.) **VWA**
Abstracted from the Washington *Evening Post.*

1757. Smith, Joseph Shuter. Trench warfare; a manual for officers and men. New York: E. P. Dutton & Co. ₁1917.₁ xvi, 144 p. illus. 16°. **VWK**
Notes on explosives, bombs, and gas warfare, p. 101–116.

1758. A **Strange** new naval weapon, idea of great scientist. illus. (Popular mechanics magazine, New York, v. 28, 1917, p. 2–3.) **VFA**
Account of an "aeromarine" torpedo, so planned as to be drawn against an enemy's ship by an aeroplane.

1759. Stroh. Les modèles actuels de torpilles automobiles. illus. (Génie civil, Paris, tome 71, 1917, p. 365–371.) **VA**
A very complete article, written to complete the history of the automobile torpedo printed in *Génie civil*, June 26, 1915. Gives valuable notes on the Whitehead and Schwartzkopff torpedoes, Kalezowksi, Whitehead, and German gyroscopes, and an interior view of a German torpedo.

1760. Submarine and kindred problems. (Engineer, London, v. 124, 1917, p. 329–330.) **VA**
Discussion of protection against submarine attack, mines and torpedoes.

1761. Torpedo running practice. illus. (Illustrated London news, London, v. 150, 1917, p. 735.) **∗DA**

1762. United States. — Engineer School. Lessons in fortification. Part 1. Effects of artillery fire. Part 2. Field fortification and the protection of batteries. Washington Barracks, D. C.: Press of the Engineer School, 1917. 2 p.l., 120 p. illus. 8°. (United States. — Engineer School. Occasional papers. no. 53.) **VWI**
Description of shells and explosives, bombs, trench mortars, trenches, and field fortifications.

1763. Vickers, Leslie. Training for the trenches; a practical handbook based upon personal experience during the first two years of the war in France. New York: George H. Doran Company ₁1917₁. xii p., 1 l., 15–127 p., 14 pl. 12°. **VWC**
Notes on the trench gun and bomb, grenades and liquid fire.

1764. Whirling disk to guard ships from torpedoes. illus. (Popular mechanics magazine, New York, v. 27, 1917, p. 802–804.) **VFA**

1765. Why not the land torpedo? illus. (Popular science monthly, New York, v. 91, 1917, p. 323.) **∗DA**

INDEX OF AUTHORS

INDEX OF SUBJECTS

Numbers refer to individual entries.

A

Aerial attack, 1471.
Aeronautics, 1501.
Aircraft in war, 1270.
American Defense Society, 1470.
"American Turtle," 1503, 1505.
Antwerp, siege of, 664, 901.
Arrows, poisoned, 1750.
Artillery, 1502.
  Fire, effect of, 1762.
  History, 1509.

B

Balloons:
  Electric-torpedo, 246.
  Torpedo, 435.
Batteries:
  Electric, 192.
  Protection of, 1762.
Battlefields, lighting of, 16, 21, 1408.
Battles, naval, in the Adriatic, 1741.
Battleships, 897.
  Design, 1288.
  German, 1627.
  Protection against submarines, 1679.
  Submarine attack, 1238.
  Torpedo room, 930.
Blockades, 1473.
Bohn & Köhler, 1187.
Bomb mortars. *See* Mortars, bomb.
Bombs, 16, 20, 22, 25, 1434a, 1599, 1664, 1677, 1758, 1762, 1763.
  Aerial, 1372, 1716, 1738, 1743.
  Dropping, 1631, 1718, 1723, 1728.
  Dropping from aeroplanes, 1335, 1418a, 1621, 1698.
  Explosive, for aeroplanes, 1623.
  Finned, 1703.
  Firing by electricity, 1736.
  German, 1343, 1632, 1735.
  Incendiary, 1343, 1406a, 1469a, 1513, 1641, 1652, 1663, 1672, 1678.
  Marten-Hall aeroplane, 1216, 1277.
  Protection from, 1648.
  Smoke, practice with, 1630.
  Throwing, 1643, 1660, 1673.
  Throwing by crossbows, 1655.
  Throwing from airships, 1696.
Bronze in torpedoes, 1419.
Brotherhood, Peter, 529.
Bullets, incendiary, for aircraft, 1739.

C

Camera and the torpedo, 264.
Camera obscura, 763.
Cannon, bomb, 1589, 1608, 1649.
Charge cases, 175.
Chariots, incendiary, 1513.
Cherbourg, experiments at, 1547.
Circuit closers, 172.
Citizen soldier, 40a.
Coast defense, 82, 762, 834, 892, 933, 1090, 1471.

College Point, experiments at, 1561.
"Columbiad" (Cannon), 1589.
Constantinople, 1513.
Convoys, protection of, 1752.
Corfu, torpedo operations, 391.

D

Dardanelles, 1334.
Detectors, microphone, 1327.
Disks, whirling, 1764.
Divers, Turkish, 1525.
Dreadnaughts vs. submarines, 1429.
Dynamite in war, 1550.

E

E. W. Bliss Co., 810.
Easthampton, L. I., 37.
Electricity:
  In submarine defense, 244.
  In submarine mining, 1339.
  In warfare, 552, 1328, 1386, 1518.
Explosions, submarine, 31, 444, 1341.
Explosives, 1111, 1664, 1726.
Explosives, military, 1500.

F

Fire, artificial, 16.
Fire, liquid, 1697, 1702, 1719, 1732, 1763.
Fire arrows, 21.
Fire barrels, 21, 37, 1513.
Fire caused by bombs, 1469a.
Fireships, 36, 40a, 519, 1508.
Fireworks, 26-28.
Flame projectors, 1702, 1708.
Fortifications, field, 1762.
Fuses:
  Mines, 1214.
  Torpedo, 100, 156, 193, 302, 1225.

G

Gallipoli, 1660.
  Torpedoplane operations, 1473.
Gas:
  Asphyxiating, 1697.
  Poisonous, 1656, 1663, 1672, 1689, 1690, 1732.
  Warfare, 1757.
  Weeping, 1690.
Grapnel, electric, 335.
Greek fire, 1509, 1513, 1642, 1697, 1706.
Grenades, 21, 22, 1344a, 1434a, 1486a, 1498a, 1611, 1618, 1639, 1647, 1654, 1656, 1657, 1664, 1668, 1671, 1676, 1681, 1701, 1707, 1709, 1710, 1724, 1734, 1737, 1747, 1763.
  Baker's, 1659.
  European war, 1315a.
  History, 1315a, 1681.
  "Mars," 1715.

U

W

Z

www.ingramcontent.com/pod-product-compliance
Lightning Source LLC
Chambersburg PA
CBHW060743100426
42813CB00027B/3033